D1644718

Po ^{Due}ial or Most-Racial?

MICHAEL TESLER is assistant professor at the University of California, Irvine, and the author of *Obama's Race*, also published by the University of Chicago Press.

The University of Chicago Press, Chicago 60637
The University of Chicago Press, Ltd., London
© 2016 by The University of Chicago
All rights reserved. Published 2016.
Printed in the United States of America

25 24 23 22 21 20 19 18 17 16   1 2 3 4 5

ISBN-13: 978-0-226-35296-1 (cloth)
ISBN-13: 978-0-226-35301-2 (paper)
ISBN-13: 978-0-226-35315-9 (e-book)
DOI: 10.7208/chicago/9780226353159.001.0001

Library of Congress Cataloging-in-Publication Data

Tesler, Michael, author.
    Post-racial or most-racial? : race and politics in the Obama era / Michael Tesler.
        pages cm — (Chicago studies in American politics)
    ISBN 978-0-226-35296-1 (cloth : alkaline paper) — ISBN 978-0-226-35301-2 (papererback : alkaline paper) — ISBN 978-0-226-35315-9 (e-book) 1. United States—Race relations—Political aspects. 2. United States—Politics and government—2009– 3. Race awareness—United States. 4. Ethnic attitudes—United States. 5. Obama, Barack. I. Title. II. Series: Chicago studies in American politics.
    E184.A1T465 2016
    305.80097309'0512—dc23

                                                                        2015027993

♾ This paper meets the requirements of ANSI/NISO Z39.48-1992 (Permanence of Paper).

TO MARY, BEST FRIENDS FOREVER

roughly twenty minutes about race and crime in the United States. Barack Obama, as the epigraph that introduced this chapter indicated, explained how the African American community was looking at the Trayvon Martin incident "through a set of experiences and a history that doesn't go away." Experiences, he detailed, which included racial disparities in the application of criminal laws and black America's regular encounters with racial profiling. Experiences, the president added, that he also frequently confronted before being elected to the United States Senate.

Many applauded the speech for doing, as Dan Balz wrote in his *Washington Post* column, what "no other American president could have done—giving voice, in calm and measured terms, to what it means still to be black in America."[6] Some commentators, however, condemned the president for emphasizing the importance of past and present encounters with white prejudice as a root cause of African Americans' emotional reactions to the Trayvon Martin incident. Rush Limbaugh used the speech to "corroborate" his 2008 claim that Barack Obama was no different from controversial civil rights leaders Jesse Jackson and Al Sharpton.[7] Bill O'Reilly carried on for several episodes of his top-rated cable news show about "Obama and the race problem," where he angrily called on "the African-American leadership, including President Obama, to stop the nonsense. Walk away from the world of victimization and grievance and lead the way out of the mess [in the black community]."[8] A few prominent conservatives even branded President Obama as a "race baiter" for his comments.[9]

The differing reactions to President Obama's comments corresponded to the large partisan and racial divisions in public opinion about the George Zimmerman trial. Ever since the earliest polling on the Trayvon Martin incident in March 2012, Democrats and African Americans had been much more likely than Republicans and white Americans to think that Zimmerman should have been arrested for murder.[10] The large racial divide in public opinion about the case should not have surprised anyone. Black and white Americans have long had "separate realities" about the criminal justice system (Peffley and Hurwitz 2010), and perceptions of O. J. Simpson's innocence were similarly split along racial lines during his murder trial in the mid-1990s.[11] The partisan divide in white Americans' responses to the Zimmerman trial was more peculiar, though. Figure I.1 shows that, although white Democrats and white Republicans responded almost identically to the O. J. Simpson verdict in October 1995, there was a forty-percentage-point gulf between white partisans in their dissatisfaction with the Zimmerman trial's outcome.[12]

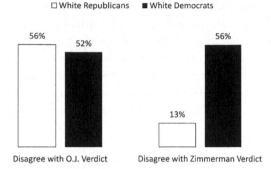

FIGURE I.I. White Partisans' Reactions to the O. J. Simpson and George Zimmerman Verdicts
Source: Gallup/CNN/*USA Today*, October 5–7, 1995 (accessed from the Roper Center's Data Archive); Pew Poll, July 17–21, 2013 (results reported by the Pew Research Center 2013b).

To be sure, there are several good reasons why those two race-infused murder trials generated such different levels of partisan polarization. A large piece of the puzzle, though, can surely be explained by the central claim of this book: *Mass politics had become more polarized by racial attitudes since Barack Obama's rise to prominence. That is, the election of President Obama helped usher in a "most-racial" political era where racially liberal and racially conservative Americans were more divided over a whole host of political positions than they had been in modern times.* A natural upshot of that growing racialization of American politics is that Democrats and Republicans increasingly viewed racial controversies like the Trayvon Martin incident through very different lenses.

* * *

How could the ascendancy of Barack Obama—a presidential candidate who once embodied the country's great hope of moving beyond age-old racial divisions—help usher in this most-racial political era? His election, as David Sears and I put it in the subtitle our 2010 book, *Obama's Race*, carried with it "the dream of a post-racial America." That election night dream, many will recall, was immortalized in Senator John McCain's 2008 presidential concession speech:

> I've always believed that America offers opportunities to all who have the industry and will to seize it. Senator Obama believes that, too. But we both recognize that though we have come a long way from the old injustices that once stained our nation's reputation and denied some Americans the full blessings

of American citizenship, the memory of them still had the power to wound. A
century ago, President Theodore Roosevelt's invitation of Booker T. Washington to visit—to dine at the White House—was taken as an outrage in many
quarters. America today is a world away from the cruel and prideful bigotry of
that time. There is no better evidence of this than the election of an African-
American to the presidency of the United States. Let there be no reason now
for any American to fail to cherish their citizenship in this, the greatest nation
on Earth.[13]

The American people generally shared in Senator McCain's hope for a
post-racial America as well. Public opinion polls taken shortly before and
after the 2008 election showed that citizens of all races were optimistic
about the effect of Barack Obama's presidency on American race relations (see fig. I.2). Black and white citizens alike were also more upbeat
about racial progress in the United States after Barack Obama's election
than they had been in recent years (Pew Research Center 2010, 2013b).[14]

But those high hopes rapidly receded. Figure I.2 shows a large dis-
connect between the percentage of Americans who thought Barack
Obama's presidency would improve race relations in 2008 and early 2009
and the percentage who thought his presidency actually had made relations better in 2010 and 2011. In fact, national surveys commissioned by
Fox News, CBS/*New York Times*, the *Economist*, and NBC News during
Barack Obama's first term in the White House all found that Americans
were more likely to think race relations had become worse since Barack
Obama took office.[15] This belief that Obama's presidency helped make
race relations worse intensified over time. Public opinion polls conducted
by *Rasmussen*, YouGov/*Economist*, and CBS/*New York Times* in 2013
and 2014 all suggested that Americans were about four times more likely
to think that race relations had deteriorated since President Obama's
first inauguration than they were to say they had improved.[16] The above-
referenced spike in the percentage of blacks and whites who thought that
conditions for ordinary African Americans had improved also quickly returned to their pre-2008 levels (Pew Research Center 2010, 2013b).

It was clear to most astute observers, then, that the first term of Barack
Obama's presidency had not marked a post-racial moment in American
politics. Moreover, any lingering doubts were all but eradicated by the
2012 election results: Barack Obama won a second term in the White
House with only 39 percent of the white vote—a slightly lower share of
white support than the 40 percent that Michael Dukakis received when he

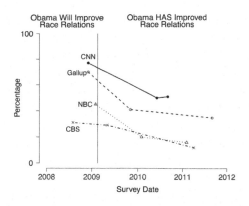

FIGURE I.2. Perceptions of Barack Obama's Impact on Race Relations, 2008–11
Source: iPOLL databank search for "race relations" and "Obama."

lost the 1988 presidential election to George H. W. Bush in a landslide.[17] With the racial and ethnic breakdown of 2012 voting factoring heavily into political commentators' postelection analyses, the 2008 election night hopes of racial unity had given way four years later to growing fears of racial polarization in American politics.[18]

Summary of Key Findings

Mass politics was indeed more polarized *by and over race* during Barack Obama's presidency than it was before his 2008 presidential campaign. In fact, this book tells the story of how and why Americans' political opinions became more heavily influenced by both racial attitudes and race in the Obama era than they had been shortly before his rise to prominence. The process documented throughout the following chapters, whereby racial considerations are brought more heavily to bear on political evaluations, is often described as racialization. Attitudes toward affirmative action and welfare, for example, are considered racialized because they are determined in large part by racial attitudes (Kinder and Sanders 1996; Sears et al. 1997; Gilens 1999; Winter 2008; Tesler and Sears 2010; De-Sante 2013). The central argument of the book, therefore, is that Barack Obama's presidency further racialized American politics, despite his administration's best efforts to neutralize the political impact of race.

The roots of that racialization, as chapter 1 explains, were in place before Barack Obama's first inauguration. That chapter documents dozens of prior academic studies, which found race-related attitudes to be significant determinants of 2008 voting behavior. Many of those studies also showed that racial and ethnocentric attitudes were stronger predictors of 2008 preferences than they had been in recent presidential elections, and much more powerful causes of Americans' vote choices than they would have been if John McCain had faced Hillary Clinton instead of Barack Obama in the 2008 election. The more interesting and politically important question for our purposes, though, is how the presence of a black president who evoked racial predispositions so powerfully affected the broader American political landscape.

The second chapter attempts to answer this question by drawing on extant social science research to put forth theoretical expectations about how, when, and why Obama's presence in the White House influenced American politics. Those theoretical expectations suggest that the unusual impact of racial considerations on mass evaluations of President Obama should have often spilled over into the broader political landscape—a phenomenon described throughout the book as the *spillover of racialization*. The spillover of racialization hypothesis, as formalized in that chapter, argues that a wide array of Americans' opinions—including their evaluations of Barack Obama's political rivals (e.g., Mitt Romney) and allies (e.g., Joe Biden), their public policy preferences (e.g., health care), their subjective evaluations of objective economic conditions (e.g., the unemployment rate), their vote choices for Congress, their partisan attachments, and even their impressions of Portuguese water dogs (the breed of the Obama family's dogs, Bo and Sunny)—should have all become more polarized by racial attitudes and race during the Obama presidency. That growing influence of racial attitudes on mass politics, chapter 2 argues, should have also been especially polarizing and contributed to the rising disdain that Democrats and Republicans had for one another in the Age of Obama.

At the same time, though, the spillover of racialization into mass politics would have occurred only if Americans continued to view Barack Obama through a racial prism. If the importance of Obama's race on public opinion about his presidency faded over time, which prior research on black mayors suggests it might have (Hajnal 2007), then the spillover of racialization should have also receded in kind. Chapters 3 and 4, therefore, examine the effects of racial and ethnocentric attitudes on public support for Barack Obama during his presidency. After detailing several reasons why racial animosity and racial sympathy should have remained

powerful determinants of opposition to, and support for, Barack Obama's
2012 presidential candidacy, those two chapters present a number of findings to support that conclusion. In particular, racial attitudes remained an
important determinant of 2012 voting behavior. Feelings toward African
Americans were not the only out-group attitude that remained an unusually strong predictor of 2012 voter choice, either. With Barack Obama
persistently painted as the "other" during his presidency (e.g., Muslim
and/or foreign born), attitudes toward Muslims were an even stronger
predictor of support for the president's reelection bid than they had been
four years earlier.

Chapter 4 goes on to show that the strong effects of racial attitudes on
public evaluations of the president were mostly unchanged by both the
2012 campaign and by various experimental treatments—experiments
that have a proven track record in the social science literature of either
enhancing or deactivating the effects of racial attitudes on political evaluations. Those results are consistent with earlier scholarly contentions that
Barack Obama's omnipresent position as a historic racial figure, and his
embodiment of race as the first African American president, make racial
attitudes a chronically accessible consideration in mass assessments of
his presidency that is difficult to either neutralize or enhance (Tesler and
Sears 2010; Kinder and Dale-Riddle 2012; Valentino et al. 2013).

The spillover of racialization hypothesis also suggests that those strong
and enduring effects of racial attitudes on public support for President
Obama spilled over into a variety of Obama-era political opinions. Chapters 3 and 4 provide some early support for that argument by showing
how evaluations that were strongly connected (e.g., perceptions of the
2012 unemployment rate and evaluations of Vice President Biden) or contrasted (e.g., Mitt Romney's favorability ratings) with President Obama's
2012 candidacy became more heavily influenced by racial attitudes than
they were beforehand.

The spillover of racialization from Barack Obama into American politics extended much further than those evaluations. Public opinion about
health care was one issue in particular that was especially ripe for racialization. After all, the intense media coverage of the 2009–10 debate over
health care reform persistently linked the president to the legislation that
would ultimately take his name, "Obamacare." Chapter 5 marshals multiple surveys to show that antiblack attitudes did in fact become a significantly stronger predictor of opposition to governmental health care
after Obama became the face of the policy. Moreover, the experiments

embedded in an original survey found health care opinions were significantly more racialized when attributed to President Obama than they
were when these same proposals were framed as President Clinton's 1993
reform efforts. The chapter also draws on recent research showing that
racial attitudes are emotionally charged in ways that nonracial ideological orientations are not (Banks and Valentino 2012; Banks 2014), to argue
that Obama's race helped make the 2009–10 health care debate so vitriolic. Consistent with that expectation, I show that anger—the emotion
most closely linked with racial resentment—was five times more prevalent in 2009–10 broadcast news stories about health care than it was during the 1993–94 health care debate. I also show that significantly fewer
Americans were angered by President Obama's 2009 health care reform
proposals when they were told that the policies were a part of President
Clinton's 1993 initiative.

The growing racialization of American politics was not limited just
to assessments of Barack Obama or to public opinion about his policies.
Chapter 6 reveals that racial attitudes spilled over into electoral outcomes
even beyond the presidential election. Results from multiple surveys indicate that white Americans' voting behavior in the 2010 and 2012 congressional elections was more racialized than it was in the pre-Obama period.
I also use aggregate election returns to show that racially conservative
congressional districts became significantly more Republican relative to
racially liberal districts in 2010 than they had been in previous midterm
elections. Like public opinion about health care, Obama's ascendancy
once again appears to have been the catalyst for this growing racialization of American politics. Evaluations of the president mediated (e.g.,
transmitted) the greater influence of racial attitudes on white Americans'
Obama-era votes for Congress, and the spillover of racialization into 2010
voting for Congress was most pronounced in congressional districts where
members of the House of Representatives voted for Obamacare. The
chapter concludes with a discussion of how the heightened emotions that
come with the enhanced racialization of congressional election outcomes
may have made it especially difficult to find common ground on legislative matters in the Obama era—a conclusion supported by new empirical
evidence presented at the end of this chapter, which shows that Republican members of Congress who represented the most racially conservative
districts were the most likely to avoid cooperating with the president on
important legislative initiatives.

Even white Americans' typically stable partisan attachments were not immune from the spillover of racialization. Chapter 7 shows that party identification was more polarized by racial attitudes in the Obama era than it was shortly prior to his ascendancy. That growing racialization of Obama-era partisanship was found in several different surveys and was found using multiple measures of racial prejudice. As expected from prior social science research, the spillover of racialization into white Americans' partisan attachments was most pronounced among poorly educated Americans who had not consistently connected their racial predispositions to their partisan attachments in the pre-Obama period. The chapter's concluding remarks detail why these findings are probably the most important in the entire book. Indeed, party identification is both the most influential and probably the most enduring of all political attitudes.

Chapter 8 transitions from the role of racial attitudes in public opinion to the growing Obama-era divide in the political outlooks of white and nonwhite Americans. Like white racial liberals and white racial conservatives, black and white Americans were more divided in their assessments of Barack Obama than their evaluations of other recent presidents. Moreover, and like the spillover of racial attitudes into white Americans' political preferences, Obama's presence in the White House helped enhance the already substantial black-white racial divide in a number of political opinions. The racial divide in support for Barack Obama's health care plan, for example, was twenty percentage points greater in 2009–10 than the black-white divide in support for Bill Clinton's 1993–94 health care initiative. Party identification also became significantly more divided by race in the Obama era, with especially large divisions opening up between whites who harbored antiblack attitudes and racially conscious African Americans who rated their own group most favorably.

Chapter 8 goes on to show that the growing divide in Obama-era party identification between Latinos and whites may have been even greater than this expanding black-white divide in partisanship. Unlike black Americans, however, the spike in Latinos' affiliation with the Democratic Party was most heavily concentrated among Hispanics who felt colder toward whites—a likely upshot of polling data showing that this group increasingly viewed Republicans as a party of and for white Americans. With the Republican Party increasingly viewed as the "party of white people" in the Obama era, attitudes about whites also seemed to be strong predictors of Asian Americans' and Native Americans' 2012 partisan attachments. The chapter concludes with a discussion of the implications of these results for a lasting nonwhite Democratic coalition in the post-Obama era.

The concluding chapter offers a number of qualifications and some potential implications for both American politics and those who research it. The qualification sections highlight results in earlier chapters on the limitations of the spillover of racialization—most notably the resistance of some issues to President Obama's racializing influence (e.g., gun control) and the fleeting nature of the spillover of racialization into others (e.g., same-sex marriage). Nevertheless, the final chapter argues that many of the book's findings may leave a lasting mark on American politics. I also present new evidence suggesting that social background characteristics of prominent political leaders aside from race (e.g., religion, ethnicity, and gender) can activate group-based considerations in the formation of mass opinions. This conclusion that group-based spillover effects are not simply unique to our first African American president should be increasingly important as the demographic composition of elected officials inevitably changes in the decades ahead.

Regardless of what the future holds, though, the findings presented throughout the book show that President Obama presided over the "most-racial" political era—one in which Americans' political orientations were more divided by and over race than they had been in modern times. That polarization of the electorate almost certainly contributed to the vitriolic political atmosphere during Barack Obama's presidency, too. It is impossible to fully understand American politics in the Obama era, then, without understanding the political impact of Obama's race.

CHAPTER ONE

Racial Attitudes and American Politics in the Age of Obama

There is a historic connection between some of the arguments that we have politically and the history of race in our country, and sometimes it's hard to disentangle those issues. You can be somebody who, for very legitimate reasons, worries about the power of the federal government—that it's distant, that it's bureaucratic, that it's not accountable—and as a consequence you think that more power should reside in the hands of state governments. But what's also true, obviously, is that philosophy is wrapped up in the history of states' rights in the context of the civil-rights movement and the Civil War and [pro-slavery and secessionist leader Senator John. C.] Calhoun. — President Barack Obama, January 2014[1]

As Barack Obama's comments above suggest, race occupied a prominent place in the modern partisan alignment long before he became the first African American president. While the two political parties largely ignored Jim Crow segregation and the plight of African Americans for generations after the Civil War and Reconstruction sharply divided Democrats from Republicans on race, the American party system once again polarized over racial issues during the civil rights era. That renewed organization of partisan politics around racial issues and race, many have convincingly argued, stemmed from elite-level differences between politicians in the two parties' support for civil rights initiatives in the 1950s and 1960s (Carmines and Stimson 1989; Kinder and Sanders 1996; Edsall and Edsall 1992; Frymer 1999; Lopez 2014).[2] Most notably, the enactment of civil rights legislation by the Democratic Kennedy and Johnson administrations, which was opposed by the Republicans' 1964 presidential candidate, Barry Goldwater, helped generate a new race-based schism between the parties.

Racial conservatism went on to divide Republican politicians from

their Democratic counterparts throughout the remainder of the twentieth century. In Congress, the two parties grew increasingly polarized over
racial issues, with Democratic lawmakers clearly establishing themselves
as the more racially liberal party (Carmines and Stimson 1989). So much
so that congressional roll call votes on racial issues were almost entirely
split across ideological and partisan lines by 1990 (McCarty, Poole, and
Rosenthal 2006; Atkinson 2012).[3] Those partisan divisions in the House
of Representatives and the Senate were further solidified by the two
major parties' presidential platforms. In particular, the Republican Party
explicitly denounced racial quotas and race-based preferences in every
one of their party platforms from the 1970s up through Barack Obama's
elections, while every Democratic platform openly endorsed "affirmative
action" during that same period (King and Smith 2011, 115).

Along with those elite-level policy differences, there was also a growing divide between Democratic and Republican politicians' racial rhetoric
in the post–civil rights era. Mayer (2002) found a consistent partisan division over race in presidential campaign appeals from 1964 to 2000 (also
see Gerstle 2002; O'Reilly 1995; and Schaller 2006); and several other
scholars and journalists documented the emergence of subtle appeals
to antiblack stereotypes by Republican candidates at all levels of government in the post–civil rights era (Edsall and Edsall 1992; Kinder and
Sanders 1996; Glaser 1998; Mendelberg 2001; McIlwain and Caliendo
2011; Lopez 2014).

These implicit racial appeals became a staple of Republican presidential campaigns when Richard Nixon deployed the "southern strategy" in
1968 to try to win over disaffected white Southern Democrats with subtle
appeals to antiblack stereotypes and racial resentments (Mendelberg
2001; O'Reilly 1995; McGinnis 1969; Lopez 2014). Or as Republican campaign consultant Lee Atwater infamously put it, "By 1968 you can't say
'nigger'—that hurts you. Backfires. So you say stuff like forced busing,
states' rights and all that stuff."[4] Ronald Reagan seemed to take that ad-
vice from Atwater, who served as political director of his 1984 presidential campaign. President Reagan was accused of similar tactics with his use
of the racially loaded term "states' rights" and his repeated invocation of
the racially stereotypical "welfare queen" anecdote (Gilens 1999; Gilliam
1999; Mendelberg 2001; Lopez 2014).[5] Reagan's vice president, George
H. W. Bush, drew even more race-based criticism after his 1988 presidential campaign, which was managed by Lee Atwater, employed provocative
materials about a violent black criminal, Willie Horton, to help attract ra-

cially conservative voters (Jamieson 1992; Kinder and Sanders 1996; Mendelberg 1997, 2001; McIlwain and Caliendo 2011; Lopez 2014).

Mass politics, in light of these elite-level developments, also grew increasingly divided by and over race in the latter half of the twentieth century. African Americans had been loyal to the Republican Party of Abraham Lincoln up until the Great Depression (Sitkoff 1978; Weiss 1983), but the 1964 presidential election solidified their bourgeoning affiliation with the Democratic Party (Dawson 1994; Tate 1994). Democrats' share of the black vote increased substantially in 1964 and has remained consistently high ever since (Kinder and Sanders 1996; see also results in chap. 8). Americans' partisan identifications also became increasingly sorted by racial attitudes in the post–civil rights era, as older citizens who came of age before the parties diverged so sharply on racial issues were gradually replaced by incoming partisans whose attachments were formed after that racial schism in American politics (Carmines and Stimson 1989; Layman and Carsey 2002; Stimson 2004; Green, Palmquist, and Schickler 2002; Valentino and Sears 2005).[6] The aforementioned differences between the two parties in both their positions on racial policies and their race-related rhetoric also help explain racial conservatism's significant independent impact on support for GOP presidential candidates from 1988 to 2004 (Kinder and Dale-Riddle 2012; Tesler and Sears 2010; Valentino and Sears 2005).

That growing influence of racial attitudes on white Americans' partisan preferences was considered a boon to the Republican Party. Race was *the* great wedge issue in post–civil rights era American politics, with unpopular racially charged policies like busing to desegregate schools, affirmative action, and welfare splintering the Democratic Party's longstanding majority coalition (Huckfeldt and Kohlfeld 1989; Edsall and Edsall 1992; Sniderman and Carmines 1997; Gilens, Sniderman, and Kuklinski 1998; Kinder and Sanders 1996; Valentino and Sears 2005). The two parties' realignment over race helped turn the once solidly Democratic South into a Republican stronghold (Valentino and Sears 2005; Green, Palmquist, and Schickler 2002; Acharya, Blackwell, and Sen 2014; Kuziemko and Washington 2015); and racially conservative "Nixon/Reagan Democrats"—Democrats who switched sides to vote for Republican presidential candidates in part because of their own party's support for unpopular racially liberal policies (Klinkner and Smith 2002, 303–5)[7]—often tipped the balance for Republican candidates in national elections held after 1964.

The two parties' respective needs to win over or retain such racially conservative swing voters also gave rise to what Donald Kinder and Lynn Sanders (1996) adroitly termed the "electoral temptations of race." The Republican Party's electoral temptation, according to Kinder and Sanders, was to appeal to culturally conservative whites (e.g., Reagan Democrats) without turning off voters by being overtly racist. Hence, their electoral temptation in the years leading up to Barack Obama's election had been implicit racial appeals like the race-coded language referenced above. The Democratic Party, however, had to maintain the loyalty of African Americans without alienating racially conservative swing voters. Hence, their electoral temptation in recent years was benign neglect or racial silence.

Both parties heeded their electoral temptations in the years leading up to Barack Obama's election. Republicans, as mentioned earlier, often made subtle appeals to racial stereotypes in local and national elections. Meanwhile, the Democratic Party increasingly answered the Republicans' racial conservatism with racial silence.[8] The Democrats' more recent party platforms have not displayed the same enthusiasm for affirmative action expressed by the Democratic Party of the 1970s (King and Smith 2011, 115–16). Bill Clinton's efforts to distance himself from controversial civil rights leaders like Jesse Jackson during the 1992 presidential campaign and his reactive "mend it, don't end it" approach to affirmative action further exemplified the Democrats' electoral temptations of racial evasion. So much so, in fact, that Klinkner and Smith (2002) found some similarities between the Democrats' unenthusiastic position on civil rights issues in the 1980s and 1990s and the Republicans' abandonment of racial equality after their party advocated for the abolition of slavery during the Civil War and for programs to help freed slaves during Reconstruction. "The Democratic record on civil rights in the 1980s and 1990s," they wrote, "has been characterized more by fairly passive resistance to conservative efforts than by any strong positive program. When the Clinton administration has found itself linked with persons identified with strong civil rights activism . . . it has quickly severed those links" (Klinkner and Smith 2002, 345).

As a result of the Democrats' fairly passive resistance to conservative attacks on race-targeted policies, the racialized issues that once dominated the national political landscape lost much of their political prominence. By the end of the 1990s, Supreme Court rulings and state ballot initiatives had limited the reach of busing and affirmative action.[9] The enactment of welfare reform by the Democratic Clinton administration in 1996—an ostensibly nonracial policy that powerfully evokes race-based opposition nonetheless (Gilens 1999; Mendelberg 2001; Winter 2008; DeSante 2013)—also neutralized this venerable racialized wedge issue. Democratic passage of the 1994 Violent Crime Control and Law Enforcement Act and plummeting crime rates during Bill Clinton's and George W. Bush's presidencies seemed to remove crime policy—another highly racialized issue (Hurwitz and Peffley 1997, 2005; Gilliam and Iyengar 2000; Peffley and Hurwitz 2010)—from the national partisan dialogue as well.

With race-based and race-evoking issues largely receding from the national political scene in the years preceding the 2008 election, there were some indicators of a declining significance of race in Americans' political preferences before Barack Obama became the Democratic nominee for president. The partisan attachments of white youths who came of voting age from 1997 to 2008 were significantly less influenced by racial attitudes than the party identifications of both their older counterparts and prior youth cohorts (Sears and Tesler 2009).[10] Kinder and Drake (2009) similarly argue that the increased focus on terrorism and national security after 9/11 reduced the impact of white racial prejudice on public opinion. And Hajnal and Lee (2011, 104) show that "in the last few decades—at least until the successful candidacy of Barack Obama—African Americans have been slowly but surely moving away from an exclusive relationship with the Democratic Party" (see also Luks and Elms 2005).

The main contention of this book, however, is that Barack Obama's presidential candidacy and victory helped breathe new life into this potentially flagging association in the American public's mind between the Democratic Party and African Americans. If, as suspected, a black president from the Democratic Party once again situated race at the forefront of the party's image, then the upshot should have been a renewed organization of mass politics around racial attitudes and race. Or so the book's argument on the spillover of racialization goes.

Racial and Ethnocentric Attitudes in the 2008 Election

Just because Barack Obama is African American, though, did not guarantee that race was an especially important determinant of how the public assessed either his presidential candidacies or his job performance as president. To be sure, pre-Obama research showed that racial attitudes were often strong determinants of white Americans' candidate preferences in biracial elections (Sears and Kinder 1971; Vanneman and Pettigrew 1972; Kinder and Sears 1981; Citrin, Green, and Sears 1990; Finkel, Guterbock, and Borg 1991; Reeves 1997; Sears, Citrin, and Kosterman 1987; Hajnal 2007). Yet, as discussed more in chapter 3, racial attitudes are not always implicated in mass opinion about black candidates for elected office (Citrin, Green, and Sears 1990; Hajnal 2007). Moreover, Americans' vote choices in presidential elections are consistently shaped by a number of different variables, most notably party identification and retrospective evaluations of the job performance of the incumbent administration (Campbell et al. 1960; Sears et al. 1980; Fiorina 1981; Kinder and Kiewiet 1981; Miller and Shanks 1996; Bartels 2000; Lewis-Beck et al. 2009; Vavreck 2009; Lenz 2012; Sides and Vavreck 2013). The profound effects of these factors on presidential elections could have overwhelmed all other considerations, leaving racial attitudes as only a minor cause of Americans' 2008 vote preferences. The same partisan attachments that have such a dominant impact on Americans' presidential vote preferences were also significantly shaped by racial attitudes and race in the pre-Obama era. There may not have been any room left, then, for racial attitudes to influence 2008 voting behavior more powerfully than they affected pre-Obama presidential contests. And, of course, many commentators viewed Barack Obama's electoral success as a sign that race did not matter in his presidential victory (Tesler and Sears 2010). So, it remained to be seen whether racial attitudes had an unusually strong impact on 2008 voting behavior.

It did not take very long, however, to see that racial attitudes had an extraordinarily large effect on Americans' 2008 vote choices. Several social science studies showed that racial attitudes were deeply implicated in mass assessments of Barack Obama throughout the election year. In fact, racial attitudes were an especially powerful predictor of white Americans' Obama evaluations even before he announced his intention to run for president (Kinder and Dale-Riddle 2012).[11] With Hillary Clinton and Barack Obama having almost identical issue positions, racial attitudes were probably the most important determinant of Americans' vote choices in the 2008 Democratic presidential primaries (Tesler and Sears 2010; Kinder and Dale-Riddle 2012). Several different racial attitudes, which included negative stereotypes, opposition to interracial marriage, favorability ratings of blacks, and racial resentment—an attitude that emphasizes blacks' lack of commitment to traditional American values—all had larger impacts on voter preferences in the 2008 Democratic presidential primaries than did Americans' policy positions and nonracial ideologies (Tesler and Sears 2010; Kinder and Dale-Riddle 2012; Jackman and Vavreck 2010; Tesler 2013b).

Many studies also showed that racial attitudes had a sizable impact on Americans' 2008 general election vote choices (Pasek et al. 2009; Windett, Banda, and Carsey 2012; Sniderman and Stiglitz 2008; Popkin and Rivers 2008; Sides and Vavreck 2013). More important, racial resentment, antiblack stereotypes, and old-fashioned racist opposition to intimate interracial relationships all had significantly stronger effects on 2008 voter preferences than they did on pre-Obama presidential contests (Tesler and Sears 2010; Weisberg and Devine 2010; Piston 2010; Kinder and Dale-Riddle 2012; Jackman and Vavreck 2012; Tesler 2013b; see also results discussed in chap. 3). These same racial attitudes were also much stronger determinants of individuals' 2008 vote preferences than they would have been had John McCain faced a white Democrat like Hillary Clinton or John Edwards instead of Barack Obama (Tesler and Sears 2010; Jackman and Vavreck 2012; Kinder and Ryan 2012; Tesler 2013b).

Consistent with those individual-level analyses of survey data, measures of racial prejudice at the level of state and media market also predicted 2008 aggregate election returns more powerfully than prior presidential election results did (Highton 2011; Stephens-Davidowitz 2013). In perhaps the most innovative study of race and the 2008 election, Stephens-Davidowitz (2013) showed that media markets with the most racist Google searches were especially likely to vote for Hillary Clinton over Barack Obama in the 2008 primaries and to have preferred John Kerry's 2004 Democratic candidacy to Barack Obama's 2008 presidential bid.

These unusually large effects of racial attitudes on Americans' 2008 vote preferences led us and others to conclude that Barack Obama's omnipresent position as a historic racial figure, and his *embodiment of race* as the first African American president, made racial attitudes a chronically accessible consideration in mass assessments of his candidacy that were difficult to deactivate (Tesler and Sears 2010; Kinder and Dale-Riddle 2012).

Attitudes about African Americans were not the only out-group sentiments activated by Barack Obama's rise to prominence, though. Impressions of Muslims were also more important determinants of 2008 voter preferences, even after controlling for racial resentment, than they had been during George W. Bush's presidency (Tesler and Sears 2010, chap. 7). Those results make sense in light of Obama's ostensibly "foreign" background and research showing that anti-Muslim attitudes are rooted in antagonism toward "a band of others" (e.g., cultural out-groups) that falls outside the mainstream of American society (Kalkan, Layman, and Uslaner 2009). Kam and Kinder (2012) provided further support for the "Obama as other" explanation by showing how the unusually strong influence of anti-Muslim attitudes on opposition to Barack Obama's 2008 presidential candidacy mediated (e.g., transmitted) the broader effects of ethnocentrism—a general tendency to partition the world into ingroups and out-groups, which these authors show was activated by Barack Obama's 2008 candidacy in part because of mistaken beliefs about his religious affiliation.

It is important to note that the outsized effects of racial and ethnocentric attitudes on voter preferences throughout the 2008 election year oftentimes cut both ways. That is, Barack Obama performed particularly poorly among racial conservatives but garnered more votes from African Americans and white racial liberals than a similarly situated white Democratic candidate like Hillary Clinton would have (Tesler and Sears 2010; Kinder and Dale-Riddle 2012). We described this phenomenon as *the two sides of racialization* because prior research primarily focused on racially resentful opposition to black candidates and racial policies (Tesler and Sears 2010). Yet, with more Americans falling on the conservative side of the racial attitude spectrum (see discussion below), most studies concluded that Obama's race cost him votes in the 2008 election. These "race penalty" estimates suggested that Barack Obama would have performed anywhere from one to seven percentage points better had he been white (Pasek et al. 2009; Lewis-Beck, Tien, and Nadeau 2010; Stephens-Davidowitz 2013; Jackman and Vavreck 2012; Sides and Vavreck 2013; Kinder and Dale-Riddle 2012; though see Kenski, Hardy, and Jamieson 2010). While it is difficult to determine just how much Obama's race may have cost him at the voting booth, the most important point for our purposes is that virtually all the evidence from the 2008 election shows that Barack Obama's candidacy *polarized* presidential vote choice by racial attitudes in 2008 more powerfully than any other presidential election on record.

That polarization of Americans' 2008 presidential vote choices by racial attitudes raises some important questions about mass politics during Barack Obama's presidency. Might these unusually large effects of racial attitudes on Americans' vote choices, for example, spill over into other political evaluations associated with Barack Obama's presidency? Or are Americans able to separate Obama's race from their assessments of his party and his policies? The spillover of racialization hypothesis, as outlined in the following chapter, suggests that a wide swath of Americans' political evaluations should have indeed become more divided by and over race in the Age of Obama than they were beforehand.

Racial Attitudes in the Age of Obama

In order to empirically test the spillover of racialization hypothesis, we must first conceptualize and measure racial attitudes. This task is much easier said than done. In fact, the conceptualization and measurement of modern racial prejudice is one of the most contentious issues in public opinion research (for a review, see Sears, Sidanius, and Bobo 2000). Fortunately, there is extensive literature on the nature of racial prejudice in contemporary American society to help guide our efforts.

Modern versus Old-Fashioned Racism

At the midpoint of the twentieth century, a substantial majority of white Americans still openly subscribed to the ideology of white supremacy. That ideology, which researchers have variously described as old-fashioned racism (OFR), Jim Crow racism, redneck racism, and biological racism, embodied three main elements (Bobo and Kluegel 1997; McConahay, Hardee, and Batts 1981; McConahay and Hough 1976; McConahay 1986; Kinder 2013): (1) desire for social distance between the black and white races, (2) beliefs in the biological inferiority of blacks, and (3) support for public policies ensuring racial segregation and formalized discrimination. Gunnar Myrdal's pivotal book, *An American Dilemma* (1944), emphasized the roots of such old-fashioned racism in the lethal combination of irrational racial prejudice and whites' self-interest in maintaining their own superior privileges. That is, OFR provided justification for the pervasive racial inequality in American Society (see also Kinder 2013; Fredrickson 1971).

A number of factors—including World War II, the new scientific consensus of *biological equality* between the races, Supreme Court cases and federal legislation dismantling Jim Crow segregation, the civil rights movement, the Cold War, and rising education levels—all helped transform white Americans' racial attitudes during the second half of the twentieth century (Chong 1991; Zaller 1992; Page and Shapiro 1992; Schuman et al. 1997; Dudziak 2011; Lee 2002). Old-fashioned racism dramatically declined during that period, accompanied by a growing acceptance of racial equality in principle. By the 1990s, in fact, white Americans' beliefs in black biological inferiority and support for de jure segregation had all but vanished from their survey reports (Schuman et al. 1997)[12]

Although the passage of civil rights legislation in the mid-1960s gradually eliminated formal segregation and discrimination, glaring racial inequality in such areas as income, education, employment, health, housing, and especially wealth remained. So, too, did substantial white opposition to government action aimed at remedying the profound socioeconomic differences between blacks and whites. As a result, new social science theories arose in the post–civil rights era to explain the decline in OFR on the one hand and continued opposition to government action to produce racial equality on the other. These "new racism" theories, which are variously described as symbolic racism (Kinder and Sears 1981; Sears 1988), modern racism (McConahay 1986), cultural racism (Kinder 2013), laissez-faire racism (Bobo et al. 1997), and this book's preferred term, "racial resentment" (Kinder and Sanders 1996), suggest that a new form of racial animus best explains the influence of antiblack sentiments in contemporary American politics.[13]

Unlike OFR, modern racism does not embrace notions of black biological and social inferiority. Instead, the new prejudice is characterized by "a moral feeling that blacks violate such traditional American values as individualism and self-reliance, the work ethic, obedience, and discipline" (Kinder and Sears 1981, 416). That is, racially resentful whites cite deficiencies in black culture, rather than innate inferiority, to explain the ongoing racial inequality in America. Or as Donald Kinder (2013, 820) described that belief system: "Racial inferiority is cultural not biological, seen in the customs and folkways of black life: idleness, violence, drug abuse, teenage mothers—the whole 'tangle of pathology' that many whites see as characteristics of life in black neighborhoods." Like OFR, then, racial resentment is used to justify the pervasive racial inequities in American society.

These racially resentful sentiments remain common in American political discourse, too. Bill O'Reilly, for instance, said in the 2014 Fox News broadcast "The Truth about White Privilege": "American children must learn not only academics but also civil behavior, right from wrong, as well as how to speak properly and how to act respectfully in public. If African-American children do not learn those things, they will likely fail as adults. They will be poor. They will be angry, and they often will be looking to blame someone else."[14] Republican vice presidential nominee Paul Ryan struck a similar cord in stating: "We have got this tailspin of culture, in our inner cities in particular, of men not working and just generations of men not even thinking about working or learning the value and the culture of work, and so there is a real culture problem here that has to be dealt with."[15] We will also see in the following sections that a majority of white Americans subscribed to symbolic racism's four specific themes: (1) African Americans no longer face much discrimination, (2) their disadvantage mainly reflects their poor work ethic, (3) they are demanding too much too fast, and (4) they have gotten more than they deserve (Henry and Sears 2002; Sears and Henry 2005).

Measuring Racial Resentment

A number of survey items over the years have been used to measure symbolic racism and racial resentment. Kinder and Sanders (1996), however, effectively standardized the measurement of modern, symbolic, and/or cultural racism with their racial-resentment scale. Racial resentment taps into the aforementioned components of the symbolic racism belief system with a battery of four questions asked in American National Election Studies (ANES) surveys from 1986 to 2012. The questions are presented as assertions, and respondents were asked to indicate whether they agreed or disagreed with the statement, and how strongly they did so. The assertions are as follows:

> Irish, Italian, Jewish and many other minorities overcame prejudice and worked their way up. Blacks should do the same without any special favors.

> Generations of slavery and discrimination have created conditions that make it difficult for blacks to work their way out of the lower class.

> Over the past few years, blacks have gotten less than they deserve.

> It's really a matter of some people not trying hard enough; if blacks would only try harder they could be just as well off as whites.

The racial-resentment scale is constructed from these statements by coding the five potential responses to each assertion from 0 to 1 in intervals of .25, with 0 being the most racially liberal response and 1 being the most racially conservative. Answers are then summed and divided by the number of items to provide an easily interpretable 0 to 1 scale.[16]

Kinder and Sanders (1996) designed the scale to distinguish between racially sympathetic Americans who see racial inequality as the result of structural causes like discrimination and racially resentful Americans who point the finger at African Americans' cultural deficiencies for their lower socioeconomic status. By this standard, a score of .50 marks the neutral point. So individuals scoring below .50 are thought to be more racially sympathetic (i.e., racial liberals), and individuals with scores above that rather arbitrary midpoint are classified as more racially resentful (i.e., racial conservatives).[17] According to these items, at least, the United States is a racially conservative country. The average racial-resentment score for whites is consistently around .65 on this 0 to 1 measure (see figs. 1.1 and 1.2).

Racial Stereotypes and Antiblack Affect

Racial resentment is the book's focal variable for explaining the changing impact of racial attitudes on mass politics during Barack Obama's presidency. Yet, because there has been considerable debate about how to best measure racial prejudice in contemporary America, I use multiple measures of racial attitudes to test the book's spillover of racialization hypothesis. The first of these measures—racial stereotypes—typically asks respondents to rate how hardworking and intelligent racial and ethnic groups are on seven-point scales, ranging from 1 (lazy/unintelligent) to 7 (hardworking/intelligent). Based on these measures, racial stereotyping is subtle but consistent (Kinder 2013). A majority of whites consistently rate their own group as more hardworking and intelligent than African Americans. Yet, almost no whites say that their racial group is categorically better than blacks. In fact, on a 0–100 stereotype scale, where a score of 50 means rating blacks and whites equally and a score of 100 represents the most prejudiced response possible, the average white American consistently scores in the mid-50s (see figs. 1.1 and 1.3).

Aside from antiblack stereotypes, the book also uses antiblack affect to measure more blatant forms of prejudice toward African Americans. Antiblack affect taps into the affective or emotional component of prejudice (Kinder 2013), typically with thermometer scales that rate various racial and ethnic groups from very cold (0 degrees) to very warm (100 degrees). In addition to those thermometer ratings, I measure antiblack affect in the General Social Survey (GSS) with nine-point scales, whereby respondents rate how close they feel to whites and blacks. These measures of antiblack affect, like the stereotypes, show a subtle but consistent pro-white bias in American society. The average antiblack affect score is typically in the mid- to high 50s on a 0-to-100 antiblack affect scale, ranging from most problack to most prowhite (see figs. 1.1 and 1.4).

Implicit Measures of Racial Prejudice

Attitudes such as old-fashioned racism, racial resentment, antiblack affect, and antiblack stereotypes are all explicit measures of racial prejudice. That is, they rely on self-reported feelings toward African Americans. By contrast, implicit measures of racial prejudice assess bias outside of our conscious awareness. These measures are quite common in social psychology research, with methods like the Implicit Association Test and the Affect Misattribution Procedure validated in dozens of academic studies (e.g., Dovidio et al. 1997; Dovidio, Kwakami, and Gaertner 2002; Fazio et al. 1995; Greenwald and Banaji 1995; Payne et al. 2005; Nosek et al. 2007). The implicit tests work by assessing how quickly (in milliseconds) respondents pair positive and negative words with black and white images. Measuring racial attitudes this way uncovers substantially more bias than our aforementioned explicit racial attitudes. More than 80 percent of whites respond faster to black-unpleasant and white-pleasant pairings than vice versa (Iyengar et al. 2009). In fact, the results from this voluminous body of research on subconscious racial attitudes are quite clear: Implicit bias against African Americans is pervasive in American society.

The impact of that implicit racial bias on white Americans' political preferences is much less conclusive, though. There is some evidence that implicit racial attitudes affected white Americans' vote choices in the 2008 election, even after controlling for explicit measures like racial resentment (Greenwald et al. 2009; Pasek et al. 2009; Payne et al. 2010). However, the best available data from three nationally representative surveys conducted during the 2008 campaign suggest that implicit racial bias had little impact on white opposition to President Obama (Kalmoe and Piston 2013; Ditonto, Lau, and Sears 2013; Kinder and Ryan 2012). Moreover, those same surveys showed that implicit racial bias failed to predict public opinion about racialized policies such as affirmative action and welfare, which have long been heavily influenced by explicit racial atti-

tudes (Kinder and Ryan 2012; Kalmoe and Piston 2013). Given those findings, the analyses that follow use only explicit measures of racial attitudes
to test the spillover of racialization hypothesis.

The Different Distributions and Political Effects of Various Racial Attitudes

Racial resentment is the focal construct for explaining the role of racial
attitudes in contemporary American politics (see Hutchings and Valentino 2004 for a review). Many studies have shown that racial resentment
is strongly associated with white Americans' opposition to race-targeted
policies. Its explanatory power over such race-related opinions typically
outweighs that of other important political attitudes like ideology, party
identification, and attitudes toward the size of the federal government,
as well as that of older and more traditional racial attitudes, such as old-
fashioned racism, negative stereotypes, and antiblack affect (Bobo 2000;
Kinder and Sanders 1996; Sears et al. 1997; Sidanius et al. 1999; see Sears
and Henry 2005 for a review). Racial resentment also significantly predicts white Americans' support for racially conservative white candidates
(Howell 1994; Kinder and Sanders 1996; Kinder and Sears 1981; Mendelberg 2001; Sears et al. 1997). And, as discussed above, racial resentment's
impact on the 2008 election was greater than in any other presidential
election on record (Tesler and Sears 2010; Kinder and Dale-Riddle 2012;
Jackman and Vavreck 2012; Weisberg and Devine 2010).

Some political scientists, however, have argued that racial resentment
confounds antiblack animus with ordinary political conservatism, so that
its effects may only reflect relatively unprejudiced aversion to liberal big
government (Hurwitz and Peffley 1998; Sniderman, Crosby, and Howell
2000; Sniderman and Tetlock 1986a, 1986b). These scholars, instead, prefer to measure prejudice with more blatant measures like antiblack affect
and negative racial stereotypes. While racial resentment is significantly
correlated with these more overt measures of prejudice ($r \approx .30–.40$),
antiblack affect and negative racial stereotypes are less confounded with
political ideology and have weaker impacts on Americans' political preferences than racial resentment. For that reason, the book also uses these
direct measures of racial prejudice in several analyses. The more blatant
nature of racial stereotypes and antiblack affect, however, is also a major
weakness. Stereotypes and thermometer ratings are especially susceptible

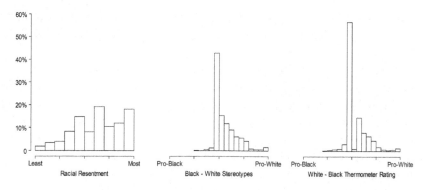

FIGURE I.I. Distribution of White Americans' Racial Attitudes
Source: 2012 American National Election Studies (ANES).

to misreporting due to social desirability pressures to rate all racial groups equally (Huddy and Feldman 2009; Sears and Savalei 2009; Iyengar et al. 2009).

Figure I.I suggests another, yet unmentioned reason the political effects of racial resentment tend to be greater than these more blatant racial attitude measures. That is, the racial resentment battery does a much better job of tapping into racial sympathy than either racial stereotypes or antiblack affect do. The display, for instance, shows that almost no whites rate blacks more favorably than their own racial group on the thermometers or the stereotypes. Rather, a large cluster of respondents evaluates both whites and blacks equally. There, unfortunately, is no way, then, to know who in that undifferentiated stack is merely unprejudiced and who is actually racially sympathetic. Kinder and Sanders's scale, in contrast, was designed to identify racially sympathetic whites who think blacks continue to face structural impediments to success in society. Not surprisingly, then, many more whites show up on the racially liberal side of that scale's distribution (approximately 20 percent) than they do on the stereotype and thermometer measures. Moreover, figure I.I shows that the racial-resentment scale encompasses the full spectrum of attitudes, ranging from the most racially sympathetic to the most racially resentful, whereas antiblack affect and negative racial stereotypes basically cover only half of the length from nonprejudiced to most prejudiced. The antiblack affect and racial stereotype measures' inabilities to tap into racial sympathy inevitably lead to underestimation of the political effects of racial attitudes, especially the political effects of racial attitudes in an

Obama era when racial liberals reacted particularly positively toward the
first black president (Sniderman and Stiglitz 2008; Tesler and Sears 2010;
Kinder and Dale-Riddle 2012).

Like past academic disputes, the inferences made from the results
in the book about how strongly racial attitudes influenced mass politics in the Age of Obama depend fundamentally on how we measure
attitudes toward African Americans. More important, though, all our
measurements—whether racial resentment, antiblack stereotypes, antiblack affect, or even old-fashioned racist desires for intimate social distance between the races—indicate that President Obama's rise to prominence helped usher in a most-racial political era.

An Obama Effect on White Racial Attitudes?

Along with the high hopes that an Obama presidency would improve race
relations—hopes documented in figure I.1 of the introduction—many
were optimistic that Barack Obama would also reduce racial prejudice.
President Obama's counterstereotypical behavior, the argument goes,
might have forced white Americans to reassess their own biases. Yet while
the 2008 presidential campaign may have temporarily reduced racial prejudice by a small amount (Goldman 2012; Goldman and Mutz 2014), most
of the evidence shows that Barack Obama's rise to prominence had a
very minimal net impact on white racial prejudice (Tesler and Sears 2010;
Hutchings 2009; Schmidt and Nosek 2010; Kinder and Dale-Riddle 2012;
Kinder 2013; Tesler 2013a; Sides and Vavreck 2013; Kinder and Chudy
2014; DeSante and Watts Smith 2014; but see Pasek et al. 2014 for an
analysis suggesting that racial resentment has increased during Obama's
presidency).

The results in figures 1.2–1.4 are also consistent with those findings.
The left panels of the three figures show white Americans' average racial
resentment, antiblack affect, and antiblack stereotype scores (0–100
scale) in repeated cross-sectional surveys—surveys of different individuals over time—carried out by the ANES and the GSS from 1992 to
2012. The right panels of the displays similarly show white Americans'
average placement on these attitudes in panel surveys—surveys that reinterviewed the exact same respondents at two or more times—conducted
for the ANES, the GSS, and the Cooperative Campaign Analysis Project
(CCAP) before and after Barack Obama became president. These figures,

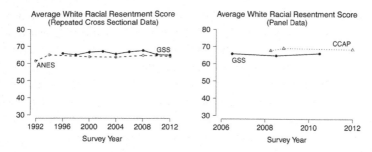

FIGURE I.2. White Americans' Average Racial Resentment Scores, 1992–2012
Source: General Social Survey (GSS) cumulative file; American National election Studies (ANES) cumulative file; 2012 ANES; 2006-2008-2010 GSS panel; 2008–12 Cooperative Campaign Analysis Project (CCAP) reinterviews.

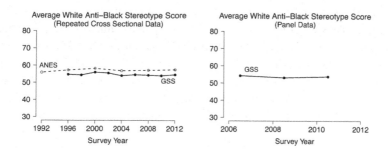

FIGURE I.3. White Americans' Average Antiblack Stereotype Scores, 1992–2012
Source: General Social Survey (GSS) cumulative file; American National Election Studies (ANES) cumulative file; 2012 ANES; 2006-2008-2010 GSS panel.

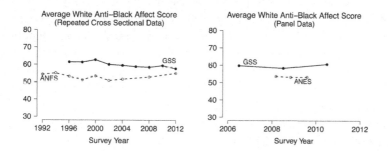

FIGURE I.4. White Americans' Average Antiblack Affect Scores, 1992–2012
Source: General Social Survey (GSS) cumulative file; American National Election Studies (ANES) cumulative file; 2012 ANES; 2006-2008-2010 GSS panel; 2008-2009 ANES.

as can be seen, uncovered no significant pre- to post-Obama changes in racial prejudice across the three different racial attitude measures and five different datasets. Or more simply put, there was no Obama effect—positive or negative—on white racial attitudes.[18]

Related research helps explain Barack Obama's minimal effects on racial attitudes by pointing to the large pre-Obama literature showing that Americans' racial attitudes are typically acquired early on in the life span and are difficult to change thereafter (Tesler and Sears 2010; Tesler 2013a; Kinder 2013; Kinder and Chudy 2014). Indeed, racial resentment is one of Americans' most stable sociopolitical attitudes (Kinder and Sanders 1996; Henry and Sears 2009; Tesler and Sears 2010). Moreover, prejudiced whites have a long history of setting aside counterstereotypical individuals like Barack Obama as atypical exceptions that prove the rule rather than as exemplars of their races (Kinder and Chudy 2014; Tesler 2013a).[19] As such, racial attitudes did not change much during Barack Obama's presidency. This strong aggregate and individual-level stability of white racial prejudice also makes us more confident that the growing racialization of mass politics documented throughout the book was not caused by changes in the underlying distribution of Americans' racial attitudes, such as greater racial liberalism or greater racial conservatism.

* * *

While Barack Obama did not noticeably reduce white racial prejudice, we would expect his rise to prominence to have increased the influence of racial attitudes on mass politics. For, as Kinder and Chudy (2014, 7–8) put it, "Obama may be an exceptional representative of black America, but he remains a black American nevertheless, and his racial identity in national life should prove sufficient to increase the importance of prejudice in shaping public opinion." This chapter has documented Barack Obama's potential to increase the importance of racial attitudes in shaping presidential vote choices. Those findings from the 2008 election certainly raised the specter of a most-racial political era during the eight years of his presidency. The next chapter formalizes that expectation, explaining how, when, and why this spillover of racialization from Barack Obama into mass politics should have taken place.

CHAPTER TWO

The Spillover of Racialization Hypothesis

The cartoon in today's New York Post is troubling at best given the historic racist attacks on African-Americans as being synonymous with monkeys. One has to question whether the cartoonist is making a less than casual reference to this when in the cartoon they have police saying after shooting a chimpanzee that "Now they will have to find someone else to write the stimulus bill." Being that the stimulus bill has been the first legislative victory of President Barack Obama (the first African American president) and has become synonymous with him, it is not a reach to wonder are they inferring that a monkey wrote the last bill. — Reverend Al Sharpton, February 2009[1]

On February 16, 2009, the police were called to the home of a Connecticut woman whose pet chimpanzee, Travis, viciously mauled her friend. The police shot and killed the chimp after Travis also tried to attack an officer. The story made national headlines, and shortly thereafter it led to a storm of racial controversy when the *New York Post* depicted the event in a cartoon that some described as racist.[2] In it, two police officers held smoking guns as they looked over the dead chimpanzee, with one cop saying to the other, "They'll have to find someone else to write the next stimulus bill."

The American Recovery and Reinvestment Act (aka, "the stimulus") had been signed into law just a few days earlier with strong backing from the Obama administration. Many, therefore, assumed that the cartoon was prejudicially portraying President Obama (the presumed author of the stimulus) as a monkey. As the epigraph that introduced this chapter indicated, Reverend Al Sharpton immediately put out a written statement that condemned the cartoonist for implying a monkey wrote the stimulus legislation that had become "synonymous" with the first black president.

The *New York Post* denied any racial intent, with the paper's editor and chief saying, "The cartoon is a clear parody of a current news event, to wit the shooting of a violent chimpanzee in Connecticut. It broadly mocks Washington's efforts to revive the economy."[3] Some of the *Post*'s employees, however, thought that the charges of racial bias were valid,[4] and the paper later apologized "to those who were offended."[5]

Regardless of the cartoonist's intent, this incident that occurred less than one month into Barack Obama's presidency instructively illustrated two points that were harbingers of things to come. First, it was hard to separate Barack Obama's legislative accomplishments from the president himself.[6] Or, as Rev. Sharpton stated, the stimulus became "synonymous" with President Obama. Second, it was difficult to disassociate Barack Obama—and his policies by extension—from race. For, as the cartoon controversy demonstrated, the stimulus package was linked to Obama's race in ways that no other prior president's policies would have been.[7] Consequently, mass politics may have become more heavily influenced by racial considerations during Barack Obama's presidency than they had been prior to his ascendancy.

The Spillover of Racialization into Mass Politics

Much more importantly, the extant social science literature also suggests that mass politics may have become more racialized because of Barack Obama's presidency. In fact, an expansive body of research focuses on how racial attitudes are activated in white Americans' political opinions. This process of *racialization*, whereby racial attitudes and race are brought to bear on political preferences, is rather straightforward for race-targeted policies like affirmative action and federal aid to minorities. Those issues are thought to readily evoke racial predispositions because there is a natural associative link between policy substance and feelings toward the groups who benefit from them (Sears 1993). Most public policies lack such clear-cut racial content, though. How, then, have racial attitudes been implicated in a wide variety of nonracial policy preferences— issues as diverse as welfare, social security, crime, taxes, gun control, and the Iraq War (Gilens 1999; Winter 2008; Kinder and Kam 2009; Gilliam and Iyengar 2000; Hurwitz and Peffley 1997, 2005; Sears and Citrin 1985; Filindra and Kaplan 2014; White 2007)?

Prior research suggests that this racialization of issues with no manifest racial content results from mass communications that heighten the association—either consciously or unconsciously (Winter 2008, 147–51)—between African Americans and political evaluations. Over-time observational studies, for example, show that the emergence of media coverage linking welfare benefits with "undeserving blacks" helped white Americans bring their racial antagonisms to bear on opposition to this policy (Gilens 1999; Kellstedt 2003; Winter 2008). Likewise, Nicholas Winter (2008) convincingly argues that media coverage connecting social security both to white recipients and to such symbolically white attributes as hard work and just rewards also made this nonracial policy about race.

Several "racial-priming" experiments[8]—experiments designed to activate racial attitudes in public opinion—provide even stronger evidence that political messages can connect racial groups to political evaluations. These studies demonstrate that race cues as subtle as coded words (i.e., "inner city" of "welfare"), black imagery, and especially some combination of the two can make racial attitudes a more central determinant of several different political preferences (Mendelberg 2001; Valentino, Hutchings, and White 2002; Hurwitz and Peffley 2005; White 2007; Winter 2008; Kinder and Kam 2009; DeSante 2013; Filindra and Kaplan 2014). Or, as Hurwitz and Peffley (2005, 109) conclude, "When messages are framed in such a way to reinforce the relationship between a particular policy and a particular group, it becomes far more likely that individuals will evaluate the policy on the basis of their evaluations of the group."[9] Those subtle race cues are thought to be especially effective in activating racial attitudes because they connect African Americans to political evaluations without audience members consciously knowing the message violates strong societal norms of racial equality (Mendelberg 2001; Valentino, Hutchings, and White 2002; Hurwitz and Peffley 2005; Winter 2008; though see Huber and Lapinsky 2006; Valentino et al. 2013; and new results in chap. 4).

Along with such established avenues, cues provided by the background characteristics of elite sources may also foster connections between governmental policies and social groups. In fact, a series of findings indicate that prominent position takers' races, religions, and genders, can all make group-specific attitudes more important in mass opinion formation. These results include the following: (1) White evangelicals' unwavering support for the Iraq War because of George W. Bush's strong identity as a born-again Christian (Jacobson 2007, 161); (2) gender attitudes influencing health care opinions in 1994 in part because of the policy's strong association with a gendered figure in Hillary Clinton (Winter 2008, 130–31); (3) experiments showing that Americans' willingness to embrace elites' views partly depends on whether the positions are attributed to black or white sources (Kuklinski and Hurley 1994; Domke n.d.; Peffley and Hurwitz 2010, 164–65); (4) attitudes about Catholics becoming stronger predictors of party identification in 1960 than they were before John F. Kennedy's presidential candidacy heightened the association between Catholicism and the Democratic Party (see fig. 9.2 in chap. 9); (5) and, finally, in what could rightfully be called the original spillover of racialization finding, Sears, Citrin, and Kosterman (1987) showed that the increased association between the Democratic Party and African Americans, which resulted from Jesse Jackson's 1984 presidential campaign, immediately accelerated the polarization of Southern partisanship by both racial attitudes and race.

If, as these studies suggest, the salient social background characteristics of elite sources have the potential to activate considerations in the realms of race, religion, and gender, then President Obama's most visible political positions should have been especially ripe for racialization. For, as Kinder and Dale-Riddle (2012) asserted about the 2008 campaign, "Whatever Obama said about society and government and about problems and policies, at the end of the day, every time American voters caught a glimpse of him, he *was* black." Given the importance of elites' background characteristics in the studies referenced above, the salience of Obama's race in public perceptions of him should also spill over into public opinion about his visible political positions.

More specifically, cues that connect racialized public figures to specific issues and political evaluations are expected to activate racial considerations in mass opinion much the way that code words and other subtle race cues have linked African Americans with political evaluations in prior research. This hypothesis, which I call the *spillover of racialization*, therefore suggests that Barack Obama's strong connection to a number of political evaluations should have led to a growing influence of both racial attitudes and race on mass politics during his presidency. In other words, the president's position as the center of the political universe strongly connected him to several different political evaluations (e.g., mass assessments of public figures, public policy preferences, vote choices for congressional candidates, party identification), many of which should have become more racialized because of their newfound association with Barack Obama.

The Conditions Ripe for Racialization

We should not expect every political position that Barack Obama staked out during his presidency to have polarized public opinion by racial attitudes and race, though. Nor would we expect every American's political views to have been influenced the same way by Barack Obama's position as the first black president. Rather, certain political evaluations and certain people were riper candidates than others for Obama-era racialization. This section, therefore, outlines the theoretical expectations for when Barack Obama's positions should have been expected to polarize public opinion by racial considerations; that is, the conditions ripe for racialization.

Barack Obama Takes a Visible Position That Is Reinforced over Time

The spillover of racialization's most straightforward necessary condition is that Barack Obama had to be easily connected, either in support or in opposition, to a political evaluation. Yet, while Barack Obama's connection to political evaluations may have been necessary for the spillover of racialization to take place, it was far from sufficient. Even issues that President Obama took clear positions on were unlikely to produce large racial spillover effects unless those positions were subjected to intense media scrutiny. Barack Obama, for instance, made clear statements in support of the legal right to an abortion. Yet, because President Obama's position on women's right to choose did not garner nearly the same media attention that his position on other issues (e.g., health care, the stimulus, taxes, and gun control) received, racial attitudes were not likely to be a more important factor in public opinion about abortion rights during his presidency.[10] For this same reason, survey experiments that ensured every respondent received the intended message about Barack Obama's positions were especially likely to produce significant racial spillover effects.[11]

The persistence of racial spillover effects should similarly depend on whether Barack Obama's position was reinforced throughout his presidency. This assertion builds on prior racialization research, which showed that mass communications connecting African Americans to specific political evaluations can have anywhere from fleeting to long-lasting effects on public opinion, depending on whether those links were persistently reinforced over time. Racial priming effects from such subtle race appeals as racialized code words and/or black imagery are thought to be short lived, losing much of their impact when communications make new considerations salient (Kinder and Sanders 1996). Mass communications can forge lasting relationships between racial attitudes and political opinions, however, by persistently framing issues in accordance with racialized attributes (e.g., the aforementioned welfare and social security studies conducted by Gilens [1999] and Winter [2008]). We should therefore expect the spillover of racialization to have more lasting effects when the mass media persistently highlighted Obama's positions (i.e., Obamacare) than it had for issues where Obama's salient stances quickly faded from the national headlines (e.g., same-sex marriage)—a proposition directly tested in chapter 5.

African Americans Were the Perceived Beneficiary of President Obama's Position

Another reason the spillover of racialization into health care was expected to have lasted longer than the spillover of racialization into same-sex marriage opinions is that Americans thought blacks benefited more than whites from Barack Obama's health care proposals. Indeed, virtually none of our respondents (2 percent) in a November 2009 original survey thought that whites would benefit more than blacks from President Obama's proposed health care reform policies.[12] Likewise, a 2010 Associated Press/Stanford poll found that 56 percent of respondents thought that the "health care law passed by Congress in March (2010) will probably cause most black Americans to get better health care than they get today," compared to just 45 percent who said the same thing about whites.[13] Since prior research suggests that mass communications activate racial attitudes in public opinion by reinforcing the relationship between particular policies and the racial groups who are affected by them, the spillover of racialization should be particularly pronounced when blacks are perceived as benefiting more than whites from Barack Obama's policies.

To be sure, this does not imply that African Americans had to be the perceived beneficiaries of President Obama's positions for the spillover of racialization to have taken place—a proposition directly tested in chapter 4. Americans' political opinions are often influenced by subconscious factors (Lodge and Taber 2013; Price and Tewksbury 1997), and Mendelberg (2001, 122) argues that implicit messages activate racial predispositions outside our conscious awareness. So, it is certainly possible and likely probable that the mere connection between Barack Obama and a political evaluation—even one where African Americans were not the perceived beneficiaries—was enough to make racial attitudes a more accessible determinant of Americans' political evaluations. Nevertheless, we would expect Obama's race to have had an especially strong impact when blacks were the perceived beneficiaries of his positions. For, as Winter (2008, 149) suggests, racial cues work best at activating racial attitudes when issues are structured to fit relevant racial considerations (e.g., a black president giving health insurance to African Americans).

The Pre-Obama Effects of Racial Attitudes Are Low, Especially Relative to Party and Ideology

Previous studies of elite cues and mass cue taking convincingly show that the signals provided to ordinary Americans by a president's issue positions often activate partisan attitudes in public opinion (e.g., Zaller 1992; Berinsky 2009; Levendusky 2009). Indeed, public opinion about foreign policy, stem cell research, social security privatization, health care reform, top-bracket tax increases, climate change, and extending the children's health insurance program are among the many issues that became more polarized by party and/or ideology after Democratic and Republican elites took dissimilar positions (Zaller 1992, 1994; Berinsky 2007, 2009; Levendusky 2009; Lenz 2012; Kriner and Reeves 2014; Tesler 2014, 2015a; McCright and Dunlap 2011; Tesler and Zaller 2014). Simply put, presidents' issue positions often activate partisan and ideological considerations in mass opinion.

Barack Obama, however, was not just a typical Democratic president. He was an African American president whose 2008 election strongly evoked racial considerations. Thus, much the way that the cues provided by past presidents' policy positions polarized the electorate by party identification, President Obama's proposals may have further divided public opinion by racial attitudes and race. The key question, then, becomes when was Barack Obama more likely to activate racial considerations than partisan attachments in public opinion and vice versa?

Formally stated, the probability that Barack Obama's positions activated such considerations as partisanship, ideology, and racial attitudes in public opinion should depend on how strongly each of these factors was implicated in mass opinion before the president's position was highlighted. This suggestion builds off of prior experimental research, which showed that subtle racial cues were less likely to activate racial attitudes in public opinion about issues that were already highly racialized (Huber and Lapinski 2006; Winter 2008). We would not expect President Obama's support for immigration reform, then, to produce significant racial spill-over effects because racial and ethnocentric attitudes were already strong determinants of Americans' pre-Obama immigration opinions (Kinder and Sanders 1996; Kinder and Kam 2009). In analogous fashion, we would not expect Barack Obama—or any other president for that matter—to further activate partisan and ideological attitudes in mass opinion about issues that were highly polarized by party and ideology before their positions were subjected to intense media scrutiny.

With party identification shaping so many contemporary political preferences (Abramowitz 2010; Pew Research Center 2012b), the pre-Obama effects of racial attitudes on public opinion tended to be small relative to such factors as partisanship and ideology. Consequently, Barack Obama's visible positions should have typically increased the modest underlying effects of racial attitudes relative to the strong pre-Obama impact of nonracial considerations. There are a few issues, however, like immigration, gun control, and racial policy preferences that are more heavily influenced by racial and ethnocentric attitudes than by nonracial factors like partisanship and ideology (Kinder and Sanders 1996; Sears et al. 1997; Kinder and Kam 2009; Filindra and Kaplan 2014; see also new results in chap. 5). We might, therefore, expect President Obama's positions to have further increased the effects of partisanship and ideology relative to racial attitudes on those rare issues—a proposition that is directly tested in chapter 5.

Americans' Pre-Obama Opinions Were Not Yet Crystallized

Along with the baseline pre-Obama effects of partisanship and racial attitudes, the spillover of racialization's reach should also depend on whether citizens' particular opinions are crystallized or strongly held. Attitude crystallization, as noted by Sears (1975, 1983, 1993), generally refers to the following: (1) the stability of an attitude over time, (2) the constraint or consistency between an attitude and different but linked objects, and (3) the power or influence that attitude exerts over new evaluations. Petty and Krosnick (1995) similarly describe "strong attitudes" as those that persist over time, resist new information, impact information processing, and guide behavior.[14] By definition, then, weakly held attitudes should be more susceptible to the spillover of racialization than less malleable crystallized and/or strong attitudes.

According to this account, we would expect the spillover of racialization into Americans' partisan attachments to be more modest than other racial spillover effects, despite the fact that Barack Obama was the de facto head of the Democratic Party for eight years, since, as discussed more in chapter 7, party identification is typically considered to be the most crystallized of all political attitudes (Campbell et al. 1960; Converse 1964; Converse and Markus 1979; Green, Palmquist, and Schickler 2002). That crystallization of mass partisanship stands in stark contrast with Americans' more weakly held policy positions (Converse and Markus 1979). Most policy positions should therefore be more susceptible to the spillover of racialization than mass partisanship. Moreover, we would also expect larger racial spillover effects to occur among Americans who did not have particularly crystallized pre-Obama political preferences—an expectation directly tested and supported elsewhere (Tesler 2015a).

* * *

All told, then, we should not expect the spillover of racialization to extend into every Obama-era political opinion or every American's political evaluations. Nor would we expect all racial spillover effects to be as strong and as long lasting as others. Rather, the ripest candidates for strong and lasting racial spillover effects were as follows: (1) issues on which Barack Obama takes a visible position that is reinforced over time, (2) issues on which Barack Obama's position is perceived as benefiting blacks, (3) political evaluations in which the pre-Obama effects of racial attitudes were low relative to the impact of party and ideology, and (4) political evaluations that were not already crystallized prior to Obama's presidency.

Anger, the Spillover of Racialization, and Political Polarization

Even if every single one of Barack Obama's positions had produced strong racial spillover effects, though, this still would not imply that racial attitudes were the most important determinant of Obama-era political preferences. Racial attitudes are merely one of many reasons why Americans hold the political beliefs that they do. In fact, nonracial factors such as ideological aversion to big government, cultural issues, and social class were especially prominent fixtures in the pre-Obama partisan alignment (Kaufmann and Petrocik 1999; Petrocik 1987; Brewer and Stonecash 2007; Edsall 2006; Bartels 2008; McCarty, Poole, and Rosenthal 2006). Moreover, moral traditionalism, religiosity, foreign-policy hawkishness, authoritarianism, cultural conservatism, patriotism, and ideological self-placement were among the many attitudes that became more closely aligned with Americans' party identifications in the years leading to Barack Obama's election (Hetherington and Weiler 2009; Layman and Carsey 2002; Levendusky 2009; Layman 2001; Leege et al. 2002; Gelman 2010; Adams 1997; Abramowitz 2010; Putnam and Campbell 2010; Citrin and Sears 2014; Pew Research Center 2012b). Or more simply put, Americans' political preferences were divided over a number of different issues and attitudes both before and after Barack Obama became president.

Americans political preferences may have been divided over a whole host of factors in the pre-Obama era, but as Marc Hetherington and Jonathan D. Weiler (2009) perceptively pointed out in *Authoritarianism and Polarization in American Politics*, not all these attitudes are created equally. Instead, intense polarization between partisans is most likely to occur over "easy issues" that are understood on the gut level (Carmines and Stimson 1980; Hetherington and Weiler 2009). Race, of course, has long been the most visceral issue in American public life, generating passionate feelings on both sides of the polarizing racial divide. Hetherington and Weiler (2009, 18) noted this potential for racial issues to polarize the electorate, writing, "An easy issue—race—forged a new party system in the 1960s (and in the 1860s for that matter)." King and Smith (2011, 11) similarly suggested that the divide between the two parties over racial issues "has contributed to the heightened polarization that wrenches apart modern American politics." And, according to Abramowitz (2014), "The roots of polarization are in our changing society . . . above all the growing racial and ethnic diversity of the American population."

Consistent with those contentions about the divisive nature of race in American politics, recent research convincingly shows that racial attitudes are emotionally charged in ways that nonracial ideological predispositions are not. Most notably, Antoine Banks's 2014 book *Anger and Racial Politics* suggests that racial resentment toward African Americans is rooted in whites' anger over blacks violating traditional American values and receiving undeserved advantages. Or as he puts it, "Seeing blacks continue to ask for assistance from the federal government while they are the ones to blame for their lower position in society evokes strong feelings of anger among many white Americans" (Banks 2014, 26). Racial liberalism is also entrenched in anger, albeit over the perceived unfair treatment of African Americans (Banks 2014). Banks supports his theory with several innovative experimental tests, which demonstrate that racial resentment and racial liberalism are rooted in anger, but race-neutral principles like aversion to big government are not strongly tied to any particular negative emotion.

In light of those findings, the hypothesized spillover of racialization from Barack Obama into mass politics could be particularly consequential. In political science literature, many debate whether the well-documented ideological polarization of Democrats and Republicans in Congress has filtered down to ordinary Americans (Fiorina 2006; Fiorina and Abrams 2008; Abramowitz 2010).[15] Although the mass public may not be as divided over ideology as political elites, it is abundantly clear from the extant evidence that rank-and-file Democrats and Republicans dislike each other more now than they did in the past—a phenomenon called "affective polarization" (Iyengar, Sood, and Lelkes 2012; Iyengar and Westwood 2015; Abramowitz 2013). The anger, which Banks demonstrates accompanies racial attitudes' enhanced influence on politics, should have contributed to partisans' growing disdain for one another in the Age of Obama and made for an especially rancorous political environment during Barack Obama's presidency. In other words, the growing influence of racial attitudes and race in mass politics should have been especially divisive—a proposition tested in chapter 5.

Ascertaining the Influence of Racial Attitudes on Mass Politics

Previous studies of elite cues and mass cue taking, as discussed above, show that the signals provided to ordinary Americans by a president's issue positions often activate partisan and ideological attitudes in public opinion (e.g., Zaller 1992; Berinsky 2009; Levendusky 2009). As also mentioned in the previous chapter, critics contend that racial resentment confounds racial animus with nonracial political conservatism. And we now know that racial resentment is emotionally charged in ways that nonracial ideology is not. These reasons make it imperative to distinguish the spillover of racialization into Obama-era mass politics from the more familiar

mechanisms of partisan or ideological activation in response to presidential position taking.

The statistical models used in the analyses that follow help separate
the effects of racial attitudes from the impact of such factors as partisanship and ideology. These regression models, which are standard proce-
dures in political science analyses, estimate what the relationship between
racial attitudes would be if racial liberals were not more likely to be liberal Democrats and if racial conservatives were not more likely to be conservative Republicans. Our statistical models' ability to hold other variables constant—or control for them—therefore helps us determine the
impact of racial resentment *independent* of those other factors.

As such, almost all the multivariate regressions include a standard
seven-category measure of party identification, ranging from strong
Democrat to strong Republican and a five-category measure of ideology
in which respondents rated their positions from most liberal to most conservative. These controls were chosen both because of their availability
in every dataset used and because past presidents' positions have tended
to activate partisan and ideological considerations rather than racial attitudes. However, at various points in the book, I employ different model
specifications when other variables are relevant and available. These additional controls include aversion to social spending (economic conservatism), tax-policy preferences, limited government attitudes, moral traditionalism, military support, religiosity, and self-interested concerns about
out-of-pocket medical expenses. As you will see, the spillover of racialization is robust even when controlling for several different factors.[16]

Testing the Spillover of Racialization: Sources of Evidence

The empirical strength of this project resides in its ability to test the spillover of racialization hypothesis with several data sources. More specifically, the book relies on three different, but complimentary, types of survey data to support its claims. These three unique sources of data, which
are described below, allow us (1) to see how the effects of racial attitudes
on public opinion changed over a long period of time, (2) to determine
how racial attitudes caused the exact same individuals' political preferences to change from before to after Barack Obama became president,
and (3) to establish whether Obama's race was actually responsible for
the enhanced over-time effects of racial attitudes on mass politics.

Repeated Cross-Sectional Surveys

Repeated cross-sectional surveys interview *different* respondents over a prolonged period. The book's repeated cross-sectional survey data come from a number of different sources. First among these is the venerable American National Election Studies (ANES). The ANES has been carried out by the Center for Political Studies at the University of Michigan's Institute for Social Research since 1948. Since then, the ANES has interviewed carefully drawn probability samples of Americans before and/or after every presidential election and included measures of racial attitudes in many of those surveys.

In addition to the ANES, I also draw on repeated cross-sectional surveys conducted by the General Social Survey (GSS), the Cooperative Congressional Election Study (CCES), and the Pew Values Survey (PVS). Like the ANES, the GSS is one of the benchmark social science surveys,[17] with particularly high quality-control standards and response rates. Also, like the ANES, the GSS's continuous assessment of racial attitudes allows us to compare the political effects of race-based predispositions over a prolonged period. So, too, does the PVS, whose series of surveys conducted between 1987 and 2012 included questions about opposition to both interracial dating and special preferences for African Americans. The CCES is an academic survey that has been carried out by the Internet polling firm YouGov since 2006. Despite its relatively short existence, the CCES's massive sample sizes of at least thirty-five thousand respondents in each of its biennial election surveys enable analyses that would simply be impossible in the smaller ANES, GSS, and Pew surveys of around two thousand Americans.

Panel Reinterview Surveys

Cross-sectional time series designs, however, are limited by interviewing different samples of people in each repeated survey. In contrast, a *panel study* interviews the exact same respondents two or more times. The panel design, as discussed in the following chapters, has a number of virtues (see Bartels 2006; Kenski and Romer 2006; Lenz 2012). Most important for our purposes, it allows us to make much stronger claims about the changing political effects of factors like racial attitudes over time by testing respondents' pre-Obama measures of racial attitudes on both their pre- and post-2008 election assessments of issues like health care reform.

The book relies on several panel surveys to test the spillover of racialization hypothesis. These include 2006-2008-2010 GSS panel and the 2008-2009-2010 ANES panel, both of which reinterviewed more than a thousand respondents who were surveyed before Barack Obama was elected president. The analyses in the following chapters, however, draw most heavily on a series of National Science Foundation funded (SES-0968830 and SES-1023942) original reinterview surveys that we fielded in November 2009, April–May 2011, and July 2012. Each of these three surveys reinterviewed *nationally representative subsamples* of at least three thousand of the twenty thousand panelists who participated in the Cooperative Campaign Analysis Project's (CCAP) 2007–8 six-wave panel of registered voters.[18]

Survey Experiments

Even if our panelists' evaluations of policies like health care were more racialized during Barack Obama's presidency than they were shortly beforehand, that still does not necessarily imply that the president's association with these issues was responsible for the increased political effects of racial attitudes. Perhaps public opinion about issues championed by the Obama administration became more racialized simply because these policies were more closely connected to the racially liberal Democratic Party than they were before Barack Obama became president. Or maybe public opinion became more racialized because the economic downturn pitted social groups against one another for scarce resources. Those explanations seem unlikely since prior Democratic presidents' positions did not racialize mass-policy preferences (Winter 2008), and racial and ethnocentric attitudes were unusually strong predictors of public opinion about Barack Obama in 2006 and 2007 before the economy cratered (Tesler and Sears 2010; Kinder and Dale-Riddle 2012). The fact that there are readily available alternatives to the spillover of racialization hypothesis, however, underscores the need to unpack the president's causal role in racializing mass political evaluations.

The most straightforward method of establishing such causality is to experimentally assign respondents different cues about who supports specific policies. Indeed, this approach of randomly assigning different contextual information about policy endorsements has been used quite effectively in previous studies to establish the causal influence of elite cues on public opinion (Druckman et al. 2010; Levendusky 2009; Tomz and Sniderman 2005; Cohen 2003; Lupia and McCubbins 1998). The book includes several survey experiments that link both Barack Obama and other Democratic politicians to specific political evaluations. These experiments test the spillover of racialization's hypothesis that President Obama's connection to various political issues should activate racial attitudes in public opinion more powerfully than white Democrats' political positions.

* * *

In sum, combining repeated cross-sectional data with panel reinterviews and survey experiments provides especially powerful tests of the spillover of racialization hypothesis. These tests help us confidently conclude that Barack Obama's presidency ushered in a most-racial political era where mass politics was more divided by and over race than it had been in modern times.

CHAPTER THREE

The Obama Presidency, Racial Attitudes, and the 2012 Election

I'm not somebody who believes that constantly talking about race somehow solves racial tensions. I think what solves racial tensions is fixing the economy, putting people to work, making sure that people have health care, ensuring that every kid is learning out there. — President Barack Obama, March 7, 2009[1]

We now know that Obama's race mattered in the 2008 election, and it mattered a lot. Chapter 1, you may recall, referenced several academic studies, which found that race-related and ethnicity-related attitudes were strong determinants of 2008 voting behavior. Those measures— whether racial resentment, antiblack stereotypes, opposition to intimate interracial relationships, ethnocentrism, anti-Muslim sentiments, or even living in areas with a high volume of racist Google searches—were also significantly more powerful predictors of 2008 preferences than they had been in recent presidential elections, or than they would have been had John McCain faced Hillary Clinton instead of Barack Obama (Tesler and Sears 2010; Kinder and Dale-Riddle 2012; Piston 2010; Windet, Banda, and Carsey 2013; Jackman and Vavreck 2012; Weisberg and Devine 2010; Kinder and Ryan 2012; Kam and Kinder 2012; Highton 2011; Tesler 2013b; Stephens-Davidowitz 2013).

The findings from the 2008 election, however, did not guarantee an equally important role for racial attitudes in Barack Obama's 2012 reelection bid. In fact, Zoltan Hajnal's (2007) groundbreaking work on black mayors showed that many African American challengers, though not all, became less-racialized public figures after winning their elections. The dynamics of that deracialization process are summarized in the following passage from his book *Changing White Attitudes toward Black Political Leadership*:

> Prior to the election of a black candidate, most white voters have little or no experience with black leadership. For this reason many whites fear that a black leader will favor the black community over the white community. They expect a black leader to redistribute income, encourage integration, and generally channel resources toward the black community. In short, they imagine that black control will have negative consequences for themselves and their neighbors. Once a black candidate is elected, however, whites gain access to better information about the policy preferences of black leaders and the effects of black leadership. They become able to judge black candidates on their records. And because the white community rarely suffers under black incumbents, those records are, in almost every case, better than white stereotypes and fears suggested they would be. When blacks have the power (or are perceived as having the power) to inflict harm on the white community and they choose not to do so, many whites are forced to reevaluate their assumptions. (Hajnal 2007, 3)

The historical trend in deactivating race-based assessments of African American mayors was apparently driven, then, by the credible information that their job performances imparted. When black mayors did not use their executive authority to disproportionately favor African American interests, whites' stereotypical fears of black political radicalism and racial group favoritism often recede in kind. Tom Bradley, the first black mayor of Los Angeles, is the quintessential example of Hajnal's "information model" in action. Racial attitudes dominated Angelinos' vote choices when Bradley ran for mayor as a challenger in 1969 and 1973. So much so, that the theory of symbolic racism was born out of explaining white opposition to Tom Bradley's mayoral candidacies (Sears and Kinder 1971; Kinder and Sears 1981). Yet, after establishing an effective and racially impartial performance record in office, race-based considerations were unimportant determinants of how white Californians felt about Bradley's reelection bids for mayor and his unsuccessful 1982 campaign for governor (Citrin, Green, and Sears 1990; Hajnal 2007).[2]

History would, therefore, seem to support the epigraph that introduced this chapter, in which Barack Obama claimed that talking about race does not solve racial tensions. "What solves racial tensions," as President Obama stated and the academic research on black mayors further suggests, "is fixing the economy"—at least when it comes to deracializing white attitudes toward black political leadership. Consequently, the improving election-year economy that Barack Obama presided over could have helped deactivate racial attitudes in 2012 voting behavior.

Along with the improving economy, this chapter discusses how aspects of Barack Obama's first-term governing behavior could have also put him on the fast track to deracialization. Most notably, the president's race-neutral rhetoric, his colorblind policy proposals, and his historically moderate legislative agenda may have all helped alleviate stereotypical fears about African American political leadership. If those common concerns about black politicians were actually assuaged, then racial attitudes probably would not have been as prominent in 2012 voting behavior as they had been in 2008.

The role of racial attitudes, however, does not always decrease during black mayors' tenures in office. In fact, Hajnal (2007) helps explain this variation in white reactions to black leaders by deploying Harold Washington—the first African American mayor of Chicago—as the archetypal case study in *unchanging* white attitudes toward black political leadership. Despite both the city's improving economy during his mayoral term and a reduced role of racial appeals in his 1987 reelection campaign, Washington won an even smaller share of the white vote (15 percent) as an incumbent than he had four years earlier as a challenger (20 percent). So, why exactly did voters' preferences remain so racialized in Chicago? A large piece of the puzzle, Hajnal (2007, 124) explains, was that "Harold Washington's tenure provided much less information to white residents than other cases of black leadership because Washington was prevented by a white-led coalition in the city council from enacting his agenda."

Aside from the parallel here between Mayor Washington's trouble with the white-led city council and President Obama's difficulties getting congressional Republicans to move on his legislative agenda, there are several additional reasons to suspect that racial attitudes continued to play a major part in white Americans' 2012 vote choices. These circumstances, which are detailed below, include the following: (1) partisan communications that reinforced prior impressions of Barack Obama; (2) the tendency of Americans—especially racially conservative whites—to alter reality in order to render President Obama's actions consistent with prior beliefs; (3) an ambiguous presidential performance record that made it even easier for voters to rely on biased information processing in evaluating Barack Obama's presidency; (4) an increased sense of white racial threat due to changing demographics; (5) a plethora of race-based appeals during the 2012 primary and general election campaigns; and (6) the easy associative link between racial attitudes and Barack Obama's historic position as the country's first black president (i.e., chronic accessibility). All these factors should have interacted with one another to cancel out the abovementioned reasons why presidential voting may have been less racialized in 2012 than it was in 2008. The chapter's main hypothesis, then, is that racial animosity and racial sympathy remained powerful determinants of opposition to, and support for, Barack Obama's 2012 presidential candidacy.

* * *

The analyses that follow support that expectation. After first establishing the theoretical reasons to believe that Obama's race remained an important consideration in how white Americans' evaluated his presidency, I show that the effects of racial attitudes on 2012 presidential vote preferences were similar to their unprecedented influence on the 2008 election. Also, like in the 2008 election, the mass public continued to evaluate Barack Obama not just as an African American but also as someone who exemplifies the more primitively frightening out-group status of "otherness." With President Obama persistently painted as the "other" (e.g., Muslim and/or foreign born) by his most ardent political foes, attitudes toward Muslims continued to be an especially potent predictor of support for and opposition to the president's reelection bid as well.

Barack Obama's Potential Path to Deracialization

Race-Neutral Rhetoric and Policy Proposals

Perhaps the most prevalent fear about black political leadership is that African American politicians will disproportionately favor the black community's interests over that of whites. Senator Obama accordingly tried to combat these concerns during the 2008 presidential campaign (Ambinder 2009; Tesler and Sears 2010; Coe and Reitzes 2010; McIlwain and Caliendo 2011; Kinder and Dale-Riddle 2012; Lopez 2014). His 2008 campaign ads overwhelmingly featured white imagery and emphasized themes of the aforementioned symbolic racism belief system like hard work, self-reliance, and American values to help "inoculate" him from those stereotypical fears (McIlwain and Caliendo 2011, chap. 7). Such deracialization strategies, however, rarely work for black challengers. Instead, white voters tend to view counterstereotypical appeals as merely the "cheap talk" of politicians who will do or say anything to get elected (Hajnal 2007). So it was not particularly surprising that the Obama Campaign's inoculation efforts failed to reduce the impact of racial attitudes on presidential vote preferences over the course of the 2008 campaign (Tesler and Sears 2010; Jackman and Vavreck 2012).

Candidate Obama's race-neutral rhetoric was much more than simply the "cheap talk" talk of campaign platitudes, though. Indeed, President Obama carefully adhered to his campaign's colorblind commitments throughout his first term in office. With few exceptions, Barack Obama avoided the subject of race during his first four years in office. According to content analyses conducted by political and communication scientists, Barack Obama actually discussed race less in his first term than any other Democratic president since Franklin Roosevelt (Gillion 2012; Coe and Schmidt 2012). Moreover, President Obama regularly downplayed accusations of race-based opposition to his presidency during his first term in the White House;[3] and he was quick to distance himself from controversial racial statements made by multiple black members of his bureaucracy.[4]

The White House even jumped the gun in pressuring an African American Agricultural Department employee, Shirley Sherrod, to resign after her comments were edited out of context to appear as if she favored blacks over whites in administering government aid. Both the White House and the Department of Agriculture later apologized to Sherrod for rushing to misjudgment, but the episode informatively illustrated the administration's eagerness to avoid any hint of racial favoritism. Or, as Sherrod herself put it, "the administration feels too that if they highlight issues of black people ... the country would perceive it as something negative."[5]

Barack Obama also adhered to a race-neutral policy agenda during his tenure in the White House. "President Obama," as political scientists Desmond King and Rogers Smith surmised in their 2011 *New York Times* op-ed, "does not openly renounce affirmative action, but he ... manages to avoid appearing especially concerned about African-Americans."[6] That detached approach to racial issues understandably drew criticism from several black politicians and public intellectuals. Maxine Waters (D-CA), for example, voiced the Congressional Black Caucus's disappointment with the White House's reluctance to directly address African American unemployment, stating in August 2011, "It's time for us to step up and note that our communities are not being dealt with and to make sure that this administration understands that we cannot continue to go on this way."[7] Yet, Waters's critique was downright tepid compared to the barrage of attacks President Obama received from famed professor Cornel West and his radio talk-show cohost, Tavis Smiley. West and Smiley were probably the most prominent critics of the administration's reluctance to confront race-specific issues, with Professor West even calling the president, "a black mascot of Wall Street oligarchs and a black puppet of corporate plutocrats."[8]

President Obama later defended his race-neutral governing approach in a meeting with African American leaders, where he reportedly asked them, "If I go out there saying 'black, black,' do you think that will help black people?" (quoted in Alter 2013, 272). The president had a point, too, as universal programs are much more politically viable than race-targeted policies (Sniderman and Carmines 1997). The more important point for our purposes, though, is that the Obama administration's color-blind agenda could have alleviated stereotypical fears about black leaders' suspected racial-group favoritism. That racially impartial approach to governing, especially when combined with President Obama's first-term reluctance to broach the subject of race, may have deactivated racial attitudes in 2012 voting behavior.

Ideological Moderation

Ideological extremism is another common concern about black political leadership (Sigelman et al. 1995; Hajnal 2007; Kenski, Hardy, and Jamieson 2010; McIlwain and Caliendo 2011). In stark contrast with this prevalent stereotype that African American politicians are too politically radical, President Obama pursued a historically moderate legislative agenda during his first term in office. Liberal politicians and political commentators often cited anecdotal evidence in defense of Barack Obama's moderation. His signature health care reform law, they frequently noted, was similar to prior legislation proposed and/or enacted by such prominent Republicans and conservatives as Bob Dole, Mitt Romney, and the Heritage Foundation.[9]

Much more importantly, the best quantitative evidence available on presidential ideology ranked Barack Obama as the most moderate Democratic president in modern times. In February 2012, political scientist Keith Poole (2012) put out an analysis of presidential ideologies

that received some media attention.[10] Poole and his colleagues' venerable DW-NOMINATE scores generate objective ideological positions for
legislatures based on who votes with whom and how often they do so
(see McCarty, Poole, and Rosenthal 2006, 2013, for much more on this
method).[11] NOMINATE can then extract ideological placements for
presidents based on the limited cases in which the White House takes a
visible position on congressional roll call votes. Poole's results from this
reliable classification system showed that Barack Obama was the least liberal president since World War II and the biggest moderate in the White
House since Dwight Eisenhower. These data, in other words, directly con-
tradicted white fears of black political radicalism. Race-based considerations may have therefore been deactivated by President Obama's counterstereotypical moderation.

An Improving Economy

The election-year economy is often *the* decisive determinant of presidential election outcomes (Fiorina 1981; Gelman and King 1993; Bartels 2008;
Vavreck 2009; Sides and Vavreck 2013). In fact, forecast models using just
real disposable income growth and incumbent party terms in office explain most of the variation in post–World War II presidential vote shares
(Bartels 2013). With real income growing by about 0.75 percent during the
election year, that forecast expected Barack Obama to easily win reelection.[12] Other economic indicators, such as growing GDP and declining unemployment, also made the president an overwhelming favorite to retain
the White House (Sides and Vavreck 2013). To be sure, the "ambiguous
record" discussion later on in this chapter makes it clear that the economy
was still in pretty poor shape going into the 2012 election. Yet, Americans'
presidential vote choices are dictated more by *trends* in the economy than
by its overall strength (Bartels 2008; Sides and Vavreck 2012; Huber, Hill,
and Lenz 2012). The positive direction in several election-year economic
indicators, therefore, augured well for an Obama reelection victory.

The improving economy also boded well for Barack Obama's deracialization prospects. We already know that booming local economies have
historically helped alleviate white fears of black mayors harming the city.
Moreover, the election-year economic gains that Barack Obama presided
over in no way privileged blacks over whites. If anything, African Americans were left behind by the economic recovery.[13] Finally, and unlike the
2008 election, President Obama owned the 2012 economy. With neither

2008 presidential candidate directly tied to the Bush administration, racial attitudes could have filled the void left by the lack of an incumbent presidential and vice presidential record to vote for or against.[14] That 2008 vacancy was occupied in 2012 by Barack Obama's performance in office, though. As such, Americans' assessments of the president's accomplishments may have drowned out racial attitudes' influence on 2012 voting behavior. Indeed, the importance of local economic conditions generally increases in importance relative to racial attitudes when black mayors run for reelection (Hajnal 2007).

* * *

Taken in isolation, President Obama's race-neutral policy agenda, his ideological moderation, and the improving election-year economy could have all offered him a viable path to deracialization. But, of course, nothing occurs in isolation when it comes to the president of the United States. And, as we will soon see, the circumstances surrounding President Obama's first-term in the White House were likely to have derailed any potential train to 2012 deracialization.

Hitches in the Road to Deracialization

Intense Opposition

It almost goes without saying that Barack Obama faced tremendous opposition during his tenure in the White House. In fact, Rush Limbaugh actually voiced his hopes for a failed Obama presidency *before* the president-elect took office in January 2009.[15] This intense opposition manifested itself in a number of ways since Barack Obama's first inauguration, including the right-wing media's unrelenting attacks on the president, the birther movement's claims that the president was not actually born in the United States, the Tea Party's fiery protests against the Obama administration and its policies (see chap. 6 for more on the Tea Party), and congressional Republicans' almost absolute obstructionism. Even such commonplace congressional actions as raising the debt ceiling to prevent the nation from defaulting on its debts and invoking cloture for Senate confirmation votes on the president's judicial nominees were the subject of bitter disputes between the White House and Congress in the Age of Obama.

This intense opposition should have been a major hitch in President Obama's potential path to deracialization. Harold Washington, as noted earlier, remained a highly racialized politician in part because of the resistance he faced from Chicago's white-led city council. Citizens inclined to think the worst of Washington and/or Obama could cite these legislative impediments as the reason why the city or nation did not completely fall apart under black political leadership. In other words, neither Mayor Washington nor President Obama had the opportunity to convey the credible information about their intentions that Hajnal's model requires for deracialization.

The fierce opposition that Barack Obama encountered from conservative politicians and pundits also confirmed the worst fears of Americans who were predisposed to distrust a black president. As Jonathan Chait astutely observed in his *New York Magazine* column, "Justifying the stance of total resistance has required Republicans to paint Obama not as simply a liberal but as a dangerous socialist bent on eradicating the best traditions of America."[16] That portrait of the president, in turn, substantiated any race-based anxieties about an Obama presidency destroying the country. Simply put, then, partisan attacks reinforced prior impressions of President Obama and inhibited the unbiased information processing that Hajnal's model requires for deracialization.

Altering Reality

Biased information processing is actually common in contemporary American politics. Building on a long line of psychological research about cognitive consistency (e.g., Festinger 1957; Abelson 1968; Kunda 1987, 1990; Ditto and Lopez 1992), Charles Taber and Milton Lodge's (2006) work on "motivated skepticism" (see also Lodge and Taber 2013) shows that political reasoning is often dictated by goals other than holding accurate beliefs. Rather, individuals—especially politically knowledgeable people who feel strongly about the issues—tend to selectively process information that is consistent with their prior opinions (i.e., confirmation bias). As a result, partisans may have completely different perceptions of political reality. Democrats (Republicans), for instance, generally think the unemployment rate and federal budget deficit are lower than Republicans (Democrats) do when one of their own is in the White House (Shani 2006; Bartels 2002, 2012; Bullock et al. 2013; Lavine, Johnston, and Steenbergen 2013; Druckman 2013). Motivated skepticism also helps explain the large partisan divide in such objective beliefs as whether the earth is getting warmer and whether Barack Obama was actually born in the United States (Tesler and Sears 2010; Berinsky 2012, 2015; Abramowitz 2011; Tesler 2014).

Barack Obama was not just a Democratic president, though. He was an African American president whose 2008 election strongly evoked racial and ethnocentric predispositions. Consequently, racial liberals and racial conservatives might also interpret objective information relating to his presidency through very different lenses. Moskowitz and Stoh's (1994) experimental findings, in fact, suggest that voters often "alter reality" in order to render black candidates' messages consistent with prior expectations and racial beliefs. In keeping with that finding, racial and ethnocentric predispositions were strong predictors of holding inaccurate factual beliefs about Barack Obama, such as thinking he was Muslim and/or foreign born (Tesler and Sears 2010; Abramowitz 2011; Kam and Kinder 2012; Kinder and Ryan 2012). Moreover, Barack Obama's increased popularity during the 2008 presidential primary was concentrated among racial liberals who were predisposed to interpret the positive press following his victory in the Iowa caucuses more favorably than racial conservatives (Tesler and Sears 2010). It may well be, then, that the aforementioned factors lining President Obama's potential path to deracialization were overtaken by race-based motivated reasoning.

Race-Neutral Policies?   Fortunately, data are available to directly test whether white Americans updated their opinions to comport with President Obama's race-neutral policy agenda, his ideological moderation, and the improving election-year economy. Figure 3.1 presents the first of that evidence, graphing ANES respondents' perceived differences between Democratic and Republican presidential candidates in their support for government aid to African Americans. Not surprisingly, the Democratic presidential candidate was rated higher on this so-called aid to blacks scale in every single survey since the question's 1972 inception. The display shows that Americans consistently placed the Democratic nominee about one point higher (approximately 17 percent of the scale's range), on average, than his Republican opponent on this seven-category measure between 1972 and 2004. That significant difference, however, nearly doubled in 2012 to more than 30 percent of the scale's range. Despite Barack Obama's race-neutral legislative agenda and presidential rhetoric, figure 3.1 shows that the American public saw a much wider 2012 disparity

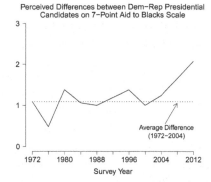

FIGURE 3.1. Perceived Differences between the Presidential Candidates' Support for Government Assistance to African Americans (1972–2012)
Note: Results subtract perceived Republican candidate support (1 is least supportive; 7 is most supportive) from perceived Democratic candidate support.
Source: American National Election Studies (ANES) cumulative file; 2012 ANES.

between Democrats and Republicans in their support for race-specific policies than they saw throughout the pre-Obama period—a finding that obviously did not augur well for a deracialized 2012 election.

Ideological Moderation?   It is important to note that this spike in public perceptions of the presidential nominees' differing positions on aid to blacks occurred without a similarly sized increase in perceived ideological disparities. Nevertheless, Barack Obama was still rated more liberal than any other Democratic president on record by ANES respondents (Sides 2013b), despite his aforementioned legislative moderation.

Figure 3.2 further shows that racial attitudes became significantly stronger determinants of Barack Obama's perceived ideological orientation than they were before he captured the Democratic presidential nomination. The left panel in the display discloses a slightly *negative* relationship between racial resentment and rating Obama at least somewhat liberal in March 2008 (after controlling for party identification and ideological self-placement). In 2012, though, racial resentment was a powerful positive predictor of these exact same panelists' perceptions of President Obama's liberalism. Racial conservatives were also significantly more likely to rate Barack Obama "very liberal" in 2012 than they had been in the spring of 2008, as the right panel of figure 3.2 illustrates. It appears, then, that racial attitudes colored white Americans' perceptions of President Obama's ideological agenda. Many white racial liberals updated

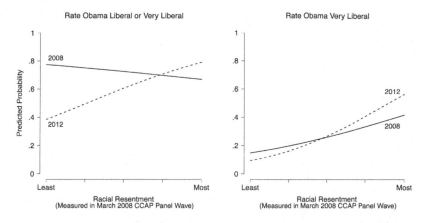

FIGURE 3.2. White Americans' Perceptions of Barack Obama's Ideology in March 2008 and July 2012 as a Function of Racial Resentment
Note: Probabilities are based on logistic regression coefficients in the online appendix. Predicted probabilities were calculated by setting party identification and ideological self-placement to their sample means.
Source: 2008–12 Cooperative Campaign Analysis Project (CCAP) panelists who were interviewed in both 2008 and 2012.

their beliefs to rate the president more ideologically moderate, whereas white racial conservatives moved in the opposite direction during Barack Obama's presidency.

An Improving Economy?   We discussed just a moment ago how booming local economies have historically helped change white Americans' attitudes toward black mayors. By that same logic, we also discussed how the improving national economy could have helped deactivate racial attitudes in the 2012 election. This assumes, however, that whites did not alter reality to render objective economic conditions consistent with their prior racial beliefs. Such unbiased information processing may be the case in mayoral elections, where local conditions are less subject to bitter partisan disputes. Yet, we know from prior research that national economic evaluations are ripe for (dis)confirmation biases, whereby Americans are more optimistic about the national economy when a co-partisan is president. With racial resentment such a strong predictor of feelings toward Barack Obama, that longstanding partisan divide in subjective assessments of objective economic conditions could have extended to racial attitudes as well.

Table 3.1 tests that expectation with data from the 2004–12 ANES and

TABLE 3.1. **(OLS) Predictors of Whites Saying Election-Year Unemployment Rate Is Getting Better**

	2004	2008	2012 ANES	2012 CCAP
Racial Resentment	−.019	.024	−.369***	−.416***
	(.070)	(.033)	(.037)	(.079)
Party Identification	.385***	.130***	−.296***	−.220**
	(.054)	(.028)	(.032)	(.068)
Ideology	.293**	.012	−.299***	−.212*
	(.096)	(.042)	(.048)	(.098)
Constant	.083	.024	1.00***	1.06***
	(.051)	(.033)	(.023)	(.057)
Observations	670	1,062	3,224	697

Source: 2004–12 American National Election Studies (ANES); 2011–12 Cooperative Campaign Analysis Project (CCAP), February 25, 2012, weekly reinterview.
Note: Dependent variable is three-point perception of unemployment over the past year (ANES) or six months (CCAP), recoded from 0 (worse) to 1 (better). All explanatory variables are coded from 0 to 1, with 1 being the most conservative response. Regression analyses use sample weights with robust standard errors that account for design characteristics.
*$p < .05$.
**$p < .01$.
***$p < .001$.

a late February 2012 YouGov poll conducted for the 2011–12 CCAP. The coefficients in the table disclose the independent effects of racial resentment, party identification, and ideological self-placement on white respondents' perceptions of whether the unemployment rate had gotten better, worse, or stayed the same over the last year (ANES) or past six months (CCAP).[17] Comparing the results in the 2004 and 2012 columns of that table is especially informative. Both George W. Bush and Barack Obama saw the unemployment rate increase by about two percentage points at various times during their first terms in office;[18] both presidents then presided over subsequent drops in the unemployment rate during the year leading up to their reelections (about half-a-point for Bush and one point for Obama).

These trends may have been similar in 2004 and 2012, but the correlates of thinking that unemployment was getting better were quite different in the two most recent reelection years. In 2004, conservative Republicans were much more likely than liberal Democrats to correctly conclude that unemployment was declining. So much so that the combined effects of party and ideology were more than the equivalent of changing from thinking the unemployment rate was static to thinking it had gotten better over the past year. In 2012, however, those large effects of ideology and party were completely reversed, with liberal Democrats now much more likely to accurately assess the unemployment rate's improvement.

More importantly for our purposes, table 3.1 indicates that racial resentment had no independent influence whatsoever on perceived trends in 2004 and 2008 unemployment. Moving on to the remaining columns of the table, however, tells us that racial attitudes had an extraordinary impact on white Americans' unemployment perceptions in 2012.[19] The coefficients for racial resentment in the third column show that the most racially liberal and conservative whites were divided by nearly 40 percent of this 0 to 1 measure's range—even after controlling for the large effects of party and ideology on economic perceptions. Moreover, the fourth and final column of the table shows a very similar negative effect of racial resentment on accurate unemployment perceptions in the 2012 CCAP. These results, therefore, suggest that race-based reactions to Barack Obama's presidency made racial liberals and racial conservatives perceive objective economic conditions like the unemployment rate much differently for the first time in recent history during the 2012 campaign.

* * *

In sum, the three major reasons to suspect voting patterns would be less racialized in 2012—Barack Obama's race-neutral agenda, his ideological moderation, and the improving election-year economy—were all influenced by biased information processing. Indeed, Americans saw a much larger divide between the Democratic and Republican presidential candidates' support for race-targeted policies in 2012 than they did throughout the pre-Obama era. Racial liberals and racial conservatives also perceived Barack Obama's ideological orientation and the state of the economy much differently during the 2012 election year. Taken together, then, these results strongly suggest that racial attitudes remained a powerful predictor of 2012 voting behavior.

An Ambiguous Record

Barack Obama's ambiguous performance record is one probable explanation why race-based motivated reasoning was so prevalent during his first term in office. The economy, as noted above, was improving fast enough in 2012 to make Barack Obama a strong favorite to win reelection. Yet, an abundance of dreadful economic indicators remained that President

Obama's opponents could reference to corroborate their claims that the recovery was not nearly as robust as it should have been: For example, the election-eve unemployment rate of 7.9 percent, while clearly declining, was higher than it was on any other presidential Election Day since the Great Depression; Americans' assets had also taken a thumping, with the average citizen's net worth cut in half since 2003; median income was still below its prerecession levels; and the federal budget deficit reached alarmingly high levels during Barack Obama's presidency.

To be sure, one could make a strong case that the inherited financial collapse was much more responsible for those dire economic conditions than the incumbent administration's policies. The ambiguity surrounding President Obama's stewardship of the economy is precisely the point, though. Racial liberals, who were disposed to like the president, could point to the declining unemployment rate and the booming 2012 stock market as proof of the president's economic acumen. Meanwhile racial conservatives, who were disposed to dislike the president, could point to mounting debt and high overall unemployment as a sign of his ineptitude. There would surely have been less wiggle room for Americans to alter reality in accordance with their prior racial beliefs if President Obama had a better or worse economic record than these conflicting indicators indicated. Indeed, table 3.1 showed that party identification and ideological self-placement had a much smaller combined effect on unemployment perceptions in 2008, when the financial collapse made it difficult for even the most passionate partisans to alter reality about the state of the economy, than they had when the economy was more ambiguous in 2004 and 2012. With the 2012 economy so open for debate, President Obama's economic performance probably failed to provide enough credible information to deactivate racial attitudes in 2012 voting behavior.

Changing Demographics

Chicago's large minority population was an important, yet unmentioned reason Harold Washington's reelection candidacy remained so racialized. It made sense, according to Hajnal (2007, 124–25), for whites to continue opposing Mayor Washington because of the precarious balance of power in the city between blacks and whites.

We might suspect that white Americans were less fearful of losing political control to minority populations in the Age of Obama because they still comprised a clear majority of the country. On the other hand, these fears could have been heightened by the fact that the United States is on the fast track to becoming a majority-minority nation.[20] Indeed, prior research suggests that whites feel more threatened by *increases* in the minority population than by its actual size (Hopkins 2010; Newman 2013).[21] Consistent with those findings, two recent political science books focused on the combustible combination of Barack Obama's presidency and America's rapidly changing demographics as an impetus for the anger and anxiety that sparked the Tea Party Movement (Parker and Barreto 2013; Skocpol and Williamson 2012).

Fears that Obama's elections were the watershed to a political era where, as Bill O'Reilly put it after Barack Obama's reelection victory, "the white establishment is now the minority,"[22] were thus another potential impediment to deracializing 2012 voting behavior.

Racialized Communications

We know from the last chapter that the impact of racial attitudes can be either enhanced or diminished depending on whether political evaluations are made in racialized or race-neutral informational environments. These previously cited studies demonstrate that subtle cues in political communications can make racial attitudes an important ingredient of mass-policy preferences. On top of those racial priming studies, a good amount of pre-Obama research shows that racialized campaign content can prime race-based attitudes in white Americans' presidential vote preferences (Kinder and Sanders 1996; Mendelberg 2001; Valentino 1999; Valentino, Hutchings, and White 2002). Perhaps most notably, George H. W. Bush's invocation of a violent black criminal, Willie Horton, to attack his Democratic opponent's liberal crime policies during the 1988 presidential campaign activated white racial resentment in support for his candidacy (Kinder and Sanders 1996; Mendelberg 2001).

David Sears and I argued in our 2010 book, *Obama's Race*, that such racialized communications should have been less of a factor in the 2008 election than they were in prior presidential campaigns. That is, Barack Obama's historic position as the first African American major party presidential nominee made racial attitudes chronically accessible in voters' preferences (see also Kinder and Dale-Riddle 2012). There was little room left, then, for campaign content to further activate race-based considerations. Even so, a renewed role for racial appeals in the 2012 campaign could have still reinforced the salience of Obama's race, thereby ensuring that racial attitudes remained accessible in white Americans' vote choices.

Racial appeals were indeed quite common throughout the 2012 election year. John McCain admirably refused to play the race card against Barack Obama in the 2008 campaign, fearing that winning under such circumstances would have delegitimized his presidency and led to urban violence (Kenski, Hardy, and Jamieson 2010, 87).[23] Barack Obama's 2012 Republican rivals, however, did not seem to be nearly as inhibited. In fact, the eventual runner-up for the Republican presidential nomination, Rick Santorum, kicked off the election year in early January by singling out African Americans as dependent welfare recipients. Senator Santorum, in fact, almost out of the blue, said, "I don't want to make black people's lives better by giving them somebody else's money; I want to give them the opportunity to go out and earn the money." This statement was criticized for conjuring up the longstanding association in both media portrayals and in public opinion between welfare recipients and "undeserving blacks" (Gilens 1999; Kellstedt 2003; Winter 2008).[24]

Republican presidential candidates' appeals to stereotypes of black dependency were just getting started, though. Newt Gingrich, who frequently faced accusations of racial bias for referring to Barack Obama as "the food-stamp president" (Lopez 2014, 131), announced only a few days after Santorum's controversial comment that he would go before the country's oldest civil rights organization, the NAACP, to "talk about why the African American community should demand paychecks and not be satisfied with food stamps."[25] Shortly thereafter, Juan Williams disapprovingly asked the former House Speaker about these statements at a debate for the South Carolina primary, adding, "Can't you see that this [comment] is viewed at a minimum as insulting to all Americans, but particularly to black Americans?" Speaker Gingrich dismissed this question from the African American Fox News contributor, and he received a standing ovation when he reiterated his statement that blacks should demand jobs not food stamps.[26] Some even suspected that this racially charged exchange fueled Newt Gingrich's stunning come-from-behind victory in the South Carolina primary—a claim bolstered by data showing that Gingrich's postdebate surge in the national polls was concentrated among the most racially conservative Republicans (Tesler 2012a).[27]

Mitt Romney was also suspected of playing the race card with welfare in the summer months of the election year when his campaign accused Barack Obama of doing away with the work requirements that accompany welfare benefits. "Under Obama's plan," one of his campaign ads proclaimed, "you wouldn't have to work, and you wouldn't have to train for a job. They just send you your welfare check." That contention was patently untrue,[28] however, leading some commentators to accuse Romney of straining the bounds of credulity to make race-infused issues a centerpiece of his campaign. Thomas Edsall, for instance, joined a chorus of left-leaning critics in stating, "The Republican ticket is flooding the airwaves with commercials . . . designed to turn the presidential contest into a racially freighted resource competition pitting middle class white voters against the minority poor."[29]

The fact that the top-three Republican presidential candidates in 2012 all anachronistically attacked Barack Obama with welfare—a racialized policy that had lost much of its political potency ever since Bill Clinton signed welfare reform legislation into law—was indicative of just how race-centric the 2012 campaign had become. *Salon* and the *Huffington Post* even ran respective countdowns called "The Most Racist Moments of the 2012 Election," with plenty more prominent examples that they could have selected. Neither of those columns included Mitt Romney's much publicized "birther" joke about no one ever asking to see his birth certificate; nor did either story mention Joe Biden's outlandish insinuation that Republicans were going to return African Americans to slavery if they retook the White House.[30]

To be sure, the prevalence of race in the 2012 campaign may well have been more of a consequence than a cause of racialized voting patterns. Either way, though, the priming and/or reinforcing role of these racial appeals was sure to keep race-based attitudes accessible in support for, and opposition to, Barack Obama's presidential candidacy.

Chronic Accessibility

As just mentioned, our central psychological explanation for the strong and stable influence of racial resentment on voter preferences over the course of the 2008 campaign was that race was a chronically accessible consideration in public opinion about Barack Obama (Tesler and Sears 2010). Chronic accessibility means that a particular predisposition is almost inevitably activated in voter preferences because there is a natural associative link between that attitude and the political evaluation in question (Sears 1993). Barack Obama's easily recognizable position as a historic racial figure was sure to foster such a strong connection between racial attitudes—both positive and negative affect toward blacks—and mass assessments of his candidacy and presidency. That accessibility of race, which may not have been quite as powerful for black mayors who do not embody the same racial symbolism as the country's first black president, should have made it difficult to alter the influence of racial attitudes in 2012 voting behavior.

Our accessibility account goes a long way in understanding the effects of racial attitudes on public opinion about Barack Obama in the 2008 campaign and beyond. Yet, this was an admittedly post hoc explanation for the results we found—one that we never directly tested. Valentino and his colleagues (2013), however, went on to fill that void and directly tested the suspected chronic linkage between racial attitudes and Obama-related evaluations. To do so, they employed various experimental manipulations that have a long track record in social science research of either priming or neutralizing racial resentment in political evaluations. Their results, which are similar to the experimental findings presented in the following chapter, showed that racial resentment's influence on Obama-oriented opinions persisted stably, even in the face of those experimental treatments. This finding is consistent with our earlier contention that the natural link between race and Barack Obama made racial attitudes a chronically accessible consideration in opinion about his presidency. One upshot of that chronic accessibility of race is that racial attitudes should have been difficult to deactivate in 2012 voting behavior.

* * *

All told, then, these six "hitches in Obama's road to deracialization" certainly suggest that race remained an important consideration in 2012 voting behavior. Unfortunately, it is impossible to parse just how much each one independently contributed to the racialized voting patterns shown below. These factors, however, should be primarily thought of as complementary, not contradictory. Take the chronic accessibility of racial attitudes in the 2008 election, for example. Would that accessibility have waned if intense opposition, an ambiguous record, and racialized communications did not make it so easy for white Americans to alter reality in order to render Obama's actions consistent with prior racial beliefs? Likewise, would opposition to the president have been so intense, had those accessible race-based reactions to Barack Obama not sparked anger and anxiety about a declining white majority? The *interplay* of these circumstances, rather than any one factor in particular, is essential to understanding the role of racial attitudes in the 2012. And this combination of factors strongly suggested that voting behavior was likely to remain racialized in Barack Obama's reelection bid.

Racial Attitudes in 2008 and 2012 Compared to Recent Presidential Elections

Our first test of that hypothesis compares the effects of racial attitudes on white Americans' vote intentions in Barack Obama's two elections to their impact on the all-white presidential contests between 1988 and 2004.[31] Those results, which use American National Election Study (ANES) data, are graphically presented in figure 3.3. The displays, as you can see, reveal a number of interesting patterns. First and foremost, racial resentment, antiblack stereotypes, and antiblack affect were all noticeably stronger determinants of presidential voting behavior in 2012 than they had been in the two decades before Barack Obama's name appeared on the national ballot.

Digging deeper into the first panel of figure 3.3 tells us that the effects of racial resentment on support for Republican presidential candidates were roughly twice as large in Obama's two elections as their average effects were between 1988 and 2004. During that pre-Obama time period, the least and most racially resentful whites were separated by about thirty-five percentage points in their presidential vote preferences (after controlling for party and ideology)—a substantively large and highly significant effect ($p < .001$) that reflected the importance of racial attitudes and race in the pre-Obama party alignment. The dashed lines in the first display, however, go on to show that this same change from least to most racially resentful was associated with a seventy-point increase in support for Obama's 2008 and 2012 Republican opponents.

The first panel of figure 3.3 also shows that the enhanced Obama-era effects of racial predispositions on 2008 and 2012 vote intention were both produced by *the two sides of racialization*. All else being equal, white racial liberals were more likely to support Barack Obama in his two presidential elections than they had been in recent all-white presidential elections. Meanwhile, white racial conservatives were noticeably more opposed to Obama than they were to his immediate Democratic predecessors.

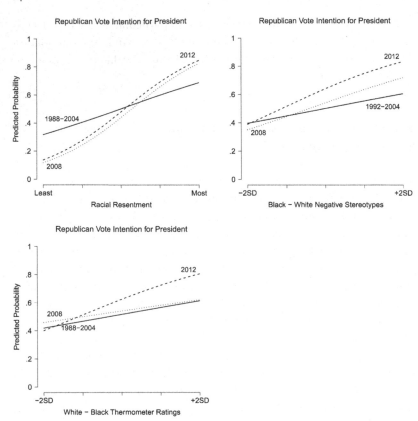

FIGURE 3.3. White Americans' Vote Intentions for President as a Function of Racial Attitudes (1988–2012)
Note: Probabilities are based on logistic regression coefficients in the online appendix. Predicted probabilities were calculated by setting party identification and ideological self-placement to the mean white respondent.
Source: American National Election Studies (ANES) cumulative file; 2012 ANES.

The remaining two panels of figure 3.3, however, suggest that the strengthened Obama-era relationships between Republican presidential support and more blatant racial prejudice measures were not produced by unusually strong racially liberal support for Barack Obama. Those differing patterns, which are illustrated on the left-hand sides of the figure's three panels, likely stemmed from the discussion in chapter 1 of the stereotype and thermometer scales' inabilities to capture racially sympathetic sentiments. Given those measures' difficulties in deciphering racially sympathetic whites from less sympathetic nonprejudiced Americans, it is not too surprising that figure 3.3 shows that the greater effects of antiblack stereotypes and antiblack affect in Obama's elections were not produced by the two sides of racialization.

Those two displays, instead, indicate that whites who scored high in antiblack stereotypes and antiblack affect were considerably more supportive of Barack Obama's opponents than they were of Republican presidential candidates between 1988 and 2004. After controlling for party and ideology, the second panel shows that whites who scored at least two standard deviations above the average antiblack stereotype score were roughly twenty percentage points more likely to vote for Mitt Romney and John McCain than prior Republican presidential nominees. The final panel of figure 3.3 goes on to disclose a similar boost in Romney support among respondents who felt warmer toward whites than blacks. This third and final panel also curiously shows that antiblack affect was not activated by Barack Obama's candidacy in the 2008 election. The effects of racial thermometer ratings, as John Sides (2009) previously documented, were similar in 2008 to their effects in elections prior to Obama's candidacy. Despite that anomalous result,[32] though, the impact of antiblack stereotypes and antiblack affect were significantly stronger in 2012 than they had been immediately prior to Obama's ascendancy; and, unlike our racial resentment results, those enhanced relationships were driven by just racially prejudiced opposition to Barack Obama's reelection candidacy.

The Effects of Racial Attitudes in 2008–12 Panel Reinterviews

The ANES results in figure 3.4 support our central claim that racial attitudes remained powerful determinants of white Americans' presidential vote preferences in the 2012 election. Some caution, however, is always required when comparing the over-time effects of attitudes on voter preferences in repeated cross-sectional surveys (e.g., Lenz 2009, 2012; Tesler 2015b). For starters, the variables in our base model used to explain attitudes toward Obama—racial resentment, party identification, and ideological self-placement—may themselves have been influenced by his rise to prominence.[33] That is, our explanatory variables could be both a consequence and a cause of Obama evaluations. In fact, the results in chapter 7 show that party identification was increasingly influenced by racial attitudes during Barack Obama's presidency. Including party identification and racial resentment in the same model may have therefore blunted the

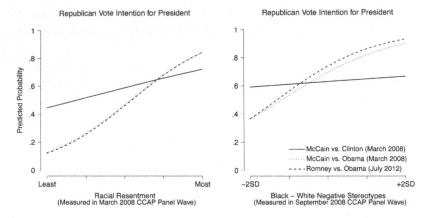

FIGURE 3.4. White Americans' Vote Intentions for President as a Function of Racial Attitudes in 2008 and 2012
Note: Probabilities are based on logistic regression coefficients in the online appendix. Predicted probabilities were calculated by setting party identification and ideological self-placement to the mean white respondent.
Source: 2008–12 Cooperative Campaign Analysis Project (CCAP) panelists who were interviewed in both 2008 and 2012.

over-time effects of racial attitudes on vote intention in repeated cross-sectional analyses.[34] There were also some differences in sample design, survey modes, and response rates between the 2012 ANES and its predecessors, which could have further complicated our over-time comparisons.[35] And interviewing different respondents at two distinct points in time naturally introduces uncertainty about how comparable our samples really were.

It is quite fortunate, then, that we can replicate our ANES results with data from the 2008–12 CCAP Panel Study. As mentioned in the prior chapter, we commissioned that July 2012 study to reinterview a nationally representative subsample of three thousand registered voters who had previously been surveyed during the 2008 campaign.[36] This panel design has a couple of notable advantages over our ANES analyses. First, we no longer have to worry about differences in sample compositions between repeated surveys because the same individuals are interviewed each time. More importantly, our panel design mitigates concerns about reverse causality by enabling us to test the effects of early measured attitudes on dependent variables from later panel waves. In other words, we can test the influence of racial attitudes—measured before Obama's presidency could have changed them and their relationship with party identification—on both 2008 and 2012 presidential vote intentions.

The results from those analyses are presented in figure 3.4. In addition to comparing the effects of racial predispositions on vote intention for Obama in 2008 and 2012, the display also graphs out the effects of those attitudes on our same panelists' support for John McCain against Hillary Clinton back in the March 2008 CCAP panel wave. That all-white trial heat is arguably more important than the pre-Obama (1988–2004) baseline effects of racial attitudes on presidential voting shown in figure 3.3. Because, unlike the 1988–2004 baseline impact, this matchup holds both 2008 conditions and the Republican candidate (McCain) constant across the Clinton and Obama comparisons. Several previous studies, in fact, used McCain versus Clinton trial heats to confidently conclude that racial resentment, antiblack stereotypes, opposition to interracial dating, anti-Muslim sentiments, and ethnocentrism were all significantly stronger predictors of support for John McCain against Barack Obama than they would have been had Hillary Clinton been his Democratic opponent in the 2008 election (Tesler and Sears 2010; Jackman and Vavreck 2012; Kam and Kinder 2012; Kinder and Ryan 2012; Tesler 2013b).

Consistent with those findings, figure 3.4 shows that racial resentment and antiblack stereotypes had a much stronger impact on support for John McCain against Barack Obama in March 2008 than they had on the exact same panelists' preferences for John McCain over Hillary Clinton. The first panel in the display, for instance, shows that moving from least to most racially resentful increased McCain's vote share by nearly thirty percentage points against Clinton, and more than seventy points against Obama. That disparity was similar to the results just presented in figure 3.3, which showed that racial resentment was more closely aligned with 2008 vote preferences than it was in the pre-Obama period. Also like those ANES results, the strengthened relationship between racial resentment and Republican presidential support against Obama was produced by the two sides of racialization. All else being equal, white racial liberals were especially more likely to prefer Obama to Clinton in 2008 trial heats against John McCain. Finally, and again like the ANES results, the effects of racial resentment on support for Obama's Republican opponents were almost identical in 2008 and 2012. So much so that the two dashed 2008 and 2012 lines almost perfectly overlap with each other in the first panel of figure 3.4.

The remaining findings from figure 3.4 have much in common with our earlier ANES results as well. The second panel of the display, in fact, shows that antiblack stereotypes were an equally strong predictor of opposition to Barack Obama in 2008 and 2012, even though those same attitudes had almost no independent effect on our panelists' support for John McCain against Hillary Clinton. In fact, moving from at least two standard deviations below the average stereotype score to at least two standard deviations above that mean increased support for Barack Obama's presidential opponents by more than fifty percentage points in both 2008 and 2012 (after controlling for party and ideology). The same change in the same panelists' stereotype scores, however, increased support for John McCain against Hillary Clinton by only about ten percentage points back in March 2008—a highly significant difference in effects.

The 2008–12 CCAP Panel results are perhaps our most convincing evidence that racial attitudes remained an unusually powerful predictor of opposition to Barack Obama in 2012. For those attitudes were at least as potent in 2012 as they were when Obama first ran, despite the fact that our analyses use 2008 measurements of racial predispositions.

The Continuing Influence of Obama as "Other" (2008–12)

Attitudes about African Americans were not the only out-group sentiments activated by Barack Obama's rise to prominence, either. As mentioned earlier, impressions of Muslims were also much more important determinants of Obama-related evaluations, even after controlling for racial resentment, than they had been during George W. Bush's presidency (Tesler and Sears 2010, chap. 7; Kam and Kinder 2012). These prior results suggest that Barack Obama was evaluated not just as an African American in 2008 but also as someone whose foreign-sounding name, Kenyan father, upbringing in Indonesia, and imagined Muslim faith marked him as distinctly "other" to many Americans.

We hypothesized elsewhere that this newfound role for attitudes about Muslims in 2008 voting behavior might lead to a surge in anti-Islamic political appeals during Obama's presidency (Tesler and Sears 2010, 141). The logic being that such appeals to religious intolerance should have been more politically relevant and resonant with a president who strongly evoked anti-Muslim predispositions in the White House. Moreover, since the American people consistently evaluate Muslims much less favorably than other racial, religious, and ethnic groups (Kalkan, Layman, and Uslaner 2009; Tesler and Sears 2010; Tesler 2011; Sides and Gross 2012), anti-Muslim appeals against Barack Obama and his party should have been more palatable than appeals to racial antagonisms, which are oftentimes criticized and thought to be correspondingly ineffective for violating strong societal norms of race equality (Mendelberg 2001, 2008).

Attacks on Obama for being "other" were indeed quite common during his presidency. "Tea Party websites," according to Christopher Parker and Matt Barreto's (2013, 197) original analysis, "are littered with rumors that Obama was a secret Muslim, that he had no valid American birth certificate, that he was anti-Christian, that he was a secret socialist or communist, and above all, he was not a real American." Many high-ranking Republicans also attacked the president for not being sufficiently American.[37] So much so that Barack Obama was compelled to release his long-form birth certificate proving he was born in the United States after the "birther" belief that he was not American born reached a critical mass in April 2011.[38] Perhaps because of these "Obama as other" attacks, the false belief that Barack Obama was a Muslim increased significantly during the first term of his presidency. In September 2008, 16 percent of the 2008–12 CCAP panelists said that Barack Obama was a Muslim. When these exact same individuals were reinterviewed in July 2012, 22 percent thought that President Obama practiced Islam.[39]

Unlike Barack Obama's race, many Americans were comfortable citing the president's supposed Muslim faith as a reason not to vote for his reelection bid. Figure 3.5 shows that our respondents in a 2012 CCES survey were generally unwilling to say that Obama's race made them less likely to vote for him.[40] Only 11 percent of Romney voters said that the president's race was a net negative. The same display, however, goes on to show that a majority of Mitt Romney's voters (51 percent) said that Obama's religion made them less likely to vote for President Obama— almost all of whom thought that Barack Obama was not a Christian. These large differences between the percentage of Romney voters who said they were less likely to vote for Obama because he was Muslim and the proportion saying they were less likely to vote for him because he was black once again attests to the relative acceptability of prejudice against Muslims in contemporary American society.

With the belief that President Obama is a Muslim increasing during his presidency, and with so many Americans citing Obama's Muslim faith as a reason not to vote for him, we would expect attitudes about Muslims to have been at least as strongly linked to 2012 vote intentions as they had been back in 2008. Consistent with that expectation, the results in figure 3.6 suggest that attitudes toward Muslims were an even stronger determinant of 2012 vote choice than they were in 2012. The first panel of

Percentage Less Likely to Vote for Obama because of his Race/Religion

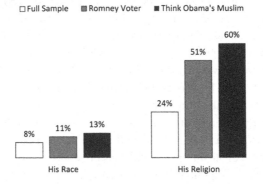

□ Full Sample ▨ Romney Voter ■ Think Obama's Muslim

FIGURE 3.5. Percentage Less Likely to Vote for President Obama Because of His Race and Religion in 2012
Source: 2012 Cooperative Congressional Election Study (CCES), Brown University Module.

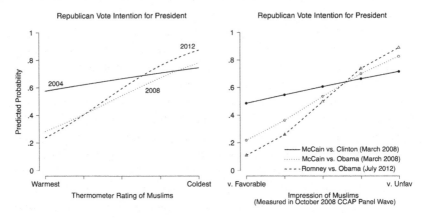

FIGURE 3.6. White Americans' Vote Intentions for President as a Function of Attitudes toward Muslims (2004–12)
Note: Probabilities based on logistic regression coefficients in the online appendix. Predicted probabilities were calculated by setting racial resentment, party identification, and ideological self-placement to the mean white respondent.
Source: 2004–12 American National Election Studies (ANES) (*left*); 2008–12 Cooperative Campaign Analysis Project (CCAP) panelists who were interviewed in both 2008 and 2012 (*right*).

the display graphs out the relationship between white respondents' thermometer ratings of Muslims and their presidential vote intentions in 2012, 2008, and 2004 (the first election year that included this measure). After controlling for racial resentment, party identification, and ideological self-placement, moving from lowest to highest in anti-Muslim affect was associated with a nonsignificant six-point increase in support for George W. Bush against John Kerry. That same change in feelings toward Muslims, however, was associated with a thirty-eight-point boost in John McCain's vote share, and fifty-three-point bump in Romney vote intention.

Perhaps more important, the right panel of figure 3.6 shows that attitudes about Muslims also became a stronger determinant of our CCAP panelists' 2012 vote preferences. Like the racial attitude results presented earlier, the solid line in this display suggests that attitudes about Muslims would have had a much smaller impact on 2008 voting behavior had John McCain faced Hillary Clinton instead of Barack Obama. As figure 3.6 shows, white panelists who rated Muslims very favorably were only slightly more likely to support Hillary Clinton over John McCain in this March 2008 trial heat than panelists who rated Muslims most negatively. Meanwhile, the same change in the same panelists' impressions of Muslims increased John McCain's vote share over Barack Obama by forty percentage points and boosted Romney's 2012 vote share by sixty points.

Thus, despite holding the most prototypically American job imaginable, President Obama continued to be evaluated as "the other" during his presidency. In fact, ethnocentric beliefs such as anti-Muslim sentiments were more powerful than they had ever been in predicting opposition to his reelection bid.

Concluding Remarks

This chapter has told the story of Barack Obama's first term in the White House through the eyes of our expectations about whether racial attitudes remained an unusually strong consideration in 2012 voting behavior. Based on the events and circumstances that were chronicled, the results presented above should not be the least bit surprising. Indeed, it was difficult to deactivate racial attitudes in 2012 voting behavior, given such factors as intense opposition to Obama, biased information processing, an ambiguous presidential record, changing demographics, racialized communications, and the president's historical racial significance. Consistent

with that expectation, the chapter showed that the effects of racial resentment, antiblack stereotypes, antiblack affect, and Muslim thermometer and favorability ratings on 2012 presidential vote preferences were
similar to their large impact on the 2008 election. It is safe to conclude,
then, that racial attitudes continued to be one of the more powerful determinants of 2012 voting behavior.[41]

The more interesting and politically important question for our purposes is how would that unusually large impact of racial attitudes on 2008
and 2012 vote preferences affect the broader American political landscape? The spillover of racialization hypothesis laid out in the previous
chapter suggests that these effects should have a profound influence on
a variety of Obama-era political opinions. That is, mass politics in general
should have been more heavily influenced by racial attitudes and race
during Obama's presidency than it was beforehand. This chapter hinted
at that conclusion, too, by showing how evaluations that were strongly
connected with President Obama's 2012 candidacy (unemployment perceptions) became more heavily influenced by racial attitudes than they
were beforehand. The spillover of racialization from Barack Obama into
American politics, as we will soon see, extended much, much further.

Racial Attitudes and Evaluations of Public Figures in the Obama Era

STEPHEN COLBERT: Why do you think [hugging Barack Obama] ended [your political career]?
CHARLIE CRIST: Number one, he was there to talk about the [American] Recovery [and Reinvestment] Act, the stimulus, as people call it. And a lot of Republicans took issue with that. So I think that was part of it. Sadly, I think another part of it was that he was Democrat—but not just a Democrat, an African-American.
COLBERT: Oh, you're not going to place the race card.
CRIST: ... I'm just trying to tell the truth. I have seen a level of vitriol directed at this president that I have never seen directed at President Kennedy or maybe President Johnson or even President Carter. — *The Colbert Report*, February 11, 2014[1]

Charlie Crist may not have employed the same terminology in this playful exchange with Stephen Colbert that I have used in the book's previous chapters. But the former Republican governor of Florida was surely making a similar argument about racial attitudes and mass political evaluations during Barack Obama's presidency. Indeed, Charlie Crist suggested on the *Colbert Report* that his political career as governor ended in large part because of the hostile, race-based, reaction to his publicized embrace of the first ever African American president. Or to use our nomenclature, Governor Crist believed that racial animus *spilled over* from Barack Obama into evaluations of his gubernatorial performance after their 2009 hug linked the two politicians in some Floridians' minds.

In another parallel with the main argument of this book, Charlie Crist did not suggest that race was the only, or even the most important, reason why so many Republicans objected to his embrace of President Obama. As the epigraph that introduced this chapter indicates, the former Florida governor also cited the president's Democratic partisanship and the pres-

ident's public policy positions as major reasons for the negative response
to his presidential hug. At the same time, though, Governor Crist echoed
the research referenced back in chapter 2 about the close linkage between
anger and racial resentment (Banks 2014; Banks and Valentino 2012)
when he singled out Obama's race as the primary reason why the opposition to his presidency was so vitriolic. Crist (2014), for example, wrote in
his memoir: "Barack Obama was the first African American in the White
House. Florida had helped to put him there. And it was impossible to
imagine an equal measure of virulence for any politician whose skin was
white."[2] Charlie Crist would later point to the tone of that opposition as
a major reason he left the Republican Party, saying in a 2014 interview,
"I couldn't be consistent with myself and my core beliefs, and stay with
a party that was so unfriendly toward the African American president."[3]

Governor Crist's statements raised two important questions about the
effects of racial attitudes on mass assessments of public figures during
Barack Obama's presidency. The first question involves the role of racial
attitudes in mass assessments of Barack Obama himself. That is, just how
important and unwavering were racial attitudes in shaping public opinion
about Barack Obama? Crist suggested that they were a prime determinant of white opposition toward Obama's presidency, and we know from
the previous chapter that they remained an important cause of 2012 voter
preferences. But were the effects of racial attitudes on public support for
President Obama altered by new events like the 2012 campaign? Or was
race such a salient feature of Barack Obama's public persona that Americans evaluated him and his presidency through a similarly strong racial
lens even when they were prompted with new information (either experimentally administered or naturally occurring) that was designed to enhance or deactivate the political influence of racial resentment?

Charlie Crist's statements also raise the second important question of
whether racial attitudes spilled over into mass assessments of political
figures who were increasingly tied to President Obama. Prior research
showed that there was, in fact, a spillover of racialization into evaluations of public figures during both the 2008 campaign and the first year of
Barack Obama's presidency. The impact of racial attitudes on mass assessments of John McCain and Hillary Clinton throughout the 2008 election
year depended in large part on how closely their candidacies were situated in opposition to Barack Obama (Tesler and Sears 2010). An August
2009 survey experiment also revealed that racial attitudes were a significantly stronger predictor of public opinion about Sonia Sotomayor's Su-

preme Court confirmation among respondents who were told at random that President Obama had nominated her (Tesler and Sears 2010, fig. 8.7). So Charlie Crist certainly seemed to be on to something. Nevertheless, it is important to determine whether the spillover of racialization into mass assessments of public figures continued throughout Barack Obama's presidency and to examine just how far those potential racial spillover effects may have extended.

* * *

The results presented in this chapter suggest that racial attitudes were a strong and stable determinant of Obama evaluations throughout the 2012 campaign. Not only did racial resentment have a similar impact on how the public evaluated Barack Obama every month of the 2012 election year but experiments designed to either prime or neutralize the influence of racial attitudes on mass assessments of President Obama did little to alter that strong relationship. Those results are consistent with our earlier contention that Obama's omnipresent position as a historic racial figure made race-based attitudes a chronically accessible consideration in mass assessments of his presidency (Tesler and Sears 2010)—one that is difficult to either deactivate or enhance. With racial predispositions strongly linked to public opinion about Barack Obama, we might expect those attitudes to have also spilled over into mass assessments of his most visible political friends and foes. Consistent with that expectation, the chapter shows that racial resentment's impact on public support for political figures during Barack Obama's presidency depended in large part on how closely these individuals were connected or contrasted with the president. Indeed, the results below indicate that racial attitudes spilled over from Barack Obama into mass assessments of Mitt Romney, Joe Biden, Hillary Clinton, Charlie Crist, and even the Obama family's dog Bo.

Racial Resentment and Obama and Romney Evaluations during the 2012 Campaign

One of the more interesting patterns that we uncovered in our analyses of the impact of racial attitudes on public opinion during the 2008 presidential election campaign was the differing effects of racial resentment on Barack Obama's and John McCain's favorability ratings at various points in the election year. Racial resentment was a strong and stable determinant of how the public evaluated Barack Obama throughout the 2008 primary and general election season (Tesler and Sears 2010; Jackman and Vavreck 2012). In stark contrast with that stability, the effects of racial attitudes on mass assessments of John McCain depended fundamentally on whether he represented the last line of defense against a Barack Obama presidency. Racial resentment had little influence on McCain's favorability ratings before he became the Republican presidential nominee. These resentment effects, however, increased dramatically during the fall campaign even though the impact of racial resentment on Republican presidential candidates' thermometer ratings had historically weakened *after* they secured the nomination. The racial resentment effects on McCain's fall 2008 favorability ratings then returned to their prenominee levels in late 2009 when his presidential contest against Barack Obama became an increasingly distant political memory (Tesler and Sears 2010, chap. 4).

If the effects of racial attitudes were as similar in 2008 and 2012 as the results in chapter suggested, then we might expect these same racialized patterns to reproduce themselves in Barack Obama's and Mitt Romney's favorability ratings during the 2012 campaign. Thankfully, we can test that expectation with the 2011–12 Cooperative Campaign Analysis Project (CCAP). This unique election study interviewed hundreds of thousands of Americans in late 2011 and then reinterviewed fresh nationally representative subsamples ($N = 1,000$) from that baseline every week of the campaign. Since racial resentment was asked in the 2011 benchmark survey, we can determine the weekly effects of racial conservatism on Barack Obama's unfavorability ratings and Mitt Romney's favorability ratings throughout the course of the 2012 campaign.

Figure 4.1 presents the results from those analyses. The lines in the display disclose the average effects of racial resentment on the two general election candidates' ratings throughout the 2012 campaign after controlling for party identification and ideological self-placement. The solid line, therefore, tells us that racial resentment was a strong and stable predictor of how white Americans evaluated Barack Obama throughout the 2012 campaign. All else being equal, the figure indicates that moving from least to most racially resentful increased Obama's unfavorability rating by 32 percent of the scale's range in February 2012, the month that the CCAP's weekly reinterview surveys first began assessing candidate favorability. That racial resentment effect, as can be seen, was nearly identical to its Election Day impact several months later. In other words, all the

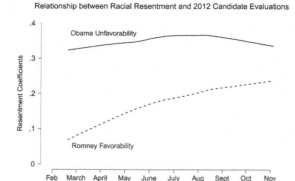

FIGURE 4.1. Relationship between Racial Resentment and White Americans' Candidate Favorability Ratings during the 2012 Campaign

Note: Lines are based on the smoothed trend (lowess) in weekly resentment coefficients, which were produced by regressing each candidate's 0 to 1 weekly favorability rating on racial resentment, party identification, and ideological self-placement for each of the thirty-eight weeks when favorability was asked from late February to November 2012. Each place on the line denotes the smoothed effect of moving from least to most racially resentful on the candidate's rating while holding party and ideology constant.

Source: 2011–12 Cooperative Campaign Analysis Project.

information imparted by the 2012 election campaign, which included racialized communications that have historically increased the association between presidential evaluations and racial attitudes (Kinder and Sanders 1996; Valentino 1999; Mendelberg 2001; Valentino, Hutchings, and White 2002; also see discussion in chap. 3), did not alter racial resentment's impact on public opinion about President Obama during the election year.

The dashed line in the display, however, indicates that the effect of racial attitudes on mass assessments of Mitt Romney changed substantially during the 2012 campaign. After controlling for partisanship and ideology, moving from least to most racially resentful increased Romney's favorability rating by only about a 7 percent of the scale's range in February 2012. Figure 4.1 goes on to show that this nonsignificant relationship steadily strengthened as Romney's candidacy was increasingly contrasted with Obama's racialized presidency. So much so that the effect of racial resentment on rating Romney favorably more than tripled by the end of the campaign to 24 percent of the favorability scale's range—an increase in magnitude that was both highly significant ($p < .001$) and almost identical to the enhanced effects of racial resentment on mass assessments of John McCain during the 2008 campaign (Tesler and Sears 2010, fig. 4.2).

Not only was the effect of racial and ethnocentric attitudes on presidential voting behavior similar in 2008 and 2012, then, but the dynamic effects of racial attitudes on public support for the two major party candidates were almost identical. As was the case in 2008, racial resentment remained a strong and stable determinant of rating Obama unfavorably throughout the campaign. Also like the 2008 campaign, racial attitudes spilled over into mass assessments of Barack Obama's general election rival after Mitt Romney's candidacy was increasingly contrasted with Barack Obama's racialized presidency.

Experimental Tests of Racial Attitudes' Influence on Obama and Romney Evaluations

These stable effects of racial attitudes on mass assessments of Barack Obama during the 2008 and 2012 campaigns, however, do not imply that the association between racial resentment and rating Barack Obama unfavorably was immutable. It could be that the potential racializing and deracializing elements of the 2012 campaign discussed in the prior chapter cancelled each other out, thereby leaving racial resentment's net impact on mass assessments of Barack Obama unchanged over the election year. It is therefore important to more directly interrogate whether and how the effects of racial attitudes on mass assessments of Barack Obama might have been altered. The following subsections present such analyses from experiments that were designed to either enhance or neutralize the impact of racial predispositions. Like the experiments conducted by Valentino and his colleagues (2013), which were discussed in chapter 3, these experiments test whether political communications could have potentially made race-based attitudes a more or less important determinant of public opinion about President Obama.

The Welfare Ad Experiment

As also discussed in chapter 3, several commentators criticized Mitt Romney's August 2012 welfare ad for playing the race card. On the basis of prior political science research (Mendelberg 2001, 2008; Valentino, Hutchings, and White 2002; Valentino 1999; Winter 2008), this televised spot had all the hallmarks of an implicit race appeal that should have activated racially resentful support for his candidacy. Indeed, the ad contained race-coded language (e.g., welfare) over racialized imagery (e.g., hardworking whites), without ever explicitly referencing race or African Americans.

With this knowledge in mind, a team of political scientists that I was fortunate to be a part of approached the survey firm YouGov to directly test the advertisement's potential racializing influence.[4] Our proposed experimental design randomly assigned half the respondents in YouGov's nationally representative weekly reinterview surveys of one thousand Americans for the 2011–12 CCAP to view the ad, with the remaining half assigned to a no-advertisement control group. YouGov very graciously agreed to field our experiment, albeit with the sensible caveat that we could not disrupt their time series of poll results by straightforwardly asking about vote intentions or candidate evaluations. We could, however, ask how the two presidential candidates' policies benefited specific groups, and then use those items to construct highly reliable instruments or proxies for candidate favorability ratings.[5]

Figure 4.2 presents those experimental findings. The Romney results in the left panel are particularly noteworthy. First, that display shows that the effect of racial resentment on Romney ratings was much stronger among the white respondents' whom we randomly assigned to see the welfare ad than they were for subjects who were assigned to the control group. All else being equal, moving from least to most racially resentful (measured in the 2011 CCAP baseline) was associated with a 5 percent increase in positive Romney ratings in the control group, and almost a 30 percent increase for the respondents who saw the ad—a difference in effects that was statistically significant ($p = .02$). While the effects of racial resentment grew stronger after seeing the ad, the impact of ideology on Romney evaluations became much weaker ($p = .002$). These results are consistent with previous racial priming research, which suggests that nonracial conservatism is not activated by implicit racial messages (Mendelberg 2001, 182).

Finally, the results in figure 4.2. show that the ad's activation of racial resentment *did not* make Romney more popular with white voters.[6] Although the most racially resentful respondents who saw the ad rated Romney significantly more favorably than their control-group counterparts, there was an even stronger backlash effect among more racially liberal whites. Romney's welfare ad may have further polarized public opinion about his candidacy by racial attitudes, but it was unlikely to net him many votes because of the two sides of racialization.[7]

The advertisement was also unlikely to net any additional votes for

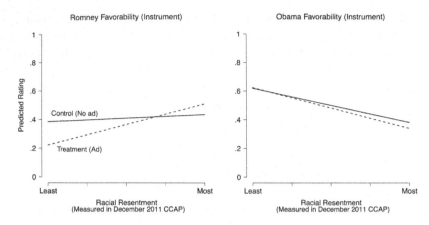

FIGURE 4.2. White Americans' Candidate Evaluations (Instrument) as a Function of Racial Resentment and Experimental Condition
Note: Predicted ratings were based on OLS regression coefficients in the online appendix. Predicted ratings were calculated by setting party identification and ideological self-placement to their sample mean.
Source: 2011–12 Cooperative Campaign Analysis Project (CCAP), August 2012 reinterview.

Mitt Romney because racial resentment was already so strongly related to mass assessments of Barack Obama. Indeed, the right panel of figure 4.2 shows that the effects of racial resentment on white Americans' evaluations of President Obama were large, and essentially unchanged, by Romney's welfare ad. Moving from least to most racially resentful decreased Obama's favorability rating by about 30 percent of this instrument's range, after controlling for party and ideology, in both the treatment and control conditions. These results are consistent with our chronic accessibility account and Valentino and colleagues' (2013) experimental results, which both suggest that subtle race appeals were unlikely to activate racial resentment in mass assessments of Barack Obama. That is, implicit racial appeals did not make racial resentment more important in white Americans' evaluations of Barack Obama because, unlike Mitt Romney and white presidential candidates before him, race was already a chronically accessible consideration in public opinion about the country's first black president.

The Racist Opposition Experiment

One particularly innovative and provocative hypothesis in political science research is that implicit messages that indirectly appeal to race (e.g., Romney's welfare ad) are more effective at activating racially resentful support than explicitly racial appeals (Mendelberg 2001, 2008; Valentino, Hutchings, and White 2002; White 2007; Winter 2008; though see Huber and Lapinski 2006, 2008). The logic here is that implicitly racial messages foster connections between racial predispositions and political evaluations without white Americans knowing that they are violating the strong societal norm of racial equality. Explicit appeals, on the other hand, can lose their political potency because even many racially resentful whites are unwilling to lend their support to a candidate who appears to be openly racist. Mendelberg (2001), for instance, famously showed that the aforementioned Willie Horton ad only activated racially resentful support for George H. W. Bush's 1988 presidential candidacy during the period when the media did not draw attention to the racial stereotypes of black criminality that many believed this advertisement was designed to tap into.[8] In fact, she found that racial resentment was deactivated in presidential preferences after the media explicitly covered the Willie Horton issue's strong racial overtones.

On the basis of those results, the "racist opposition experiment" tests whether racial resentment could have been deactivated in disapproval of Barack Obama's presidency by making opposition to his presidency explicitly racial. This experiment, which was embedded in our July 2012 CCAP reinterviews, randomly assigned half the respondents to receive the following prompt before we asked them whether they approved or disapproved of Barack Obama's presidency: "As you may know, some people claim that race is a factor in opposition to President Obama. How much if anything, have you heard about RACE-BASED OPPOSITION to Obama's presidency?" The remaining half of the sample, meanwhile, was just asked whether they approved or disapproved of Obama's job as president without this "explicit prompt" drawing attention to race-based opposition to his presidency.

Figure 4.3 presents the first set of results from that experiment. Like the welfare ad experiment, which was designed to prime racial resentment, this experiment that was intended to deactivate racially conservative opposition did not alter the relationship between racial resentment and white Americans' Obama evaluations. As can be seen, racial resentment was strongly related to Obama disapproval, regardless of whether our panelists received the "explicit prompt." These findings are once again consistent with Valentino et al.'s (2013) experimental results, which showed that explicitly racial messages did not neutralize racial resentment in Obama-oriented evaluations.

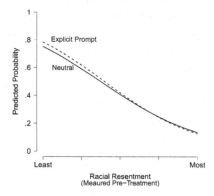

FIGURE 4.3. White Americans' Presidential Approval as a Function of Racial Resentment and Experimental Condition
Note: Probabilities based on logistic regression coefficients in the online appendix. Predicted probabilities were calculated by setting party identification and ideological self-placement to their sample mean.
Source: 2008–12 Cooperative Campaign Analysis Project (CCAP) panel, July 2012 reinterviews.

At the same time, though, the results in figure 4.4 suggest that drawing attention to racist opposition toward Barack Obama activated old-fashioned racist desires for intimate social distance between the races in presidential disapproval ratings. Those displays show that old-fashioned racism (OFR)—measured here with a reliable two-item additive index that gauged opposition to interracial dating and support for close relatives marrying spouses of the same race[9]—had a significantly stronger negative effect on Obama approval among white panelists' who were assigned to receive the "explicit prompt." As can be seen, those statistically significant differences in OFR's effects between experimental conditions were present regardless of whether we controlled for racial resentment ($p = .04$ and $p = .02$, respectively). And like the Romney racial priming result presented in figure 4.2, this experiment did not activate party and ideology in mass assessments of Barack Obama.[10]

How did an experiment designed to deactivate racially resentful opposition to Barack Obama result in priming old-fashioned racism? One likely explanation is that white Americans who are uncomfortable with intimate interracial relationships are not nearly as burdened by the norm of racial equality as are many racially resentful whites.[11] After all, if they had internalized this norm, then they should have been fine with their

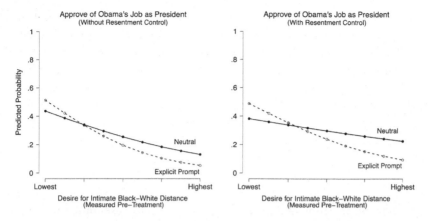

FIGURE 4.4. White Americans' Presidential Approval as a Function of Old-Fashioned Racism and Experimental Condition

Note: Probabilities based on logistic regression coefficients in the online appendix. Predicted probabilities were calculated by setting party identification, ideological self-placement, and racial resentment (*right*) to their sample mean.

Source: 2008–12 Cooperative Campaign Analysis Project (CCAP) panel, July 2012 reinterviews.

close relatives marrying someone of a different race. Drawing attention to Obama's race by highlighting accusations of racist opposition to his presidency might have, therefore, made this racially inegalitarian group even more opposed to the president than they already had been.

The racially egalitarian side of the OFR spectrum also helps explain our results. The old-fashioned racism measure suffers from the same problems that the racial thermometers and stereotypes do in discerning low-scoring racially sympathetic whites from their equally low-scoring race-neutral counterparts (see discussion in chap. 1). Comparing the results in figures 4.3 and 4.4, in fact, shows that individuals who scored low in old OFR were considerably less supportive of Barack Obama than racially sympathetic whites who scored low in racial resentment—a likely upshot of the Kinder and Sanders (1996) scale's aforementioned ability to tap into racial sympathy. Less sympathetic whites, who scored low in OFR but disapproved of Obama, may have become more supportive of the president after receiving the "explicit prompt," because racist opposition to President Obama violated the norm of racial equality. The upshot is that drawing attention to race-based opposition polarized public opinion about Barack Obama by whether white Americans were okay with intimate interracial relationships.

To be sure, much more work is needed to determine whether explicit racial appeals consistently prime old-fashioned racism in public opinion, and if so, what mechanism is responsible for that activation of OFR. For the time being, though, it appears that accusations of race-based opposition to Obama's presidency, which were frequently found on such liberal media outlets as MSNBC and the *Huffington Post* in the Obama era, further divided old-fashioned racists from their more racially egalitarian counterparts in mass assessments of Barack Obama's presidency.

* * *

In sum, our experimental results suggest that racial resentment was difficult to either deactivate or prime when it came to Barack Obama. At the same time, though, political evaluations that were not as naturally linked with racial resentment as mass assessment of Barack Obama (e.g., Mitt Romney's favorability ratings), as well as racial attitudes that were less powerful in public opinion about the president (e.g., OFR), were still primed by political communications in the Age of Obama.

Racial Attitudes and Evaluations of Democratic Vice Presidential Candidates, 1988–2012

These strong and stable effects of racial attitudes on public opinion about Barack Obama suggest that the spillover of racialization into mass assessments of public figures may have extended further than evaluations of his general election rivals. Aside from John McCain and Mitt Romney, whose 2008 and 2012 presidential candidacies represented the last lines of defense against Barack Obama's two presidential victories, no public figure was as strong of a candidate for the spillover of racialization as Joe Biden. After all, vice presidential candidates are intrinsically linked to their presidential running mates. The American public has accordingly used similar criteria to evaluate both presidential candidates and their vice presidential nominees (Weisberg and Rusk 1970). So we would expect racial attitudes to have been an unusually strong predictor of public opinion about Joe Biden during the 2008 and 2012 elections.

Table 4.1 tests that expectation with American National Election Studies (ANES) data collected from 1988 to 2012. The racial resentment coefficients in the table disclose the independent effects of moving from least

TABLE 4.1. **(OLS) Predictors of Whites' Thermometer Ratings of Democratic Vice Presidential Candidates**

	1988	1992	2000	2004	2008	2012
Racial Resentment	−8.10**	−7.63**	−10.1**	−11.8**	−21.1***	−19.1***
	(3.10)	(2.30)	(3.56)	(3.87)	(3.28)	(1.98)
Party Identification	−12.7***	−26.4***	−21.3***	−33.3***	−20.4***	−38.7***
	(2.17)	(1.73)	(2.49)	(3.16)	(2.96)	(2.92)
Ideology	−.410	−13.6***	−8.77	−17.0**	−16.6***	−30.2***
	(4.20)	(3.02)	(4.65)	(5.31)	(4.25)	(2.22)
Constant	64.5***	81.5***	77.6***	87.6***	84.0***	92.4***
	(2.52)	(2.52)	(2.50)	(2.27)	(2.27)	(1.49)
Observations	959	1450	908	670	813	3167

Source: American National Election Studies (ANES) cumulative file; 2012 ANES.
Note: Dependent variable is ninety-eight-category thermometer rating, ranging from 0 to 97. All explanatory variables are coded from 0 to 1, with 1 being the highest and/or most conservative value. Regression analyses use poststratification weights with robust standard errors that account for design characteristics.
*$p < .05$.
**$p < .01$.
***$p < .001$.

to most racially resentful on white Americans' 0–100 thermometer ratings of Democratic vice presidential candidates. After controlling for ideology and partisanship, the table shows that moving from least to most racially resentful consistently decreased support for Democratic vice presidents by about 10 percent of the thermometer scale's range in the twenty years preceding Barack Obama's presidential election. That same change in racial resentment, however, was associated with roughly a 20 percent decrease in support for Joe Biden in both 2008 and 2012. Or more simply put, the negative effect of racial resentment on Joe Biden's thermometer ratings was twice as strong as it had been for previous Democratic vice presidential candidates—a highly significant difference in pooled overtime effects ($p < .001$). It appears, then, that racial attitudes spilled over into mass assessments of Joe Biden because of his close association with Barack Obama.

Spillover of Racialization into Mass Assessments of Hillary Clinton

Our initial idea that racial attitudes spilled over from Barack Obama into related political evaluations began in early 2008 by merely observing how racially liberal and racially conservative Democrats seemed to change their opinions about Hillary Clinton during the 2008 presidential primaries. Racially resentful Democrats appeared, to us at least,[12] to have grown warmer toward Hillary Clinton during her divisive contest against Barack Obama, whereas racial liberals seemed to be increasingly hostile to the former First Lady. Consistent with that observation, the effect of racial resentment on Democrats' evaluations of Hillary Clinton changed rather dramatically from before to after her 2008 primary campaign. From 1992 through 2004 racially liberal Democrats rated Hillary Clinton significantly more positively than their more racially conservative Democratic counterparts. That longstanding negative relationship between racial resentment and rating Hillary Clinton favorably completely reversed itself during the 2008 primaries, though. In March 2008, racially conservative Democrats now evaluated Hillary Clinton significantly more favorably than their fellow partisans (Tesler and Sears 2010, fig. 2.5). A similar effect occurred with race, too, as African Americans rated Senator Clinton thirty percentage points less favorably in May 2008 than they did shortly before her primary contest against Barack Obama (Pew Research Center 2010, 2012a).

Hillary Clinton, however, was a loyal member of Barack Obama's cabinet throughout his first term in the White House. As a result of that harmonious relationship, we would expect the negative effects of racial resentment on Hillary Clinton's favorability ratings to have grown stronger from before to after she served as President Obama's secretary of state. Fortunately, the 2008–11 and the 2008–12 CCAP panel studies, which assessed the exact same panelists' opinions of Hillary Clinton at both the height of her contest with Barack Obama in March 2008 and then again in 2011 and 2012 when she was riding a wave of record popularity as secretary of state, are ideal for testing that expectation.

Figure 4.5 presents the results from those tests. The first panel of the display graphs out the relationship between racial resentment and rating Hillary Clinton favorably in the March 2008 and April 2011 waves of the 2008–11 CCAP panel study. As can be seen, there was a modest, but statistically significant ($p = .02$), *positive* relationship between racial resentment and Hillary Clinton's favorability ratings in March 2008. After controlling for party identification and ideological self-placement, moving from least to most racially resentful increased white support for Hillary Clinton by twelve percentage points. That positive relationship was almost certainly the byproduct of her divisive primary contest against Barack Obama, as racial resentment had long been negatively associated

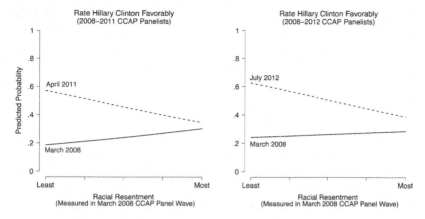

FIGURE 4.5. White Americans' Support for Hillary Clinton as a Function of Racial Resentment, 2008–12
Note: Probabilities based on logistic regression coefficients in the online appendix. Predicted probabilities were calculated by setting party identification and ideological self-placement to their sample mean.
Source: 2008–11 Cooperative Campaign Analysis Project (CCAP) panel; 2008–12 CCAP panel.

with support for Hillary Clinton (Tesler and Sears 2010). By 2011, though, racial resentment was once again a highly significant negative predictor of these exact same panelists feelings toward Secretary Clinton ($p = .001$).[13] The second panel of the display, which uses a different baseline sample for the 2008–12 CCAP reinterviews, reveals a very similar result. That display shows that the impact of racial resentment on Hillary Clinton's favorability ratings also changed from positive in March 2008 to significantly negative in July 2012.

It is worth mentioning a few additional points about the dynamics of public support for Hillary Clinton during her time as President Obama's secretary of state. First, the combined over-time effects of party and ideology did not increase in either the 2008–11 or 2008–12 CCAP panels. At the same time, though, the independent impacts of racial and gender attitudes on Hillary Clinton's favorability ratings *both* increased significantly from 2008 to 2011 when these measures were included in the same model (McThomas and Tesler forthcoming, table 1). Those findings suggest that Americans with conservative feelings about gender and race did not update their feelings toward Secretary Clinton despite the mostly positive press about her job performance as secretary of state and her record popularity during Barack Obama's presidency. Although gender traditionalists were apparently unlikely to reevaluate their prior opinions of Hillary Clinton because of their aversion to women in powerful positions (McThomas and Tesler forthcoming), racial conservatives were presumably unwilling to increase their over-time support for Hillary Clinton because she went from an adversarial to a cooperative relationship with Barack Obama.

Meanwhile, white racial liberals and African Americans naturally became more favorably disposed toward Hillary Clinton than they had been when she was Barack Obama's main rival for the 2008 Democratic nomination. All else being equal, white racial liberals rated Hillary Clinton thirty percentage points more favorably in both 2011 and 2012 than they had back in March 2008. Both African American CCAP panelists and black Pew Poll respondents also rated Clinton at least thirty percentage points more favorably during Barack Obama's presidency than they had when the two were rivals for the 2008 Democratic nomination (Pew Research Center 2010, 2012a).[14]

All told, then, the effects of racial attitudes and race on mass assessments of Hillary Clinton from 2008 to 2012 depended in large part on her relationship with Barack Obama. When she was the last line of defense against Barack Obama winning the Democratic Party's presidential nomination, racial liberals and African Americans increasingly disliked her. Their historically strong support, however, more than rebounded after the divisive 2008 primary and propelled Hillary Clinton's popularity to record levels when she was closely aligned with President Obama as his secretary of state.

Spillover of Racialization into Portuguese Water Dogs

The results presented thus far, however, cannot tell us why racial attitudes spilled over from Barack Obama into mass assessment of public figures. Did this spillover of racialization, for instance, occur because Americans thought public figures who were aligned with (or against) President Obama disproportionately favored (or opposed) policies aimed at helping black people? Or was it simply the case that any direct link to President Obama was sufficient to racialize mass opinion about public figures? The spillover of racialization hypothesis, as elaborated in chapter 2, suspects that both processes were at play during Barack Obama's presidency, with racial spillover effects thought to be especially large and long lasting for issues in which African Americans were the perceived beneficiaries of the president's positions. Yet, if connecting an apolitical public figure to President Obama still polarized public opinion by racial attitudes and/or race, we could at least conclude that racial policy congruence is not a necessary condition for racial spillover effects to have taken place.

To test that conjecture, I surveyed a nationally representative sample of a thousand YouGov respondents in March 2012 about something with no manifest political content whatsoever—feelings toward Democratic politicians' dogs. Individuals were first shown a picture of the Clintons' former chocolate Labrador, Buddy, and then asked to rate how favorably they felt toward him. This evaluation of Buddy Clinton provides an important baseline for how respondents used their racial attitudes to rate an easily identifiable Democratic politician's pet.[15] These same respondents were then shown a picture of the Obamas' Portuguese water dog Bo, but with an important twist: A random half of the sample was told that the picture was of Bo Obama, and the remaining half was told that it was a picture of Ted Kennedy's dog, Splash—a design enabled by the fortuitous fact that Kennedy actually had a Portuguese water dog named Splash. The idea here is that any differences in evaluations of Bo Obama and Splash Kennedy should have been caused by their respective Democratic owners rather than their pictures.[16]

Figure 4.6 presents the results from this experiment. The display plots the probability of rating Buddy Clinton more favorably than Bo Obama and Splash Kennedy as a function of racial resentment. The solid line in the display, therefore, indicates that racial resentment had a slightly negative impact on rating Buddy more favorably than Splash. Moving from lowest to highest in racial resentment decreased white respondents' probability of rating Buddy higher than Splash by about five percentage points (after controlling for party and ideology). That same change in racial resentment, however, made our respondents about twenty points more likely to rate Buddy Clinton higher than Bo Obama—a statistically significant impact ($p < .05$). Although those increased effects of racial resentment on white respondents' Buddy-Bo evaluations were not quite significantly different than their impact on Buddy-Splash evaluations ($p = .13$), racial resentment was a significantly stronger predictor of Buddy-Bo evaluations when controlling for race in the full sample of one thousand respondents.[17]

We can confidently conclude, then, that the spillover of racialization even extended into evaluations of Portuguese water dogs.[18] This example,

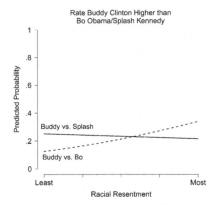

FIGURE 4.6. White Americans' Evaluations of Democratic Politicians' Dogs as a Function of Racial Resentment
Note: Probabilities based on logistic regression coefficients in the online appendix. Predicted probabilities were calculated by setting party identification and ideological self-placement to the average respondent.
Source: 2012 Cooperative Campaign Analysis Project (CCAP), March 30–April 1, 2012, re-interview survey.

while meant to add levity to an otherwise serious subject matter, also proves an important point about the spillover of racialization into mass assessments of public figures. Individuals need not think that public figures allied with Barack Obama will be more supportive of African Americans for the spillover of racialization to have taken place. Indeed, strongly connecting an apolitical public figure to President Obama should have also polarized public opinion by racial attitudes, as it did with Bo Obama.

Was Charlie Crist Right about the Spillover of Racialization?

This chapter began with Charlie Crist's assertion that racial animus spilled over from Barack Obama into Floridians' evaluations of his gubernatorial performance after the two politicians' embraced. On the basis of the results above, which showed that racial attitudes became more closely associated with mass assessments of Hillary Clinton, Joe Biden, and even Portuguese water dogs after they were increasingly tied to the president, Governor Crist's contention certainly seems plausible.

We can do better than that, though, and directly test whether the growing opposition to Charlie Crist's job performance from 2008 to 2010 was most pronounced among racially conservative respondents in re-peated cross-sectional surveys conducted for the Cooperative Congres-sional Election Study (CCES). The CCES, which included representative samples of 2,816 and 4,547 Floridians in 2008 and 2010, respectively, asked about affirmative action for blacks and gubernatorial job performance in both of those surveys. Opposition to affirmative action is a viable measure of racial conservatism but by no means a perfect one. Many Americans oppose this policy for reasons that have nothing to do with race (Snider-man and Piazza 1993; Kinder and Sanders 1996; Sniderman and Carmines 1997). Nevertheless, racial resentment is consistently the strongest pre-dictor of white opposition to race-targeted policies (Kinder and Sanders 1996; Sears et al. 1997), and the correlation between racial resentment and opposition to affirmative action in the 2010 and 2012 CCES surveys was very high ($r = .68$). A major critique of symbolic racism and racial resent-ment, in fact, has long been that its measurement is too close in content to affirmative action to validly explain racial policy preferences (Snider-man, Crosby, and Howell 2000; Carmines, Sniderman, and Easter 2011; Schuman 2000). For our purposes of estimating the effect of racial con-servatism on public opinion about Charlie Crist, though, the strong con-ceptual and quantitative link between symbolic racism and racial policy preferences makes opposition to affirmative action an outstanding proxy for racial resentment.[19]

That being said, figure 4.7 displays Charlie Crist's job approval rat-ings as a function of opposition to affirmative action in the 2008 and 2010 CCES surveys. Consistent with Crist's contention at the beginning of this chapter, racially conservative Americans were particularly less supportive of his job as governor after he hugged Barack Obama than they were be-forehand. In 2008, opposition to affirmative action had a slight, but non-significant, positive relationship with Crist approval. After controlling for partisanship and ideological self-placement, the graph shows that chang-ing from strongly supporting affirmative action to strongly opposing it in-creased Crist's approval rating by eight percentage points in 2008. That same change in affirmative action opinions, however, significantly de-creased white Floridians' approval of Governor Crist by sixteen percent-age points in 2010 ($p = .001$). Those differing effects of affirmative action opposition from 2008 to 2010 were also statistically significant ($p = .002$).

It is important to note that these results could have also been driven in part by the fact that Governor Crist changed his party affiliation in 2010 to run for the United States Senate as an Independent candidate.[20]

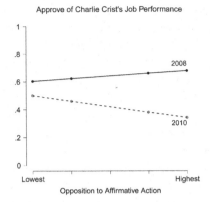

FIGURE 4.7. White Floridians' Support for Charlie Crist as a Function of Affirmative Action Opposition, 2008–10
Note: Probabilities based on logistic regression coefficients in the online appendix. Predicted probabilities were calculated by setting party identification and ideological self-placement to the average white Floridian.
Source: 2008 and 2010 Cooperative Congressional Election Study (CCES).

Indeed, the growing disapproval of Crist's job performance from 2008 to 2010 was also pronounced among conservatives and Republicans. Yet, given the pervasive spillover effects of racial attitudes into mass assessments of public figures in the Age of Obama—effects that included the spillover of racialization into mass assessments of John McCain, Hillary Clinton, Sonia Sotomayor, Mitt Romney, Joe Biden, and Bo Obama—it appears that Crist's embrace of President Obama contributed to the increased negative effects of racial conservatism on white Floridians disapproval of his job performance from 2008 to 2010.

Concluding Remarks

This chapter has shown that racial resentment was a strong and mostly stable predictor of public opinion about Barack Obama during the first term of his presidency. Neither the 2012 campaign nor experimental treatments that have a proven track record of changing racial attitudes' impact on mass assessments of public figures altered the negative relationship between racial resentment and support for President Obama. As a result of that important and enduring relationship, mass assessments of prominent public figures in the Obama era depended in large part on how closely these individuals were linked or contrasted with the president. So much so, that racial resentment even spilled over from Barack Obama into public opinion about his dog Bo.

As we will see in later chapters, this spillover of racialization into mass assessments of public figures had electoral consequences. Chapter 6 shows that racial attitudes had a stronger influence on congressional elections during Barack Obama's presidency than they had previously. And in an even stronger parallel with the results presented above, we will soon see that the spillover of racialization into congressional elections was most pronounced in districts where Democratic members of Congress were most supportive of President Obama's legislative agenda.

Along with the importance of this chapter's findings for the growing racialization of congressional elections during Barack Obama's presidency, the results should also have implications for the 2016 presidential election. In particular, they suggest that the impact of racial attitudes on mass assessments of the 2016 Democratic nominee for president will depend in part on how closely he or she is associated with Barack Obama. To be sure, presidential candidates from the incumbent party often try to distance themselves from the sitting president in open-seat contests like the 2016 election (Vavreck 2009; Johnston et al. 2004; Kenski, Hardy, and Jamieson2010). And given Barack Obama's underwater approval ratings at the time of this writing, the 2016 Democratic nominee will probably try to detach him- or herself from the president. Despite those earnest efforts, though, evaluations of the outgoing president inevitably come to influence open-seat presidential contests (Abramowitz 1988, 2008; Hillygus and Jackman 2003; Johnston, Hagen, and Jamieson 2004; Tesler and Sears 2010). It is unlikely, then, that the 2016 Democratic presidential nominee will be able to separate him- or herself too much from Barack Obama. Consequently, the results in this chapter suggest that racial attitudes may spillover even further into mass assessments of the 2016 presidential candidates and hence Americans' voting behavior in this first post-Obama presidential election.

CHAPTER FIVE

The Spillover of Racialization into Public Policy Preferences

What I'm saying is this debate that's taking place [over health care reform] is not about race, it's about people being worried about how our government should operate. — President Obama, *Meet the Press*, September 2009[1]

Health care reform dominated the national political landscape during much of Barack Obama's presidency. From the spring of 2009, when the president's proposals first began to surface, up until the Affordable Care Act (ACA) was signed into law on March 23, 2010, health care reform shined especially bright in the media spotlight. In fact, the highly visible debate over the government's role in providing health care touched off by the White House's proposal of policies like universal health insurance coverage and a government-administered public health care option was one of the most reported on news stories in America every single week from early July 2009 through the remainder of the calendar year.[2]

Of course, the stringent opposition from Barack Obama's political opponents to those proposed reforms drove much of the media's interest. Republican lawmakers, libertarian interest groups, Fox News commentators, Tea Party activists, and rank-and-file conservative Americans vehemently objected to the administration's health care reform efforts. Their disapproval was powerfully voiced to congressional Democrats at angry town hall meetings throughout the summer of 2009 and helped fuel the Tea Party's early protest rallies against Barack Obama's presidency in 2009 and 2010. The acrimonious atmosphere surrounding the 2009–10 health care debate was perhaps best personified by Congressman Joe Wilson (R-SC), who yelled, "You lie!" at the president during a September

2009 joint session of Congress where Barack Obama laid out his health care proposals.

Barack Obama was by no means the first president to propose a greater role for the federal government in providing health coverage. Health care reform had been hallmarks of the Democratic Party's presidential platforms and legislative agendas ever since Harry Truman proposed national health insurance in the 1940s (Morone 2010; Blumenthal and Morone 2010). Nor was Barack Obama the first Democratic president whose health care reform proposals faced formidable obstacles in Congress. Congressional opposition ultimately derailed Bill and Hillary Clinton's efforts to enact health care reform legislation sixteen years earlier. At the same time, though, the emotionally charged vitriolic response to President Obama's health care proposals—a response that was prominently displayed at angry town hall meetings and Tea Party protest rallies throughout the second half of 2009—seemed to be substantially different than the tone surrounding those prior legislative debates.

And indeed it was. As discussed in greater detail below, the percentage of broadcast news stories about health care, which mentioned the words "anger" or "angry," was five times greater in 2009 and 2010 than it was during the 1993–94 health care debate prompted by the Clintons' legislative proposals.[3] Or more simply put, the 2009–10 legislative debate stirred up angry emotions in ways that prior health care proposals had not.

While there were a number of plausible reasons why the 2009 health care debate was so heated,[4] many liberal Americans were quick to point to Obama's race as the primary cause of the visceral opposition. These political commentators saw the angry reaction to health care reform as an expression of racist opposition to the first black president's most significant policy proposal. Paul Krugman, for instance, wrote in his August 2009 *New York Times* column: "The driving force behind the town hall mobs [opposing health care reform] is probably the same cultural and racial anxiety that's behind the "birther" movement, which denies Mr. Obama's citizenship."[5] The *Huffington Post* published a similar story in July 2009, entitled "Opposition to Obama Health Care Reform Driven by Racism Not Fear of Increasing Debt."[6] And President Jimmy Carter provocatively proclaimed during September 2009's rancorous health care debate that "an overwhelming portion of the intensely demonstrated animosity toward President Barack Obama is based on the fact that he is a black man, that he's African-American."[7]

As a result of those conspicuous charges of racial bias, news stories

citing accusations of racist opposition to the president's health care proposals were quite common during the 2009–10 health care debate. There
were hundreds of broadcast news stories about alleged racist opposition
to health care.[8] Those reports of health care racism reached their high-
point in the immediate aftermath of the ACA's passage when health
care protestors purportedly shouted racist slurs at black congressmen
on their way to vote for the bill.[9] By contrast, explicit mentions of race
were entirely absent from the 1993–94 health care debate. A quick Lexis-
Nexis search revealed *no broadcast news stories* that referenced racist or
prejudiced opposition to the Clintons' health care reform legislation in
1993 and 1994.[10] Consequently, race was more closely linked to Barack
Obama's health care reform efforts in the news media than it had been
for previous presidents.

Not surprisingly, then, the belief that racism undergirded opposition
to Obamacare gained some public traction during the prolonged 2009–
10 health care debate. Google searches for *health care racism*, which were
also nonexistent in the pre-Obama period, spiked in the summer of 2009,
reached their height the month that the ACA was signed into law (March
2010), and persisted throughout most of Barack Obama's presidency.[11]
In keeping with those Google search patterns, 40 percent of adults said
they had heard "a lot" about "charges that racism is a factor in criticism
of President Obama" by September 2009 (Pew Research Center 2009a).
And according to a November 2009 Pew Poll, 54 percent of respondents
thought that race was at least a minor reason why "people oppose Barack
Obama's policies," with 52 percent of African Americans saying it was a
major factor (Pew Research Center 2010).

The president, along with many other political figures, came to a much
different conclusion. As the epigraph that introduced this chapter indicated, Barack Obama repeatedly rebutted claims that hostility toward his
health care plan was rooted in racial animus. He, instead, insisted that the
media was merely pursuing the prejudiced opposition narrative because
race continues to evoke such powerful emotions in American society.[12]
The president even jokingly answered charges of racist opposition against
his health care reform plan on the *Late Show with David Letterman*, saying in September 2009, "I think it's important to realize that I was actually
black before the election."[13]

Republican lawmakers, who understandably took offense at being
branded as potential racists for their opposition to Obamacare, were even
more vociferous in countering such claims. Senator Ron Johnson (R-WI),

in one particularly telling incident, voiced those collective sentiments of his party when he erupted at Senator Jay Rockefeller (D-WV) for saying that some people opposed the Affordable Care Act because the president is "the wrong color." "I didn't object to [the ACA] because of the race of the president," Senator Johnson said to his Democratic colleague with his voice rising in anger. "I objected to this [health care reform legislation] because it was an assault on our freedom."[14]

It is important to note that the impassioned public exchange between Senators Johnson and Rockefeller took place in May 2014, nearly five years after charges of racist opposition to President Obama's health care reform proposals first appeared in the press. Rockefeller's claims of racist opposition to Obamacare and Johnson's counterclaims instructively illustrated the enduring nature of this debate about the role of racial prejudice (or lack thereof) in public opinion about the ACA. Yet, their exchange also demonstrated another durable feature of the debate about racism and public opposition to health care as well. Neither side of the dispute provided any evidence in support of their contrasting positions about racial attitudes and mass health care opinions. Indeed, prominent liberals and conservatives debated the role of racism in public opposition to health care throughout Barack Obama's presidency—and will likely continue doing so into the immediate future—without marshaling much, if any, corroborating evidence beyond personal anecdotes.

* * *

This chapter helps fill that empirical void by documenting the impact of racial attitudes on health care opinions before and after Barack Obama's strong association with the policy. The findings presented show that racial attitudes were both an important determinant of white Americans' health care opinions in the fall of 2009 and that their influence increased significantly *from before to after* President Obama became the face of health care reform. Moreover, results from a nationally representative survey experiment show that racial attitudes had a significantly greater impact on health care opinions when framed as part President Obama's plan than they had when the exact same policies were attributed to President Clinton's 1993 health care initiative. The effects of racial resentment on public opinion about the 2009 stimulus package and top-bracket tax increases were also significantly stronger when these policies were experimentally framed as Barack Obama's proposals than they were when they were ascribed to less racialized Democratic politicians. At the same time, though, the spillover of racialization from Barack Obama into other policy preferences was not nearly as strong and/or as lasting as the spillover of racialization into health care. In fact, this chapter highlights the resistance of some issues to President Obama's racializing influence (e.g., gun control) and the fleeting nature of the spillover of racialization into others (e.g., same-sex marriage). Nevertheless, the results presented indicate that health care's strong association with President Obama both effectively racialized public opinion about this especially important policy and contributed to the unusual anger exhibited toward the president's proposals during the bitter 2009–10 health care debate.

Racial Attitudes and Health Care Opinions 1988–2012

Public opinion about health care offers a critical test of the spillover of racialization hypothesis. After receiving little media attention during the first half of 2009, the debate over health care reform was one of the most reported on news stories in America every single week from early July through the remainder of the calendar year.[15] As a result of that sustained media coverage, up to 49 percent of Americans reported following the health care reform debate "very closely" in 2009 (Pew Research Center 2009b). Of course, health care reform legislation was so closely linked to President Obama that the ACA eventually became better known to the American public by its other name, "Obamacare." If, as the spillover of racialization hypothesis contends, Barack Obama's connection to the issue helped racialize white Americans' policy preferences, then the impact of racial attitudes on their issue opinions should have increased from before to after his reform plan was subjected to such intense media scrutiny.

My first test of that hypothesis compares the over-time relationship between racial resentment and health care opinions in American National Election Study (ANES) surveys. Since 1988, the ANES has regularly measured both respondents' preferences for governmental health insurance and their racial resentment levels in the same surveys. Likewise, every ANES presidential election year survey since 1992 has contained both racial stereotype measures and this longstanding health care item. That standard ANES health care question asks respondents to place themselves on a seven-point scale ranging from strongest support for private insurance to strongest support for governmental health care (see online appendix for exact question wording).[16] We can, therefore, use these repeated cross-sectional data to compare the relationship between racial attitudes and health care opinions during Barack Obama's presidency to their association in pre-Obama ANES surveys.

Figure 5.1 presents the results from that test. The solid line in the left panel shows the relationship between racial resentment and white Americans' support for government medical insurance (e.g., those who placed themselves between 5 and 7 on the ANES seven-point scale) in the pre-Obama health care era from 1988 to 2008. As can be seen, the most racially resentful whites were modestly more likely than their least resentful counterparts to oppose government involvement in health insurance. Moving from lowest to highest on the racial resentment scale decreased white Americans' support for government insurance by about twelve percentage points in the 1988–2008 ANES surveys after controlling for party and ideology. The dashed line in the left panel of figure 5.1 shows that this pre-Obama negative relationship increased substantially in the 2012 ANES survey. All else being equal, strong racial liberals and strong racial conservatives were separated by more than thirty percentage points in their support for government medical insurance. That nearly threefold increase in the effects of racial resentment from before to after Barack Obama became president was highly significant as well.[17]

So, too, were the changing effects of antiblack stereotypes on white

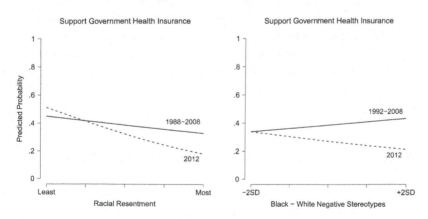

FIGURE 5.1. White Americans' Support for Government Health Insurance as a Function of Racial Attitudes

Note: Predicted probabilities based on logistic regression coefficients in the online appendix. Probabilities were calculated by setting ideology, partisanship, to the mean white respondents.

Source: American National Election Studies (ANES) cumulative file; 2012 ANES.

Americans' health care opinions. The right panel in figure 5.1 shows that racial stereotypes actually increased support for government medical insurance before Barack Obama became president. That slight, but significant ($p < .05$), *positive association* in the pre-Obama era changed to a modest, but significant ($p < .05$), *negative association* in 2012. The graph goes on to show that, all else being equal, white Americans who scored at least two standard deviations above the average antiblack stereotype score were over twenty percentage points less supportive of government health insurance in 2012 than they had been in ANES surveys conducted before Barack Obama became the face of the policy.

The over-time comparisons in figure 5.1 suggest that racial attitudes were more closely aligned with health care opinions during Barack Obama's presidency than they were in earlier surveys. They also suggest that the declining support for government health insurance during Barack Obama's presidency was driven by racially conservative defections. Yet, while the negative effects of racial attitudes on governmental health insurance support during Obama's presidency were significantly larger than they were in the pooled ANES, it is important to again note that sampling, mode, and response differences between the 2012 ANES and its predecessors might bias the over-time comparisons.[18] And, as we discussed earlier, comparing the pre- to post-Obama effects of racial attitudes on political opinions in repeated cross-sectional data can produce misleading results.

All told, then, figure 5.1 offers a potentially informative snapshot of the differing racial dynamics in support for governmental health insurance during Barack Obama's presidency; but much more work is needed to confidently determine both whether racial attitudes were a significantly stronger predictor of health care opinions after Obama's issue position was highlighted and whether that racialization was caused by the president's race or another factor.

Racial Attitudes and Health Care Opinions in Panel Data 2007–12

The 2008-2009-2010 ANES panel study is particularly well suited to address the former of those two concerns. Not only did that study gauge the exact same panelists' preferences for governmental medical insurance before (March 2009) and after (September 2009) the debate over Obama's proposals heated up in the summer of 2009,[19] but it contained excellent measures of limited government attitudes and self-interested anxiety about out-of-pocket medical costs—control variables not consistently available in the figure 5.1 comparisons.

The results from these March 2009 and September 2009 ANES panel waves are presented in table 5.1. The first column of that table shows that, with partisanship, ideology, limited government preferences, and medical cost anxiety held constant, moving from least to most racially resentful decreased white support for government involvement in health insurance by about 9 percent of the scale's range in March 2009. That same change in racial resentment, however, nearly doubled to a 17 percent change in opposition to government health insurance in September 2009—a highly significant difference in over-time effect sizes ($p = .003$). The remaining columns of table 5.1 further show that antiblack stereotypes, which had no independent influence whatsoever on health care support in March 2009,

TABLE 5.1. **(OLS) Predictors of White Support for Government Health Insurance, March–September 2009**

	March 2009	Sept. 2009	Diff.	March 2009	Sept 2009	Diff.
Racial Resentment	−.093**	−.174***	−.080**			
	(.027)	(.027)	(.027)			
Party Identification	−.175***	−.161***	.013	−.189***	−.177***	.012
	(.023)	(.023)	(.024)	(.023)	(.023)	(.024)
Ideology	−.103***	−.145***	−.042	−.119**	−.175***	−.056
	(.028)	(.028)	(.029)	(.028)	(.028)	(.029)
Limited Government Scale	−.377***	−.355***	.023	−.390***	−.378***	.013
	(.029)	(.029)	(.027)	(.030)	(.029)	(.027)
Medical Cost Anxiety	.196***	.183***	−.013	.188***	.172***	−.016
	(.025)	(.025)	(.025)	(.025)	(.026)	(.025)
Antiblack Stereotypes				.005	−.124**	−.129**
				(.044)	(.043)	(.045)
Antiwhite Stereotypes				.058	.085	.028
				(.057)	(.058)	(.060)
Constant	.525***	.563***	.039	.457***	.497***	.041
	(.027)	(.027)	(.025)	(.033)	(.033)	(.032)
Observations	1604	1604	1604	1604	1604	1604

Source: 2008–9 American National Election Studies (ANES) panelists interviewed in both March and September 2009.

Note: Dependent variable is a two-item, fourteen-category government insurance scale, recoded from 0 (least support) to 1 (most support). All variables are coded from 0 to 1. Racial resentment and antiblack stereotypes were measured in August 2009; party and ideology were measured in October 2008; limited government was measured in November 2008; and medical cost anxiety was measured in March 2009. Regression analyses use weights with robust standard errors that account for design characteristics.

*$p < .05$.
**$p < .01$.
***$p < .001$.

were also a significantly stronger predictor of government health insurance preferences in September 2009 than they had been just a few months earlier ($p = .004$).

The significant over-time racialization results in the ANES panel study were replicated in the November 2009 Cooperative Campaign Analysis Project (CCAP) reinterviews. These panelists were originally asked in the December 2007 CCAP whether health care should be provided by the federal government, subsidized by the government, or voluntarily left up to individuals. Figure 5.2 examines whether the impact of racial resentment on this pre-Obama baseline assessment of health care opinions increased in November 2009. The display plots the probability of saying health care should be voluntarily left up to individuals as a function of racial resentment at these two points in time.[20] Consistent with the results in figure 5.1 and table 5.1, health care opinions were more racialized after Barack Obama became the most visible spokesperson for reform. With partisanship, ideology, and tax policy preferences (used here as a proxy for limited government) held constant, moving from least to most racially resentful increased the predicted proportion of white respondents saying that health care should be left up to individuals by just over thirty

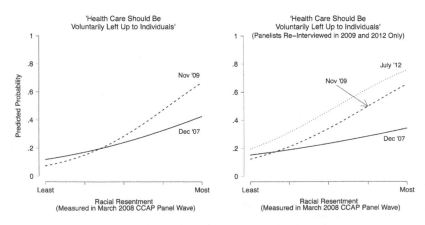

FIGURE 5.2. White Americans' Health Care Opinions as a Function of Racial Resentment
Note: Predicted probabilities based on logistic regression coefficients in the online appendix. Probabilities were calculated by setting ideology, partisanship, and tax policy preferences to their sample mean.
Source: Cooperative Campaign Analysis Project (CCAP) panelists interviewed in December 2007 and reinterviewed in the March 2008 and November 2009 panel waves (*left*). CCAP panelists interviewed in the December 2007, March 2008, November 2009, and July 2012 panel waves (*right*).

percentage points in December 2007. The same change in these panelists' resentment levels, however, increased their support for private insurance by nearly sixty percentage points in November 2009—a statistically significant difference in over-time effects ($p = .01$). Like the results in figure 5.1, this display also shows that the enhanced effects of racial attitudes were particularly pronounced among the most racially conservative respondents, whose support for private insurance increased substantially from 2007 to 2009.

These racialization results persisted, too, at least throughout the first term of Obama's presidency. The right-hand panel of figure 5.2 presents results for the 2007–8 CCAP white panelists whom we reinterviewed in both 2009 and 2012 ($n = 798$). Among this subsample of panelists, we again see a strong increase in the effects of racial resentment on support for private insurance from before to after Barack Obama became president. After controlling for March 2008 measures of party identification, ideological self-placement, and tax-policy preferences, the effects of racial resentment more than doubled from December 2007 to November 2009. As can also be seen, that increased effect remained intact during the first term of Obama's presidency. The effect of racial resentment, as measured in March 2008, on health care preferences was nearly identical in both November 2009 and July 2012 among these CCAP panelists.[21]

Interestingly enough, the effects of partisanship and ideology did not grow significantly stronger over that same time period in any of our panel surveys. In fact, their impacts were nearly identical in both the 2007 and 2009 CCAP panel waves.[22] Despite the wide schism between Democratic and Republican elites in support of health care during the latter half of 2009, table 5.1 also showed that the effects of party and ideology on ANES panelists' health care opinions were similar in March and September of that year. Only racial resentment and antiblack stereotypes were stronger predictors of white Americans' health care opinions in September 2009 than they were six months earlier. Those results stand in stark contrast with prior research on how past presidents' most visible policy positions tended to polarize public opinion by partisanship and ideology (e.g., Zaller 1992; Berinsky 2009; Levendusky 2009).[23]

In sum, whether using ANES panel data from March and September 2009 or CCAP reinterviews from December 2007, November 2009, and July 2012, the debate over President Obama's health care proposals appears to have altered the ingredients of mass opinion about this issue. Racial attitudes became more important in white Americans' beliefs about health care relative to nonracial considerations like partisanship, ideology, medical cost anxiety, and aversion to big government.

* * *

It is also worth mentioning that these results were not even the strongest health care racialization findings found in panel data. Data from the January 2008 and July 2010 ANES panel waves suggest that racial attitudes were entirely unrelated to health care opinions in January 2008, but became a very strong predictor of the exact same respondents' feelings toward the president's health care proposals in July 2010. However, those corroborating results are relegated to the online appendix because the questions were not identically worded in both waves.[24] More importantly, Henderson and Hillygus (2011) found that the effect of racial resentment on opposition to universal health insurance tripled from September 2008 to September 2010 among panelists whom they reinterviewed from the 2008 Associated Press/Yahoo! Election Survey. Also like the results presented in this chapter, Henderson and Hillygus's racialization findings were primarily driven by the most racially resentful panelists, whose predicted opposition to universal health care increased by about forty percentage points from 2008 to 2010. The results from both their data and the 2008–10 ANES panel findings presented in the online appendix should make us all the more confident that racial attitudes and health care opinions became more closely aligned after Obama's strong association with the policy.[25]

Racialization of Public Policy Preferences in Survey Experiments

The Health Care Experiments

The president's racial background, however, is certainly not the only explanation for that pre- to post-Obama health care racialization. One plausible alternative is that Barack Obama's party affiliation was responsible for polarizing public opinion by racial considerations. After all, partisan politics at both the elite level and among the mass electorate was increasingly divided by racial issues before Obama became president (Carmines and Stimson 1989; Laymen and Carsey 2002; Stimson 2004; Valentino and Sears 2005; King and Smith 2011, 2014). Racial attitudes may have been stronger determinants of health care opinions during Obama's presidency, then, because the policy was more closely connected to the racially liberal political party than it was before the visible reform debate. That party-specific hypothesis seems unlikely to fully account for the increased effects of racial attitudes and race in the fall of 2009, though. Winter (2008, 132), for example, found that thermometer ratings of African Americans were not implicated in health care opinions during the Clintons' 1993–94 reform efforts. Yet, the fact that there are readily available alternatives to the spillover of racialization from a black president into his policies underscores the need to unpack the causal effects of Obama's race in polarizing public opinion by racial considerations.

So with that in mind, we randomly assigned our November 2009 CCAP respondents to receive three different cues about who proposed specific health care reform policies.[26] These survey groups are described as (1) the neutral condition, (2) the Clinton-framed condition, (3) and the Obama-framed condition. Respondents in all three conditions were asked whether they favored or opposed the federal government guaranteeing health care for all Americans (i.e., universal coverage) and if they supported or opposed a government-administered health insurance plan to compete with private insurance companies (aka, "the public option"). Individuals in the neutral condition, however, were told only that "some people" had proposed these policies. The Clinton-framed condition, in contrast, explained that these policies were a part of President Clinton's 1993 reform efforts; and the Obama-framed condition described the initiatives as President Obama's current health care proposals.[27] We then asked each group four follow-up questions about the consequences of passing these two policies, which the questions explained were proposed by either "some people," President Clinton, or Barack Obama. A final question asked the subjects whether passing these proposals would make them feel happy, hopeful, angry, and/or afraid. Taken together, the seven health care questions form a highly reliable twenty-six-category support scale.[28]

As mentioned earlier, this approach of randomly assigning different contextual information about policy endorsements has been effectively used in previous studies to establish the causal influence of elite cues on public opinion (Peffley and Hurwitz 2010; Levendusky 2009; Tomz and Sniderman 2005; Lupia and McCubbins 1998; Kuklinski and Hurly 1994). Similarly, telling one group of respondents that Bill Clinton proposed universal coverage and the public option in 1993 and another one that the exact same initiatives were Barack Obama's proposals is especially important for our purposes because it varies the race of these policies' presidential sponsor. The partisan cues provided in both conditions, however, are held constant because Clinton and Obama are easily identifiable Democrats. Any difference in the effects of racial attitudes between the Obama and Clinton conditions, then, cannot simply be attributed to health care's increased association with the more racially liberal political party.

The chapter's second major hypothesis, therefore, is that racial attitudes should have been brought more heavily to bear on health care opinions among respondents who were told that policies like universal coverage and the public option were a part of President Obama's reform efforts. This hypothesis test, however, is complicated by the fact that many respondents surely did not need the Obama cue to connect the president—and their racial attitudes as a consequence—to health care reform. We saw above that with Obama's health care plan dominating the headlines at the time of our November 2009 survey, our CCAP panelists' opinions about governmental health insurance were already strongly influenced by racial resentment, even without additional information about Obama's position. "This baseline racialization," as Winter (2008, 66) discusses with an analogous case, "creates a ceiling effect that limits the additional framing that might be possible in the race condition." Ceiling effects might have thus inhibited the experimental cues provided in the Obama condition from further enhancing the impact of racial attitudes on health care opinions (see also the discussions in chap. 2 and below). As a result, any differences produced between conditions were likely conservative estimates of Obama's causal potential to racialize public policy preferences.

That being said, the experiments embedded in our November 2009 CCAP reinterviews still yielded significantly stronger racial attitude effects on health care opinions in the Obama condition. Those results are displayed in figure 5.3. The points on the display denote the respective impacts of racial resentment and antiblack stereotypes on the aforementioned seven-item, twenty-six-category health care support scale (recoded from 0 to 1) in all three experimental conditions. That is, each dot represents the change in health care support scores associated with moving from most racially liberal to most racially conservative with partisanship, ideology, and tax-policy preferences held constant. The coefficients presented on the left-hand side, therefore, show that moving from least to most racially resentful decreased support for health care by 23 percent of the scale's range in the Clinton condition and 40 percent in the Obama condition—a statistically significant difference in effects ($p = .01$). The

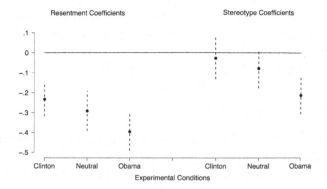

FIGURE 5.3. Impact of Racial Attitudes on White Americans' Health Care Support Scores by Experimental Condition

Note: The points on the display are based on OLS regression coefficients reported in the online appendix with partisanship, ideology, and tax-policy preferences included in the model. Each point represents the change in health care support scores (coded 0 to 1) associated with moving from least to most racially conservative, and the dashed lines denote the 95 percent confidence interval around the point estimates. Racial resentment, partisanship, and ideology were measured in both March 2008 and November 2009 and averaged across waves. Tax preferences were only measured in March 2008, and stereotypes were only measured in November 2009.

Source: Cooperative Campaign Analysis Project reinterviews, November 2009.

negative relationship between antiblack stereotypes and health care support was also significantly larger in the Obama group than it was in the Clinton condition ($p < .01$), as shown on the right side of figure 5.3.

Figure 5.3 further indicates that differences in racial attitude effects were not as pronounced between the Obama and neutral conditions as they were between the Obama and Clinton conditions. Racial resentment's impact on health care opinions among Obama-group respondents was not quite statistically different from its neutral-condition impact ($p = .14$), although antiblack stereotypes had a significantly stronger negative relationship with health care support in the Obama condition than they had for neutral-group respondents ($p = .05$). The most plausible reason why both measures of racial attitudes had larger effects on health care opinions in the neutral condition than they had in the Clinton condition is that neutral-group respondents already connected President Obama to their health care opinions even when no cue was provided.[29] Indeed, recall from table 5.1 and figure 5.2 that racial attitudes were a more powerful determinant of ANES and CCAP panelists' preferences for private health insurance *after* the 2009 summer months in which President Obama's reform efforts dominated the news. The Clinton frame, however, should have caused some respondents to shift their point of reference on health care reform from Obama to the less racialized Clinton, thereby *deactivating* the impact of racial attitudes on their opinions.

The Stimulus Experiment

An additional three-condition experiment from our November 2009 CCAP reinterviews—one of whose experimental groups framed the $787 Stimulus Package as legislation passed in 2009 by Congressional Democrats—produced an even more dramatic pattern of deracialization. With President Obama's stimulus package receiving heavy media coverage during the first half of that year (see discussion in chap. 2), the left panel of figure 5.4 predictably shows that racial resentment was a powerful independent determinant of opposition to the policy among respondents who received the Obama-framed and neutral versions of this stimulus question. Those substantial resentment effects, however, almost completely vanished in the second panel of the display for the subset of respondents who were asked if they thought the economic stimulus package *approved by Congressional Democrats* was a good or bad idea. In fact, racial resentment had a significantly larger negative impact on stimulus support in *both* the Obama and neutral conditions than it had among the Congressional Democrat (Cong Dems) group respondents. Shifting the responsibility for the stimulus away from President Obama toward these much less racialized Democrats (Tesler and Sears 2010, fig. 8.2), therefore, appears to have decreased the influence of racial attitudes on public opinion about this policy.

That deactivation in figure 5.4 is reminiscent of how counterstereotypical cues in previous racialization experiments (i.e., white criminals or white welfare recipients) neutralized the impact of racial predispositions on political evaluations (Gilliam and Iyengar 2000; Mendelberg 2001; Valentino, Hutchings, and White 2002). Combining those prior results with the deracializing impact that the Clinton and especially the congressional Democrat cues had on support for two of Obama's most visible policy proposals—health care reform and the stimulus package—seem to offer an important corollary to the spillover of racialization hypothesis. Much the way that Barack Obama's association with legislative proposals activated racial considerations, shifting responsibility for those policies away from Barack Obama to less racialized political actors like Bill Clinton and

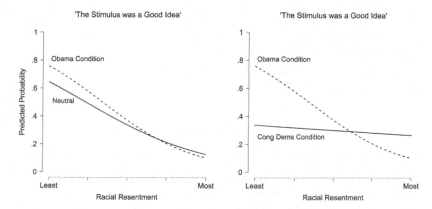

FIGURE 5.4. White Americans' Opinions about the Stimulus as a Function of Racial Resentment and Question Frame

Note: Predicted probabilities based on logistic regression coefficients in the supplemental online appendix. Probabilities were calculated by setting ideology, partisanship, and tax-policy preferences to their sample means. Racial resentment, partisanship, and ideology were measured in both March 2008 and November 2009 and averaged across waves. Tax-policy preferences were only measured in March 2008.

Source: Cooperative Campaign Analysis Project reinterviews, November 2009.

congressional Democrats should have dampened the effects of racial predispositions.

Dampening the effects of racial predispositions, however, did not necessarily mean greater public policy support. Recent research, as discussed earlier, suggests that racialization can be brought about not only by racially conservative opposition to policies and candidates but also by racially liberal support (Hurwitz and Peffley 2005; Winter 2008; Tesler and Sears 2010; Kinder and Dale-Riddle 2012). These two sides of racialization are particularly noticeable in figure 5.4, where predicted support for the stimulus was considerably higher among racial liberals in the Obama condition than it was for the Cong Dems group but weaker amongst the most racially resentful. President Obama's activation of racial liberals also helps explain why health care support was not statistically higher in the Clinton condition than it was in the Obama condition, despite the fact that health care opinions were significantly more polarized by racial attitudes when these policies were attributed to President Obama.[30]

Finally, and consistent with the results from the observational data, the effects of such nonracial factors as partisanship and ideology were not larger in the Obama condition than they were in the other two experimental groups. Respondents, therefore, used different considerations in expressing their health care and stimulus package opinions, depending on whether specific policy proposals were attributed to President Clinton, President Obama, or no one in particular: The Obama-framed questions caused racial attitudes to be a more important determinant of public policy preferences relative to nonracial considerations.[31]

Tax Increase and Assault Weapons Ban Experiments

Not all of Barack Obama's positions, however, were expected to increase the effects of racial attitudes relative to nonracial considerations. As chapter 2 suggested, Barack Obama's policy positions were unlikely to have increased the effects of racial attitudes on public opinion about issues that were already highly racialized. Instead, we might expect Obama's position to further increase the effects of partisanship and ideology relative to racial attitudes in public opinion about those policies.

Fortunately, we can test that expectation with the same experimental data used in the health care and stimulus experiments. Along with those treatments, the November 2009 CCAP survey included two additional three-condition experiments that randomly assigned respondents to Clinton-framed questions, Obama-framed questions, and a neutral condition. Respondents in all three conditions were asked whether they favored or opposed raising taxes on wealthy Americans, and if they supported or opposed banning semiautomatic assault weapons. Individuals in the neutral condition, however, were only told that "some people" had proposed these policies. Meanwhile, the Clinton-framed condition explained how President Clinton had previously signed these initiatives into law; and the Obama-framed condition described top-bracket tax increases and the assault weapons ban as President Obama's current policy proposals.

Based on the "ceiling effects explanation" proffered in chapter 2, we would expect the Obama-framed condition to have had different racializing effects on public opinion about taxes and the assault weapons ban. Support for top-bracket tax increases is characteristic of most public policy positions, whereby party and ideology have greater effects than racial attitudes. The assault weapons ban, however, is one of the few issues where racial resentment and nonracial political conservatism had similar effects on public opinion before the policy was experimentally associated with Barack Obama (Filindra and Kaplan 2014).[32] Thus, if the extent to which partisan/ideological activation and the spillover of racialization depends on the respective pre-Obama baseline effects of party/ideology and racial attitudes, then the Obama-framed condition should have mostly activated racial attitudes in tax-policy opinions and primarily activated partisan/ideological attitudes in public opinion about gun control.

Figure 5.5 tests that expectation. The two panels on the left-hand side graphically display support for top-bracket tax increases and the assault weapons ban in each of the three experimental conditions as a function of racial resentment (holding party/ideology constant). Likewise, the right-hand panels show respondents' support for these policies as a function of party and ideology (holding racial resentment constant). Consistent with

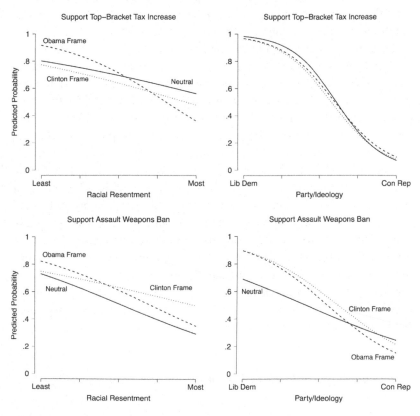

FIGURE 5.5. White Americans' Support for Top-Bracket Tax Increases and the Assault Weapons Ban as Functions of Racial Resentment, Party and Ideology, and Experimental Condition
Note: Predicted probabilities based on logistic regression coefficients in the online appendix. Probabilities calculated by setting party/ideology (*left*) and racial resentment (*right*) to their sample means. Racial resentment, partisanship, and ideology were measured in both March 2008 and November 2009 and averaged across waves.
Source: 2008–9 Cooperative Campaign Analysis Project reinterviews.

our expectations, the top-left panel shows that framing top-bracket tax increases as Barack Obama's policy activated racial resentment. After controlling for party and ideology, racial resentment had a noticeably stronger effect on opposition to increasing taxes in the Obama-framed condition than it had in the neutral and Clinton-framed conditions.[33] The top-right panel of figure 5.5, however, shows that the huge baseline effects of party and ideology were not further activated by experimentally connecting the policy to such well-known Democratic presidents as Bill Clinton and Barack Obama. As can be seen in that display, party/ideology had similarly sizable effects on tax-policy opinions across all three conditions. Like the health care and stimulus experiments, then, the Obama-framed condition enhanced the impact of racial attitudes on tax policy opinions without further activating the already large effects of party and ideology.

The result was quite different when these exact same respondents were asked about the assault weapons ban, though. The bottom-left panel of figure 5.5 shows that the large baseline effect of racial resentment on opposition to the assault weapons ban was not further activated by the Obama-framed condition. Instead, the bottom-right panel of figure 5.5 shows that our two-item political conservatism scale was a significantly stronger predictor of opposition to the assault weapons ban in the Clinton and Obama conditions than it was in the neutral condition.[34] Unlike our health care, stimulus, and tax experiments, connecting the assault weapons ban to President Obama activated party and ideology without significantly increasing the already large baseline effects of racial resentment on opposition to gun control. These results therefore suggest that, if racial attitudes had a stronger pre-Obama effect on public opinion than party identification, then Barack Obama's positions were unlikely to further racialize public policy preferences. Instead, President Obama was more likely to activate party and ideology in those rare cases.

The (Fleeting) Spillover of Racialization into Same-Sex Marriage Opinions

Barack Obama made history on May 9, 2012, by becoming the first sitting president to openly support marriage equality for gays and lesbians. This historic announcement dominated the news for a few days, but this media attention surrounding the statement soon gave way to other campaign events.[35] With President Obama's newly announced support for same-sex marriage quickly vanishing from the headlines, we would expect any racial spillover effects into public opinion about this issue to have also receded in kind. Fortunately, the 2011–12 CCAP's unique design allows us to test that expectation. As mentioned earlier, this election study interviewed hundreds of thousands of Americans in late 2011 and then reinterviewed fresh nationally representative subsamples ($N = 1,000$) from that baseline every week of the campaign. Since support for gay marriage was asked in several of these weekly reinterview surveys, we can confidently determine (1) whether Barack Obama's announcement caused racial attitudes to spill over into same-sex marriage opinions and (2) whether that suspected spillover of racialization faded after Barack Obama's support for same-sex marriage gave way to other campaign news.

Figure 5.6 tests those expectations. The dots on the display disclose the effect of moving from least to most racially resentful on opposition to same-sex marriage after controlling for partisanship, ideology, and panelists' prior opinions about same-sex marriage. As can be seen, racial resentment had a modest but significant effect on same-sex marriage opinions in 2012 surveys conducted before Barack Obama's historic announcement. After controlling for party, ideology, and 2011 opinions about marriage equality, moving from least to most racially resentful decreased support for same-sex marriage by 7 percent of the scale's range. That preannouncement impact of racial resentment, however, was nearly 2.5 times larger in the CCAP survey conducted the week after President Obama made his statement in support of marriage equality—a highly significant increase in over-time effects as shown by the barely overlapping confidence intervals in the display. Those increased effects of racial resentment on white Americans' policy preferences occurred without enhancing the effects of partisanship and ideology, either. Perhaps more importantly, though, the significant spillover of racialization effect shown in figure 5.6 immediately vanished. As can be seen in the display, the effects of racial resentment on same-sex marriage opinions quickly returned to their pre-Obama levels immediately after news of the president's announcement faded from the national headlines.

These results again show that Barack Obama's positions altered the ingredients of Americans' policy positions. Like the health care, stimulus, and tax results presented above, Barack Obama's historic announcement made racial attitudes a more important determinant of white Americans' same-sex marriage opinions. Unlike Barack Obama's longstanding association with the health care reform legislation that took his name, however,

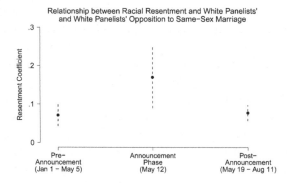

FIGURE 5.6. Relationship between White Racial Resentment and Opposition to Same-Sex Marriage in 2012
Note: Results based on OLS regression coefficients in the online appendix with 2011 measures of ideology, partisanship, and opposition to same-sex marriage included in the model. Each dot denotes the effect of moving from least to most racially resentful on opposition to same-sex marriage. Dashed lines are 95 percent confidence intervals.
Source: 2011–12 CCAP.

the president's connection to gay marriage was much more tangential. As such, the spillover of racialization into health care persisted long after the spillover of racialization into Americans' same-sex marriage preferences vanished.

Racial Attitudes and Health Care Anger

That pervasive and prolonged spillover of racialization into health care likely contributed to the especially angry tone of the 2009–10 debate over health care reform legislation. As mentioned earlier, race is probably the most divisive issue in American public life, and Banks's (2014; Banks and Valentino 2012) groundbreaking experimental work shows that racial resentment is linked to the emotion of anger in ways that such nonracial attitudes as ideological self-placement and support for limited government are not. Unfortunately, though, it is simply impossible to quantify how much racial animus might have contributed to the emotional nature of the 2009–10 health care debate.

Nevertheless, we still can glean some important insights into the emotional tenor of the 2009–10 health care debate by looking at whether our November 2009 CCAP panelists were angered more by President Obama's health care proposals than they were when the exact same policies were attributed to President Clinton. Moreover, we can determine whether the emotion of anger was particularly prevalent during Barack Obama's presidency by comparing media coverage of President Obama's health care plan in 2009–10 to broadcast news stories about Bill and Hillary Clinton's 1993–94 health care reform efforts.

Figure 5.7 presents the first of those two tests. As mentioned earlier, one of the seven questions in our November 2009 health care experiments asked respondents to check the emotions they felt toward health care proposals like universal health coverage and the public option. If, as suspected, Obama's race contributed to the emotional nature of the 2009–10 debate, then we might suspect that fewer respondents were angered by these proposals when they were attributed to President Clinton. That expectation is borne out in figure 5.7. White CCAP panelists expressed similar levels of anger toward these health care reform proposals in both the Obama and neutral experimental conditions—a likely upshot of the strong connection between President Obama and government health care at the time of the November 2009 survey. As can be seen in the figure, 35 percent of our white panelists said they were angered by these health care reform proposals in the Obama-framed and neutral condition. Only 28 percent of whites, however, were angered when the exact same proposals were attributed to President Clinton—a statistically significant difference in proportions as shown by the non-overlapping confidence intervals in figure 5.7.

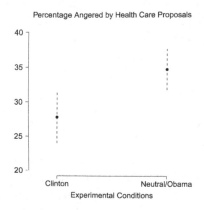

FIGURE 5.7. Percentage of Whites Angered by Health Care Proposals in Experimental Conditions
Source: Cooperative Campaign Analysis Project reinterviews, November 2009.

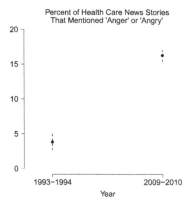

FIGURE 5.8. Percentage of Broadcast News Stories about Health Care That Mention "Anger" or "Angry" in 1993–94 and 2009–10
Source: LexisNexis search for broadcast news stories with "health care" in the headline and "anger" or "angry" in the body.

With more Americans angry about Barack Obama's health care proposals than Bill Clinton's health care initiatives in our experimental data, it is not surprising that anger was a much more prevalent emotion in the 2009–10 health care debate than it had been sixteen years earlier. Figure 5.8, for instance, presents the percentage of broadcast news stories about health care that contained the words "anger" or "angry" in both 1993–94 and 2009–10. Only 3 percent of broadcast news stories about health care mentioned these words during the debate over the Clintons' health care proposals. In 2009–10, however, more than 16 percent of broadcast news stories about health care contained the words "anger" or "angry." As many commentators observed, and the results in figure 5.8 further suggest, the debate over Barack Obama's health care proposals was more emotionally charged than the debate over the Clintons' health care reform legislation.

Along with figures 5.7 and 5.8 analyses, I searched for questions from 1993 and 1994 surveys to try to assess how much angrier white Americans were about Barack Obama's health care proposals than they had been sixteen years earlier about the Clintons' plan. Yet, while there were twenty-four different polls in the iPOLL databank that asked whether respondents were angered by Barack Obama's health care proposals in 2009 and 2010, there was not a single question that gauged respondents' anger toward President Clinton's health care reform plan in 1993 and 1994.[36] Since the pervasiveness of poll questions tends to reflect the actual dynamics of public opinion (Lee 2002), these results also speak volumes about the angrier tone of the debate over Barack Obama's health care plan in 2009 and 2010.

Taken together, the results in this chapter suggest that the spillover of racialization into health care contributed to the angry opposition toward Obamacare. We know, for example, that racial attitudes were a stronger predictor of public opinion about Barack Obama's health care plan than Bill Clinton's initiative. We also know that the public was less angered by Bill Clinton's plan than Obama's in survey experiments; and finally, we know that the emotion of anger is tied to racial resentment but unrelated to nonracial ideological predispositions (Banks 2014; Banks and Valentino 2012). Given that knowledge, it is safe to assume that Obama's race played an important part in the especially angry opposition to his health care reform plan.

Concluding Remarks

The results presented in this chapter have shown that Barack Obama's association with both health care reform legislation and other policies like the stimulus package and top-bracket taxes altered the ingredients of public opinion. Racial attitudes became a more important predictor of health care opinions during the Obama presidency, whereas the influence of partisanship, ideology, limited government attitudes, and self-interested anxiety about medical costs remained rather stagnant. That ingredients alteration, as just mentioned, almost certainly helped make the 2009–10 health care debate so vitriolic. To be sure, this does not mean that every Obamacare opponent was a racist or that racial attitudes were even the dominant determinant of health care opinions during Obama's presidency. The results in table 5.1 suggest that nonracial attitudes explained much more of the variation in opposition to governmental health care than racial attitudes did.

Nor do the health care findings suggest that every position Barack Obama staked out during his presidency polarized public policy preferences by racial attitudes. According to the theoretical conditions specified in chapter 2, health care opinions were especially ripe for racialization. Indeed, (1) Barack Obama took a very visible position on this issue, (2) his position was reinforced over time, (3) Americans did not have particularly well-developed positions about health care prior to Obama's presidency,[37]

(4) racial attitudes were not strong determinants of public support for governmental health insurance in the pre-Obama era, and (5) Americans thought blacks would benefit more than whites from Obamacare.[38] The spillover of racialization into public policy preferences that did not meet these conditions, as we saw with the assault weapons ban and same sex-marriage in this chapter, was not as large and/or not as long-lasting as the spillover of racialization into health care.

That being said, some very important takeaways from the spillover of racialization into health care still remain. The ACA was the most significant legislation of the Obama era, and it will likely remain an important political issue after Barack Obama leaves the White House. The Republican Party has made repealing Obamacare a focal point of its legislative agenda, and participation in certain ACA provisions such as expanding Medicaid for individuals who make up to sixteen thousand dollars a year remains a hotly debated issue in several states. With racial attitudes such a strong and stable predictor of feelings toward Obamacare,[39] the continued prominence of the ACA in American politics could help maintain the racialization of mass partisan politics in the post-Obama era. In fact, we'll see in the next chapter that the spillover of racialization into 2010 congressional elections was most pronounced in districts where Democrats in the House of Representatives voted for Obamacare. We will also see in chapter 6 that Republican members of the House who voted against ending the 2013 government shutdown unless the ACA was defunded or delayed from taking full effect came disproportionately from the most racially resentful congressional districts. The spillover of racialization into health care, therefore, could continue influencing the American political landscape even after Barack Obama leaves the White House.

CHAPTER SIX

Racial Attitudes and Voting for Congress in the Obama Era

I'm not recommending for every future President that they take a shellacking like I did last night. I'm sure there are easier ways to learn these lessons. But I do think that this is a growth process and an evolution. And the relationship that I've had with the American people is one that built slowly, peaked at this incredible high, and then during the course of the last two years, as we've, together, gone through some very difficult times, has gotten rockier and tougher. — President Obama's postelection press conference, November 3, 2010[1]

It was inevitable that the Democratic Party would suffer substantial losses in the 2010 midterm elections. After all, the political party who controls the White House almost always loses seats in midterm contests for the House of Representatives. The president's party, in fact, lost an average of twenty-four House seats in midterm elections held between 1946 and 2006.

A number of factors suggested that the 2010 elections would be even worse for Barack Obama and the Democratic Party than that historical average. For starters, Democrats in the House had outperformed their recent vote and seat-shares by large margins in 2006 and 2008, picking up numerous Republican-leaning seats during those two election years when the prevailing political winds were at their backs. Indeed, the Democrats held forty more seats going into the 2010 midterms than they had averaged since 1994 (Jacobson 2011). That unusually high Democratic seat-share would have been hard for the party to sustain even under favorable campaign circumstances; and it figured to cost them dearly if and when the political pendulum swung back to the right (Campbell 2010a; Jacobson 2011).

The political pendulum was almost certain to swing back to the right in

2010 given the dreadful economy that Barack Obama presided over during the first two years of his presidency. Theories of retrospective voting cast national elections as referenda on how the president is handling the economy (Fiorina 1981). It is not too surprising, then, that objective measures of economic performance like GDP growth and real disposable income gains loom large in forecast models predicting how many votes or seats the president's party will lose in the midterms (Kramer 1971; Tufte 1978; Campbell 2010b). These forecasts suggest that the president's party should win upward of fifty more seats in the very best economies than they should under the poorest economic conditions (Jacobson 2004, 155). With a stagnant economy and nearly double-digit unemployment in the aftermath of the Great Recession, the Democratic Party was bound to suffer serious setbacks in 2010. The real question heading into the election, then, was just how big their losses would be.

Along with the economy, feelings about the incumbent president are also important determinants of midterm elections. For, as Erikson, MacKuen, and Stimson (2002, 279) explain, "Approval of the president serves to predict congressional outcomes because *Approval* is a general proxy for the performance aspect of voters' partisan evaluations, including economic perceptions." Consequently, presidents with less than 50 percent approval on Election Day lost an average of thirty-six House seats in midterm elections held between 1946 and 2006 compared to just fourteen seats lost by presidents who were supported by a majority of Americans (Jones 2010).

Unfortunately for 2010 Democratic congressional candidates, President Obama was on the wrong end of this 50 percent divide. The president's 2009 honeymoon support gradually eroded over time, leaving him with an approval rating around 45 percent on the eve of the election.

Or as President Obama put it in the epigraph that introduced this chapter, his relationship with the American people had become "rockier and tougher" since its Inauguration Day apex. To be sure, much of that rockier relationship with the American public was due to the sluggish economy. Yet, presidential popularity is a strong predictor of midterm vote loss even after accounting for the relationship between economic conditions and support for the incumbent president. Barack Obama's underwater approval ratings were thus guaranteed to be a further drag on his party's prospects of retaining congressional control after the 2010 elections.

These fundamental causes of congressional election outcomes, however, still failed to predict just how large the Democratic losses were in

2010. The average political science forecast model underestimated the sixty-three members of the House that the Democrats lost in 2010 by over twenty seats. There is strong evidence that Democratic congressional candidates' support for Obama administration policies, especially the Affordable Care Act (ACA), contributed to their worse than expected showing (Nyhan et al. 2012; Brady, Fiorina, and Wilkins 2011). Relatedly, the 2010 elections were unusually nationalized—meaning Republicans and allied interests effectively used national conditions like intense opposition to the president and his policies to make the midterm election a referendum on support for Barack Obama (Jacobson 2011; Aldrich al 2013; Abramson, Aldrich, and Rohde 2011). That nationalization is another reason why the Republican tidal wave was so big in 2010.

As nationalized as the 2010 midterm elections were, President Obama's influence on the 2012 congressional elections was sure to be even stronger given his position at the top of the ballot. Consistent with that expectation, Gary Jacobson (2013), one of the leading authorities on congressional elections, found that "the relationship between presidential and House and Senate voting patterns was extraordinarily strong [in 2012], making it the most partisan, nationalized, and president-centered election in at least 60 years."

We would expect from the results presented in the prior chapters that the unusually strong influence of the president and his policies on 2010 and 2012 voting behavior made these two Obama-era congressional elections especially ripe for the spillover of racialization. Kinder and Dale-Riddle (2012) even speculated that racialized responses to President Obama and his party might be responsible for the Democrats' failure to do as well as the political science forecast models predicted in 2010: "The models used to forecast the 2010 elections share three things in common," they wrote, "all presume that the fate of the president's party at the midterm depends upon economic conditions. All ignore the fact that the president in 2010 is of African descent. And all seriously underestimate the magnitude of the Democratic midterm disaster" (153).

* * *

This chapter explores the role of racial attitudes in the 2010 and 2012 elections for the House of Representatives. After first documenting how the Tea Party's ascendancy within the Republican Party may have further enhanced the influence of racial attitudes in white Americans' vote preferences, I present evidence that voting behavior in the 2010 and 2012 congressional elections was significantly more racialized than it was in the pre-Obama era. At the individual level, racial resentment and especially antiblack stereotypes predicted vote preferences for the House of Representatives more powerfully in 2010 and 2012 than they had in congressional elections over the last quarter century. And at the aggregate level, racially conservative congressional districts became significantly more Republican in 2010 than they had been in previous elections; the most racially liberal districts, meanwhile, maintained the same high levels of Democratic support that they exhibited in previous midterm elections. Barack Obama's ascendancy once again appears to have been the catalyst for this racialization. The results below reveal that evaluations of the president transmitted the greater influence of racial attitudes on white Americans' Obama-era votes for Congress and that this spillover of racialization was most pronounced in districts where members of Congress voted for Obamacare. Perhaps most importantly, the chapter includes an empirical analysis of congressional roll call votes to end the sixteen-day government shutdown that took place in October 2013. The results suggest that Republicans from the most racially conservative congressional districts were the most unwilling to cooperate with President Obama during his tenure in the White House. The concluding remarks go on to discuss how the spillover of racialization into Obama-era congressional elections continued through the 2014 midterms and may well affect American politics even after Barack Obama leaves office.

The Tea Party Movement and the Racialization of Congressional Elections

The Tea Party Movement (TPM) will forever be linked with the GOP landslide in the 2010 midterms. After making national headlines with their large 2009 rallies in protest of the president's proposed tax and health care reform legislation, the Tea Party quickly organized itself into a formidable power within the Republican Party. By Election Day 2010, there were more than one hundred TPM-backed House candidates, all of whom represented the Republican Party. In retrospect, these Tea Party candidates did not noticeably outperform their non-TPM Republican counterparts after controlling for other district-level variables (Sides 2010; Jacobson 2011). Nevertheless, the Tea Party's relentless criticism of the president helped nationalize the election, and their energy surely contributed to the enthusiasm gap between Republicans and Democrats in 2010 midterm voting (Aldrich et al. 2014; Jacobson 2011). As Jacobson (2011, 2) again put it, "The Tea Party movement, which promoted, articulated, and focused the opposition to Obama and his policies, played a major role in turning the election into a national referendum on the administration." After the 2010 midterms, the Tea Party constituted a formidable power in Congress, with more than fifty members of their caucus who were especially opposed to compromising with President Obama.

Fairly or unfairly, the Tea Party Movement will also probably be forever linked with racial prejudice. Liberal political commentators took it as a matter of fact that this right-wing movement was driven by racism toward Obama's presidency. The *Huffington Post*—perhaps the most popular progressive news outlet of the time—even devoted a whole index page to the subject heading "Tea Party Racism," cataloging upward of fifty stories on this topic from 2011 to 2012.[2] Several factors, including racist comments made by Tea Party leaders and activists, racially insensitive images of President Obama at their rallies, and the prevalent belief advanced by many Tea Partiers that the president is the "other" (i.e., foreign born and/or Muslim) all contributed to this popular narrative since the election of Barack Obama (Parker and Barreto 2013, 7–8). Accusations of TPM racism reached their peak, though, when the country's oldest civil rights organization, the NAACP, called on the Tea Party to repudiate racist elements within their ranks in July 2010 and then released a report later that year contending that the TPM is "permeated with concerns about race."[3] The media was also quick to pick up this storyline. A simple LexisNexis search reveals more than 1,200 broadcast news stories in 2010 with the words "Tea Party" and "racist" in them. Not surprisingly, then, one-third of Americans sampled in a July 2010 Pew Poll reported hearing at least "a fair amount" about the NAACP's condemnation of Tea Party racism.[4]

There is good deal of social scientific evidence to support claims that both Tea Party members, and those who sympathize with them, were driven at least in part by racial conservatism. Williamson, Skocpol, and Coggin (2011, 34) deduced from their in-depth interviews with Tea Party members that "racial resentment stokes Tea Party fears about generational societal change, and fuels the Tea Party's strong opposition to President Obama" (see also Skocpol and Williamson 2011). Consistent with that conclusion, an April 2010 CBS/*New York Times* poll found that

Tea Party supporters were nearly twice as likely as the general public to endorse the symbolic racist belief that "too much has been made of the problems facing black people in recent years" (52 percent to 28 percent).[5] Parker and Barreto (2013) offer more quantitative evidence for the link between racial conservatism and the Tea Party, finding TPM sympathizers scored significantly higher in racial resentment even after controlling for several other plausible causes of Tea Party support. And political psychologists Howard Lavine and David Perkins experimentally found that Tea Party supporters reacted more negatively toward a black man who irresponsibly took on a mortgage he could not afford than they did towards a white man who did the same thing.[6]

To be sure, it would be unfair and overly simplistic to broadly condemn the Tea Party as racists. Tea Party activists joined the movement for a variety reasons, only one of which may have been racial conservatism (Skocpol and Williamson 2011; Williamson, Skocpol, and Coggin 2011). Regardless of their motivations, though, the Tea Party's fierce opposition to President Obama and the media's frequent reporting on instances and accusations of Tea Party racism surely led some Americans to believe that the movement was motivated by racial animus. In fact, nearly half the respondents in an April 2010 ABC News/*Washington Post* poll said that at least some support for the Tea Party is based on racial prejudice against President Obama.[7] We would, therefore, expect impressions of the TPM to have been unusually racialized heading into the 2010 midterm elections.

Consistent with that expectation, table 6.1 shows that racial attitudes had a stronger impact on white Americans' Tea Party opinions than they had on their assessments of the GOP in the July 2010 wave of the American National Election Studies (ANES) panel. We will see in the next two chapters that perceptions of the two major political parties were already becoming more racialized by the 2008 election. Yet, despite that growing influence of racial attitudes in white Americans' feelings toward the Republican Party, the coefficients in the table reveal that racial resentment was even more powerfully linked to white respondents' Tea Party opinions. The coefficients in the first column, for instance, indicate that moving from least to most racially resentful decreased Tea Party favorability by 40 percent of the seven-point scale's range, even after controlling for several other plausible sources of TPM support like limited government, authoritarianism, patriotism, gun rights, and religious fundamentalism. That effect, as can be seen in the second column of the table,

TABLE 6.1. **(OLS) Predictors of White Support for the Tea Party and the Republican Party**

	Tea Party	GOP	Tea – GOP	Tea Party	GOP	Tea – GOP
Racial Resentment	.409***	.217***	.191***			
	(.037)	(.039)	(.037)			
Subtle Prejudice				.178***	.101*	.077
				(.040)	(.041)	(.045)
Limited Government	.469***	.265***	.203***	.565***	.323***	.242***
	(.036)	(.039)	(.038)	(.036)	(.038)	(.037)
Patriotism	.073**	.135***	−.062*	.116***	.156***	−.039
	(.026)	(.026)	(.030)	(.028)	(.026)	(.031)
Gun Control	−.075**	−.022	−.053*	−.096***	−.039	−.057*
	(.025)	(.024)	(.024)	(.027)	(.025)	(.024)
Authoritarianism	.114***	.093**	.021	.161	.125***	.036
	(.028)	(.029)	(.029)	(.028)	(.028)	(.029)
Bible Literalism	.071***	.133***	−.062*	.088***	.148***	−.060*
	(.022)	(.024)	(.027)	(.025)	(.025)	(.027)
Constant	.332***	.240***	.092*	.443***	.298***	.144**
	(.039)	(.040)	(.041)	(.044)	(.042)	(.045)
Observations	1,204	1,205	1,204	1,186	1,187	1,186

Source: 2008–10 American National Election Studies panel.
Note: Dependent variables in first two columns are seven-point likability scale, recode from 0 (extreme dislike) to 1 (extreme like). Dependent variable in the third column is the difference between Tea Party and Republican Party likability recoded on a −1 to 1 scale. All explanatory variables except limited government are coded from 0 to 1, with 1 taking on higher values (limited government is coded from −1 to 0).
$*p < .05$.
$**p < .01$.
$***p < .001$.

was nearly twice as large as the relationship between racial resentment and opinions about the Republican Party. The third column, therefore, indicates that racial resentment was a powerful and highly significant predictor of which respondents liked the Tea Party more than the Republican Party. The remaining columns of the table show that Pettigrew and Meertens's (1995) subtle prejudice scale—measured here by how often one feels sympathy and admiration for African Americans—was also a sizable predictor of TPM support and was a marginally significant ($p = .08$) predictor of liking the Tea Party more than the Republican Party.[8]

The large influence of racial attitudes on white Americans' evaluations of the Tea Party does not imply that the group was *primarily* driven by racial animus. In fact, limited government attitudes were similarly strong predictors of both Tea Party support and of which respondents liked the Tea Party more than the Republican Party. For our purposes, though, the greater effects of racial resentment on Tea Party favorability than GOP support are still quite consequential. The Tea Party strongly backed one-

quarter of the Republican candidates for the House and helped nationalize the 2010 and 2012 congressional elections into a referendum against a
most-racial president. The strong link between racial attitudes and TPM
evaluations, as well as the movement's fervent opposition to President
Obama and their influence on Obama-era congressional elections, all
likely caused racial attitudes to further spill over into white Americans'
2010–12 vote preferences.

Racial Attitudes and Congressional Voting (1986–2012)

The first test of this chapter's main hypothesis that Barack Obama's presidency helped racialize white Americans' 2010 and 2012 voting behavior for Congress compares the impact of racial attitudes on Republican
vote preference for the House of Representatives in 2010 and 2012 to
their average effects on congressional vote choices in the pre-Obama era
(1986–2004). Figure 6.1 graphically presents that over-time comparison.
The solid line in the first panel of the display discloses a modest, but statistically significant ($p < .01$), relationship between racial resentment
and support for Republican congressional candidates in the two decades
before Obama became president. After controlling for party identification
and ideological self-placement, moving from least to most racially resentful was associated with about a twelve-percentage-point increase in Republican vote share among white ANES respondents surveyed between
1986 and 2004. As you may recall, that effect was considerably smaller
than the pre-Obama relationship between racial resentment and support
for Republican presidential candidates shown back in figure 3.3—a likely
upshot of the fact that Congress members are oftentimes more insulated
from national party positions than presidential candidates.

Those modest 1986–2004 effects nearly tripled in a pair of pooled 2010
preelection ANES surveys, though.[9] The dashed line in the top-left panel
of figure 6.1, for instance, shows that the same change from least to most
racially resentful was now associated with a thirty-five-percentage-point
increase in 2010 Republican vote preferences. Moreover, this greater
effect was particularly pronounced amongst the most racially resentful,
who all else being equal, supported Republican candidates at higher rates
than they had in pre-Obama congressional elections.

With Obama on the ballot and the relationship between presidential and congressional vote larger in 2012 than any other time on record

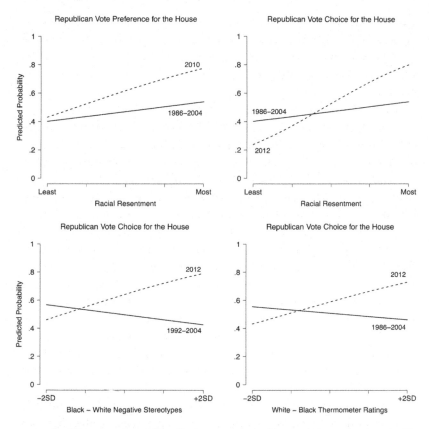

FIGURE 6.1. White Americans' Vote Preferences for the House of Representatives (1986–2012) as a Function of Racial Attitudes

Note: Probabilities based on logistic regression coefficients in the online appendix. Predicted probabilities were calculated by setting party identification and ideological self-placement to the mean white respondent.

Source: American National Election Studies (ANES) cumulative file; July 2010 ANES panel study; October 2010 ANES's Evaluation of Government and Society Survey; 2012 ANES.

(Jacobson 2013), we would expect the spillover of racialization into that year's elections for the House of Representatives to have been even greater than it was in 2010. The top-right panel in figure 6.1 confirms that expectation. The figure shows that the least and most racially resentful were separated by over fifty percentage points in their 2012 congressional vote choices after controlling for party and ideology—nearly five times the average 1986–2004 pre-Obama effect. Unlike the 2010 results displayed in the top-left panel of figure 6.1, these greater effects were produced by the two sides of racialization. After controlling for party and ideology, the display shows that racial conservatives were more likely to vote for Republicans than they had been in the pre-Obama era, whereas white racial liberals were less supportive of the GOP than their historical average.

The two sides of racialization in 2012 congressional voting behavior were less apparent, though, with more blatant racial prejudice measures— antiblack stereotypes and antiblack affect—which as discussed earlier are not nearly as good at capturing racial sympathy as the measure pioneered by Kinder and Sanders (1996).[10] The differing effects of those racial attitudes on white Americans' vote choices for the House before and after Obama was elected were still quite informative, nonetheless. The bottom-left panel of figure 6.1 shows that there was actually a modest, but significant ($p < .05$), *negative relationship* between antiblack stereotypes and Republican vote share for the House in the pooled 1992–2004 ANES survey. Moving from at least two standard deviations below the average antiblack stereotype score to two standard deviations above the mean was associated with a fourteen-percentage-point decrease in white support for GOP congressional candidates over that time period. That same change in stereotype scores, however, was now associated with a thirty-five-percentage-point *increase* in the Republican Party's 2012 vote share for the House of Representatives.

The bottom-right panel of figure 6.1 shows nearly identical results for antiblack affect. Much like the 1992–2004 stereotype results, there was a slight, but significant ($p < .05$) negative relationship between feeling warmer toward whites than blacks and Republican vote share in the House among white ANES respondents interviewed between 1986 and 2004. Also like the stereotype results, that pre-Obama negative effect turned into a highly significant ($p < .01$) positive relationship between antiblack affect and white support for GOP House candidates in 2012. And finally, the greater effects of antiblack stereotypes and antiblack affect in 2012 voting behavior were both particularly concentrated among racially conservative respondents who either felt warmer toward whites than blacks or were more willing to endorse negative stereotypes about African Americans than their own racial group.

* * *

All told, then, the relationship between racial attitudes and white Americans' vote choices for Congress were stronger in the Obama era than they were in the two decades prior to his ascendancy. That spillover of racialization into congressional voting behavior was not limited to racial resentment, either. In fact, more blatant forms of prejudice that were not implicated in support for Republican candidates prior to Obama's presidential candidacy were powerfully activated in white Americans' 2012 congressional voting behavior.

Racial Attitudes and Congressional Voting in Panel Data (2008 and 2012)

The results presented in figure 6.1 are certainly consistent with this chapter's main hypothesis that Barack Obama's presidency helped make racial attitudes a more important factor in recent congressional elections. At the same time, though, they are far from definitive causal evidence. As was the case with the repeated cross-sectional results presented in the previous chapters, sampling and mode differences between the pre- and post-Obama ANES surveys could complicate our over-time comparisons.[11] Moreover, it is possible that racial attitudes and/or party and ideology were changing to comport with congressional vote preferences rather than vice versa. It is quite fortunate, then, that we can once again employ panel data from the 2008–12 Cooperative Campaign Analysis Project (CCAP) to help get a better handle on how the relationship between white Americans' racial attitudes and their House vote preferences changed from before to after Obama became president. The comparison here is still not perfect because Barack Obama's presence on the ballot in 2008 likely enhanced the effect of racial attitudes above their pre-Obama baseline.[12] Nevertheless, the especially close link between a sitting president and congressional candidates of his party should have increased the impact of racial attitudes even further in 2012.

Figure 6.2 tests that expectation by graphing out the impact of racial and ethnocentric attitudes on congressional vote preferences among white CCAP panelists ($n \approx 1,500$) who supported one of the two major party nominees for the House in both 2008 and 2012. The first panel compares the relationship between racial resentment, as measured in March 2008, on the exact same panelists' vote preferences for the House in 2008 and 2012. As can be seen, there was already a substantial effect of racial resentment on white support for Republican candidates in 2008 with Barack Obama on the ballet. All else being equal, the most racially resentful whites were forty-five points more supportive of the Republican

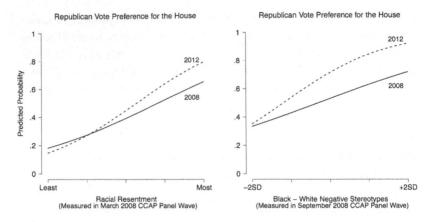

FIGURE 6.2. White Americans' Vote Preferences for the House of Representatives in 2008 and 2012 as a Function of Racial Attitudes
Note: Probabilities based on logistic regression coefficients in the online appendix. Predicted probabilities were calculated by setting party identification and ideological self-placement to the mean white respondent.
Source: 2008–12 Cooperative Campaign Analysis Project (CCAP) panelists who expressed a preference for one of the major party candidates in both November 2008 and July 2012.

candidate in 2008 than their least resentful counterparts. That large effect grew even larger amongst the exact same respondents in 2012, though. After controlling for 2008 measures of party and ideology,[13] moving from lowest to highest on the March 2008 racial resentment scale increased our white panelists' support for GOP House candidates by sixty-five points in 2012.

The right panel of figure 6.2 suggests that Obama activated antiblack stereotypes even more powerfully than racial resentment in white Americans' congressional vote choices, much like the results presented earlier in figure 6.1. In fact, the logistic regression coefficient on antiblack stereotypes (measured in September 2008) nearly doubled from 2008 to 2012 (1.6 to 2.8, respectively). And after controlling for party and ideology,[14] the display shows that nearly 90 percent of white respondents who scored at least two standard deviations above the average antiblack stereotype score supported their district's Republican candidate for Congress in 2012, compared to roughly 70 percent back in 2008. Like the ANES results, then, it appears that the declining fortunes of Democratic candidates for the House of Representatives from their 2008 apex in which they won the national popular vote by eleven percentage points was due in part to defections from racially conservative white Americans—a conclusion further bolstered by the results presented in the following sections.

District-Level Racial Conservatism and Aggregate Midterm Vote Tallies (2002–10)

Along with that individual-level panel data, we can also examine how the effects of district-level racial conservatism on aggregate midterm election returns changed from before to after Obama became president.[15] This approach leverages the enormous sample sizes of the 2006, 2008, and 2010 Cooperative Congressional Election Study (CCES; pooled $n = 123,721$) to calculate reliable racial conservatism scores for all 435 congressional districts.[16] Unfortunately, racial resentment was not asked in the CCES until the 2010 survey. So, our aggregate measure of racial conservatism was estimated instead by each district's level of opposition to affirmative action for African Americans in the three CCES surveys.[17] As discussed back in chapter 4, though, this opposition to affirmative action measure in the CCES is an excellent proxy for racial resentment.

Figure 6.3 graphs out the relationship between this district-level measure of racial conservatism and election returns for the House of Representatives in 2006 and 2010. Those displays, which plot each contested district's Republican vote share in 2006 and 2010 according to its racial conservatism, reveal a number of interesting patterns. First, and perhaps most importantly, the relationship between district-level racial conservatism and Republican vote share grew stronger in 2010 than it had been in 2006. As the predicted vote share equations at the bottom of the panels indicate, 2010 Republican candidates performed ten percentage points better, on average, in the most racially conservative districts than they did back in 2006. The most racially liberal districts, meanwhile, supported the Democrats at the same overwhelming rates in 2010 that they had before Barack Obama became his party's presidential nominee.

District-level racial conservatism also explained more of the variation in 2010 election outcomes. The R^2 numbers at the bottom of the panels indicate that district-level opposition to affirmative action explained 42 percent of the variation in 2006 election returns compared to 60 percent of the voting differences across districts in 2010. Or more simply put, electoral returns were better organized around district-level racial conservatism in 2010 than they were in 2006. Most of this enhanced explanatory power resulted from racially conservative districts who voted Democratic in previous years moving to the Republicans in 2010. In fact, 90 percent of Republican candidates from districts that scored in the top quartile in racial conservatism won in 2006, compared to 75 percent in 2006.

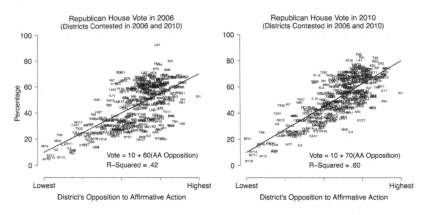

FIGURE 6.3. House Election Returns in 2006 and 2012 as a Function of District-Level Racial Conservatism

Note: Results limited to the 354 districts contested by the two major parties in both 2006 and 2010.

Source: District-level racial conservatism calculated by the average opposition to affirmative action across the 2006, 2008, and 2010 Cooperative Congressional Election Study surveys. House election returns in 2006 and 2010 were accessed from the census's *Statistical Abstract*.

Republicans who ran elsewhere, however, were no more likely to win in 2010 than in 2006 (41 percent in both midterm election years). Those results, which are consistent with the individual-level findings presented earlier, again suggest that racial conservatives were moving away from the Democratic Party in Obama-era congressional elections.

Of course, there are several other factors correlated with district-level racial conservatism that may have also been responsible for these changes in aggregate vote tallies between 2006 and 2010. Table 6.2 addresses these potential confounding variables by estimating the relationship between our aggregate measure of racial conservatism and House voting returns while controlling for several important district characteristics. Those models include aggregate measures of party and ideology (measured in the 2006–10 CCES surveys), as well as each district's black population percentage, their Democratic presidential vote proportion in 2004,[18] and their Republican vote share for the House of Representatives in the prior midterm election. Including the lagged dependent variable of prior midterm vote share allows us to assess the impact of the remaining predictors on the *change in Republican vote share* from the prior midterm election. In other words, this is a model of vote change. The coefficient on affirmative action opposition in the first column of table 6.2, therefore, indicates that the most racially conservative districts grew thirteen percentage points

TABLE 6.2. **(OLS) Predictors of District-Level Election Returns for House of Representatives**

	2010	2006
Opposition to Affirmative Action	.128***	−.004
	(.031)	(.040)
Party Identification	−.035	−.010
	(.048)	(.062)
Ideology	.044	−.015
	(.046)	(.059)
Black Population Percentage	−.000	.001
	(.000)	(.000)
Kerry Vote Proportion	−.579***	−.550***
	(.061)	(.071)
Prior Midterm Vote Proportion	.393***	.564***
	(.031)	(.034)
Constant	.545***	.444***
	(.058)	(.070)
Observations	354	320

Source: House election returns in 2006 and 2012 accessed from the Census's *Statistical Abstract*. House elections in 2002 were provided by Gary Jacobson, University of California, San Diego. District-level opposition to affirmative action, party identification, and black population were calculated from the 2006-2008-2010 Cooperative Congressional Election Study (CCES).
Note: Dependent variable is the Republican proportion of the two-party vote in districts contested by both major parties, with 0 representing 100 percent of the vote going to the Democrat and 1 representing 100 percent of the vote going to the Republican. All variables except actual black population percentage are coded from 0 to 1. Opposition to affirmative action, party, and ideology were measured in the 2006–10 CCES.
$*p < .05.$
$**p < .01.$
$***p < .001.$

more Republican than their most racially liberal counterparts from 2006 to 2010 after controlling for the other variables in the model—a highly significant relationship ($p < .001$).

Perhaps more importantly, the coefficient on affirmative action opposition in the second column of the table shows that *there was absolutely no relationship* between district-level racial conservatism and changes in Republican vote share from 2002 to 2006. It appears, then, that the independent relationship between how racially conservative a congressional district is and how much more supportive its constituents were of Republican candidates for the House of Representatives than they had been in prior elections was a unique feature of the Obama era.

Obama Evaluations as a Mediator of Racialization

The results presented thus far indicate that racial attitudes—whether measured at the individual or district level—became a more important factor in white Americans' vote choices for Congress than they were before Barack Obama was elected. They do not tell us, however, why racial attitudes became more important determinants of House vote choices in the Obama era. That explanation should seem obvious after the theoretical expectations and results presented in previous chapters. Nevertheless, it is important to establish more directly whether President Obama's position atop of the Democratic Party was responsible for these more racialized voting patterns.

Experimental results presented elsewhere suggest that Obama's presidency was, in fact, making racial and ethnocentric attitudes more important in Americans' congressional vote preferences. Those findings indicate that experimentally connecting Barack Obama to Democratic candidates for Congress significantly increased the influence of both anti-Muslim sentiments and old-fashioned racism on 2010 candidate preferences (Tesler 2011, 2013b). At the same time, though, this experiment failed to enhance the effects of racial resentment on evaluations of Democratic candidates for Congress, which were already heavily influenced by racial resentment in that October 2010 survey. More work is needed, then, to establish whether Obama's presidency was responsible for the greater effects of racial resentment and opposition to affirmative action on 2010 and 2012 voting behavior that we saw earlier in this chapter.

In the absence of such experimental evidence, one strategy to establish whether Americans' votes became more racialized because of the country's first black president is to test whether Obama evaluations mediated the enhanced effects of racial attitudes on their congressional vote choices. Mediation occurs when an explanatory variable's influence (in this case racial resentment) on a dependent variable (congressional vote choice) is transmitted through an intervening variable (hypothesized here to be evaluations of President Obama) (Baron and Kenny 1986). Thus, if the mediational pathway specified above is correct, then the relationships between congressional vote preferences and racial resentment should become negligible after controlling for white respondents' assessments of the president.

The results presented in figure 6.4 are quite consistent with that expectation. The first panel of that display shows that the large effects of racial resentment on 2012 House vote intention shown in figure 6.2 were almost completely mediated by evaluations of Barack Obama. In fact, including a five-category measure of Obama favorability in our base model with ideology and party identification reduced the effect of racial resentment on white support for GOP House candidates by more than a factor of four.

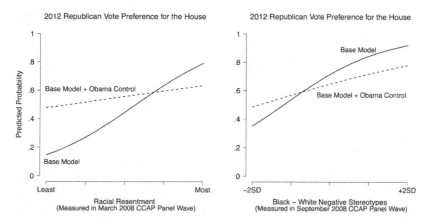

FIGURE 6.4. White Americans' Vote Preferences for the House of Representatives in 2012 as a Function of Racial Attitudes

Note: Probabilities were based on logistic regression coefficients in the online appendix. Predicted probabilities were calculated by setting party identification and ideological self-placement and Obama favorability (dashed lines only) to the mean white respondent.

Source: 2008–12 Cooperative Campaign Analysis Project (CCAP) panelists who expressed a preference for one of the major party candidates in both November 2008 and July 2012.

Likewise, the effect of racial resentment on 2010 midterm voting shown in figure 6.1 was reduced all the way down to zero after including a seven-category measure of Obama likability in our base model. Those mediating effects were not quite as large for antiblack stereotypes, as the second panel of figure 6.4 illustrates. At the same time, though, the once large effects of negative racial stereotypes on support for Republican congressional candidates in 2012 was reduced to nonsignificance after controlling for mass assessments of President Obama.

Much of the large effects of racial attitudes on white Americans' 2010 and 2012 congressional vote preferences were, therefore, transmitted by evaluations of Obama—a finding entirely consistent with this chapter's contention that Barack Obama's presidency helped make racial attitudes a more important determinant of white Americans' congressional vote choices.

Obamacare Vote as a Moderator of Racialization

Mediational analyses, however, often run the risk of overstating the causal effects of intervening variables like Obama evaluations in figure 6.4

(Green, Ha, and Bullock 2010). It is important to augment those results, then, with an additional test of how directly connecting President Obama to Democratic candidates for Congress activated racial attitudes in white Americans' voting preferences. Thankfully, the House of Representatives' final vote on the Affordable Care Act provides somewhat of a natural experiment for establishing how directly connecting Democratic candidates to Barack Obama may have increased the effects of racial attitudes in white Americans' 2010 vote preferences.

The Obamacare vote, as mentioned earlier, loomed large in 2010 voting behavior; Democrats who voted for the ACA performed significantly worse at the ballot booth in 2010 than their fellow partisans who voted against the bill (Nyhan et al. 2012; Brady, Fiorina, and Wilkins 2011). We would also expect the spillover of racialization into white Americans' vote choices to have been more pronounced for those congressional Democrats who voted for Obamacare. After all, this health care vote provided a clear opportunity for Congress members to stand with or against the president on his administration's signature legislative accomplishment. Put in more technical terms, we would expect the Obamacare vote to have *moderated* the influence of racial attitudes in the 2010 elections, with the effects of racial resentment on 2010 vote preferences stronger in districts where Democratic members voted for the bill ($N = 219$ districts) than it was in districts where Democrats voted against the ACA ($N = 34$ districts).

Figure 6.5 tests that expectation, thanks again to the CCES's enormous sample size. As expected, the display shows that the negative effect of racial resentment on white support for 2010 Democratic candidates was significantly larger in districts where Democrats voted for Obamacare. After controlling for party and ideology, the relationship between racial resentment and Republican vote choice was about 50% larger in districts with Democratic candidates who voted for Obamacare—a statistically significant difference in effects ($p = .02$). Moreover, figure 6.5 shows that the diminished Democratic support for candidates who voted against Obamacare found in prior research (Nyhan et al. 2011; Brady, Fiorina, and Wilkins 2011), was concentrated among white Americans who scored high in racial resentment. All else being equal, the most racially resentful were nearly twenty points more likely to support a 2010 Democratic candidate who voted against the ACA than one who voted for Obamacare.

It is still possible, however, that the patterns produced in figure 6.5 were due to naturally occurring selection effects. That is, white Americans

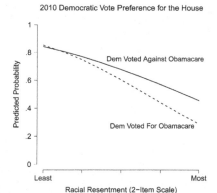

2010 Democratic Vote Preference for the House

FIGURE 6.5. White Americans' Vote Choice for the House of Representatives in 2010 as a Function of Racial Resentment and District's Obamacare Vote
Note: Probabilities based on logistic regression coefficients in the online appendix. Predicted probabilities were calculated by setting party identification and ideological self-placement to their sample means.
Source: 2010 Cooperative Congressional Election Study.

in districts with Democratic candidates who voted against Obamacare might have always used racial attitudes less in their congressional vote preferences.[19] The results in figure 6.6 help rule out that alternative explanation, though. Those two displays graph out the relationship between opposition to affirmative action and Democratic vote choice for the House in 2008 and 2010 separately, depending on whether Democratic members of Congress voted for or against the ACA.[20] The left panel shows that the negative impact of this racial conservatism measure on Democratic vote choice in districts that voted for Obamacare was more than 50 percent larger in 2010 than it was 2008—a highly significant difference in effects ($p < .001$).

Once again, these greater racial attitude effects were concentrated among the most racially conservative Americans. The left panel of figure 6.6, for instance, shows that white Americans' who strongly opposed affirmative action were especially likely to defect from 2008 to 2010 in districts where Democrats voted for Obamacare. That significant racialization effect from 2008 to 2010, however, was not reproduced in the thirty-four congressional districts where Democrats voted against the ACA. As can be seen in the right panel of the figure, the negative effect of opposition to affirmative action on Democratic vote was virtually unchanged from 2008 to 2010 in those Democratic districts.

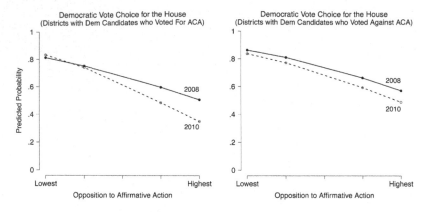

FIGURE 6.6. White Americans' Vote Choice for the House of Representatives in 2008 and 2010 as a Function of Opposition to Affirmative Action and District's Obamacare Vote
Note: Probabilities based on logistic regression coefficients in the online appendix. Predicted probabilities were calculated by setting party identification and ideological self-placement to their sample means.
Source: 2008 Cooperative Congressional Election Study (CCES); 2010 CCES.

The results in figures 6.5 and 6.6, therefore, suggest that the highly publicized House of Representatives vote on President Obama's signature piece of legislation moderated the effects of racial attitudes on congressional vote choices in 2010, with the spillover of racialization only occurring in districts where Democratic members of Congress voted with the president on his signature health care reform legislation.

District-Level Racial Resentment and Roll Call Votes to End the Government Shutdown

The congressional politics of Obamacare did not end with the 2010 midterm elections, though. The new Republican majority, who took control of the House of Representatives in January 2011, voted well over fifty times to repeal the ACA during Barack Obama's presidency.[21] Those roll call votes were merely symbolic, as the Democratic Party's majority in the Senate through 2014 and Barack Obama's veto power both made repealing Obamacare impossible. Some Republican lawmakers, therefore, turned to other strategies to prevent the law from taking effect. More specifically, the GOP-led House of Representatives refused to pass a continuing resolution to fund the United States government unless that bill included language delaying or defunding the health care exchanges created by the ACA from taking effect on October 1, 2013. Or more simply put, the government would shut down unless Obamacare was defunded or delayed.

President Obama refused to negotiate over the ACA's implementation. He, instead, announced his firm position on the first day of the shutdown, saying in a press conference, "I will not give in to reckless demands by some in the Republican Party to deny affordable health insurance to millions of hardworking Americans."[22] With the Democratic and Republican leadership at an impasse, most routine governmental operations officially shut down from October 1 to October 16, 2013.

Much like the 2009–10 health care reform debate discussed in the previous chapter, several liberal political commentators asserted that the 2013 government shutdown was rooted in racist opposition to President Obama.[23] Actors Chris Noth and Robert Redford even joined in the accusations, with Noth tweeting, "[The] highest level of racism was shown yesterday when Republicans forced a shutdown of our government. Mostly because our President is black."[24] Conservatives were understandably quick to dismiss such charges of racial bias, as they had also regularly done throughout Barack Obama's presidency. Or as Mitt Romney's chief strategist Stuart Stevens put it, "There's certainly racism left in America, but liberal pundits claiming it's driving the government shutdown make a mockery of the real thing."[25]

Of course, neither side again provided much evidence to support their contrasting claims about the role of racial prejudice in the government shutdown. Nor is it possible to quantify how much, if at all, Barack Obama's race may have mattered in the budget standoff. Nevertheless, we can still glean some insights into the racialized dynamics of shutdown negotiations by examining who in Congress voted against the eventual bill to reopen the government (H.R. 2775)—a bill that was supported by every Democratic member of the House of Representatives but opposed by a majority of Republicans ($N=$ 144) because it did not delay or defund Obamacare. More specifically, we can test whether GOP members of the House who represented racially conservative congressional districts were more likely to vote against the bill than their other Republican colleagues.

Like the results in figure 6.3, this analysis leverages massive academic surveys, the 2012 CCES ($N = 54,535$) and the 2012 CCAP ($N = 44,000$), to calculate reliable racial resentment scores for each congressional district. The first panel of figure 6.7 then shows how likely each Republican

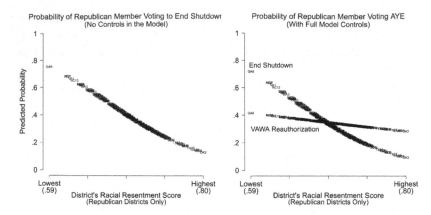

FIGURE 6.7. Probability of Republican Members of the House of Representatives Who Voted to End the Shutdown and Reauthorize the Violence against Women's Act as Functions of District-Level Racial Resentment

Note: Probabilities based on logistic regression coefficients in the online appendix. Predicted probabilities in the second panel were calculated by setting legislature's ideological ideal point and district-level partisanship, ideology, religiosity, percentage black, and percentage Latino to the average Republican district. District-level estimates based on the 2012 Cooperative Congressional Election Study and the 2012 Cooperative Congressional Analysis Project.

in the House was to vote yes on the bill to end the shutdown, given their district's estimated level of racial resentment. As figure 6.7 shows, Republican members from districts scoring high on racial resentment were considerably more likely to vote against H.R. 2275 than other Republicans. Republicans from House districts that had the highest levels of racial resentment (such as OK2, MO8, and LA1) were about sixty percentage points less likely to vote for the deal to end the shutdown than Republicans from districts with low levels of racial resentment (such as GA6, AR2 and FL27).

The right-hand panel of figure 6.7 shows that this relationship held up once other factors were taken into account. As can be seen, the relationship between district-level racial resentment and voting against the shutdown deal persisted after accounting for some important attributes of congressional districts, including their partisanship, their ideological orientation, their religiosity, and their minority population percentages. The results were also not affected by controlling for Republicans' own individual ideologies, as measured by their previous roll call votes in the 113th Congress.[26]

Perhaps more importantly, district-level racial resentment did not independently predict the votes of Republican members of the House of Representatives to reauthorize the Violence against Women Act (VAWA) in 2013—legislation that, like the shutdown deal, passed with a minority of Republicans (eighty-seven members of the House) supporting it. As can be seen, the "VAWA reauthorization" line in figure 6.7 shows that Republicans from the most racially resentful districts were only slightly less likely than their fellow partisans to oppose that legislation. It appears, then, that the relationship between district-level racial resentment and the shutdown vote was not merely partisan politics as usual. Rather, it was specific to a bill that was closely associated with President Obama and his administration's implementation of the Affordable Care Act.

To be sure, these results do not imply that the shutdown was primarily driven by racial prejudice against the president. Indeed, prior ideological voting records were by far the strongest predictor of Republicans' House votes on the shutdown. At the same time, though, the results suggest that Republicans from the most racially conservative congressional districts were the most unwilling to cooperate with President Obama during his tenure in the White House—a logical upshot of the growing racialization of congressional elections shown in this chapter.

Concluding Remarks

This chapter has shown that racial attitudes became a bigger factor in white Americans' Obama-era congressional voting behavior than they were beforehand. That racialization occurred at both the individual-level and district-level, and it extended to subtle and more blatant forms of racial prejudice. In fact, racial attitudes that were not consistently implicated in congressional support for Republican candidates prior to Obama's presidential candidacy, namely antiblack stereotypes and antiblack affect, became significant predictors of GOP vote choices during Obama's presidency.[27] President Obama's mere presence in the White House seems to have been the driving force behind this spillover of racialization. Evaluations of Barack Obama almost completely mediated the large effects of racial resentment in congressional vote choices, and the Obamacare vote significantly moderated the effects of racial conservatism on 2010 voting. These racial spillover effects from the president to congressional voting likely contributed to Democrats' declining fortunes in Obama-era congressional elections, too, as the enhanced effects of racial attitudes were primarily concentrated amongst those with conservative predispositions.

Those declining fortunes eventually reached their nadir in the 2014 midterm elections. The Democrats' seventy-seven-seat majority in the House of Representatives when Barack Obama took office had become a fifty-nine-seat minority following the 2014 elections. Not surprisingly, the racialized voting patterns presented in this chapter for the 2010 and 2012 congressional elections solidified themselves even further in the 2014 midterm elections. New analyses from the 2014 CCES indicate that the impact of racial resentment on white Americans' vote choices for the House of Representatives was quite similar to its effects in the 2010 and 2012 elections;[28] and at the aggregate level, the Republican Party expanded its House majority in primarily white working-class congressional districts from 20 seats prior to the 2010 midterms to a whopping 125 seats when the 114th Congress was sworn in on January 6, 2015 (Brownstein 2015).

The growing racialization of American politics in the Obama era, therefore, was not just limited to assessments of Obama and his presidential rivals, as shown in chapters 3 and 4. Nor was it limited to public opinion about complicated fiscal policies that Americans did not have particularly stable preferences about, as shown in chapter 5. Rather, this chapter revealed that racial attitudes spilled over into electoral outcomes even when Barack Obama was not on the ballot. It is important to note that unlike the results in the prior chapters, ideology was also now a more important factor in congressional voting behavior—a likely upshot of the growing relationship between partisanship and ideology (Levendusky 2009), as well as the salience of limited government rhetoric and attitudes in the Obama era (e.g., table 6.1), and the unusual nationalization of 2010 and 2012 congressional elections.

Nevertheless, the spillover of racialization into white Americans' congressional voting behavior should still have some important implications going forward. Once elected, members of Congress are rarely voted out. Typically, 90 percent of House incumbents run for reelection and 90 percent of them win (Jacobson 2004). With the same candidates running election after election, the racialized voting patterns produced in the 2010 and 2012 elections could reproduce themselves long after Obama leaves office. Indeed, familiar voting patterns are one likely reason why racial attitudes did not strongly influence white Americans' votes for the House of Representatives in the pre-Obama era, despite the fact that roll call voting on racial issues in the House of Representatives was well sorted along party lines by 1986 (Carmines and Stimson 1989; McCarty, Poole, and Rosenthal 2006; Atkinson 2012).

The most important potential implication of this spillover of racialization, though, is once again polarization. As discussed earlier, racial attitudes are emotionally charged in ways that nonracial ideological considerations are not. To be sure, these emotionally charged racial issues have long been incorporated into the partisan/ideological dimension that explains most of Congress's roll call voting behavior (McCarty, Poole, and Rosenthal 2006; Atkinson 2012). Yet, it is unclear whether racial issues were simply subsumed by the left-right ideological divide over economic issues, which has long defined the partisan cleavage in Congress, or if such ideological voting in the House became racialized after the parties effectively sorted themselves into racially liberal and racially conservative coalitions (see King and Smith 2011 for a discussion).

The results presented in figure 6.1 would suggest the former, as racial attitudes had little independent influence over white Americans' vote choices for Congress in the pre-Obama era. With more racialized constituencies in the Obama-era elections, and the heightened emotions that come with that racialization, it may be even more difficult to find common ground on legislative matters in the years ahead—a conclusion bolstered by the results in figure 6.7 showing that members of Congress from the most racially conservative districts were the least likely to cooperate with Barack Obama during his presidency.

CHAPTER SEVEN

The Growing Racialization of Partisan Attachments

There's also a dark vein of intolerance in some parts of the [Republican] party. What do I mean by that? What I mean by that is they still sort of look down on minorities. — General Colin Powell, *Meet the Press*, January 13, 2013[1]

General Colin Powell's above-referenced statement that there is "a dark vein of intolerance" within some parts of a Republican Party that "still sort of look[s] down on minorities" quickly made national headlines.[2] Intraparty criticism is typically viewed as more newsworthy and credible than the more familiar forms of interparty sniping (Baum and Groeling 2009). So Powell, a self-identified Republican who had long been widely respected by Americans of all races and racial predispositions (Kinder and McConnaughy 2006; Kinder and Dale-Riddle 2012), breathed a new air of interest and authority into the commonplace charge of Republican racial insensitivity during Barack Obama's presidency.

General Powell's January 2013 comments may have made news, but as we now know, they were hardly anything new. The prior chapters documented several similar charges against high-ranking members of the Republican Party throughout Barack Obama's tenure in office. As we have discussed, those allegations against the GOP for racial intolerance and appealing to white voters' racial stereotypes extended all the way up to the three leading candidates for the Republican Party's 2012 presidential nomination—Mitt Romney, Rick Santorum, and Newt Gingrich.

At least some members of the public also appeared to be paying attention to this alleged turn toward Republican racial conservatism. Google searches for "Republican racism," which were virtually nonexistent in the pre-Obama period, spiked in 2008 and steadily continued throughout his time in the White House.[3] More importantly, there was a notable increase in the percentage of Americans who thought the Republican Party was "generally doing a bad job these days of reaching out to blacks, Hispanics, and other minorities." Exactly half the participants in a July 2010 CNN poll said the Republican Party is doing a "bad job" with their minority outreach, compared to just 33 percent the last time that question was asked in 2000.[4] And perhaps most important, the gap in perceived differences between Barack Obama and Mitt Romney on the American National Election Studies' (ANES) "aid to blacks" scale was nearly twice as large in 2012 as it had been in the pre-Obama era from 1972 to 2004 (see fig. 3.1). That perceived distance between the two major party's 2012 standard bearers on racial issues could have been particularly consequential since differences in the 1964 presidential nominees' support for civil rights legislation have been widely cited as the reason for the realignment of American partisanship around racial attitudes and race in the post–civil rights era (Carmines and Stimson 1989; Edsall and Edsall 1992; Kinder and Sanders 1996; Frymer 1999; also see discussion in chap.1).

White Americans' partisan attachments would, therefore, seem especially ripe for Obama-era racialization. After all, we had a Republican Party that was seen by some Americans as less supportive of minorities and their interests than they had been in the recent past; and the Democratic Party, of course, was being led during this time period by an African American president who strongly evoked racial predispositions. Moreover, we have now seen racial attitudes spill over into political evaluations that were similarly associated with Barack Obama, such as economic evaluations, public policy positions, mass assessments of public figures, and Americans' vote choices for Congress.

At the same time, though, mitigating factors could have made it harder for racial attitudes to have spilled over into mass partisanship during Obama's presidency. Party identification (PID), for starters, has long been considered the most stable of all political attitudes (Campbell et al. 1960; Converse 1964; Converse and Markus 1979; Miller and Shanks 1996; Green, Palmquist, and Schickler 2002). Americans' vote choices for national offices often vary from one election to the next (Campbell et al. 1960; Fiorina 1981; Zaller 2004), and their vote preferences can change dramatically over the course of an election campaign (Gelman and King 1993; Erikson and Wlezien 2012).[5] Public policy preferences are even more notoriously fickle—especially opinions about complicated issues like health care reform—and will frequently change depending on the context in which they are assessed (Converse 1964; Zaller 1992; Kinder 1998; Cohen 2003; Lenz 2012; Tesler and Zaller 2014; Tesler 2015b). Partisan attachments, by contrast, are much less susceptible to short-term influences like feelings about specific presidential candidates and presidents (Campbell et al. 1960; Miller and Shanks 1996; Green, Palmquist, and Schickler 2002). In fact, once acquired, party identification tends to persist rather stably throughout the lifecycle (see Sears and Levy 2003 for a review). Few Americans may have changed their crystallized party identifications, then, in response to Barack Obama's position atop the Democratic Party.

Along with that established stability, the prominent role of race in the pre-Obama partisan alignment could have also made it more difficult for racial attitudes to further influence white Americans' Obama-era party identifications. As mentioned throughout the book, elected officials from the two major political parties were well sorted into racially liberal and racially conservative camps long before Barack Obama's rise to prominence (Carmines and Stimson 1989; McCarty, Poole, and Rosenthal 2006; King and Smith 2011, 2014; Atkinson 2012). We also know that this elite-level polarization filtered down to the mass electorate. That is, racially conservative Americans were significantly more Republican than their racially liberal counterparts were throughout much of the post–civil rights era (Carmines and Stimson 1989; Sears and Funk 1999; Layman and Carsey 2002; Stimson 2004; Valentino and Sears 2005; Hetherington and Weiler 2009). There might be limitations, then, on how much more racial attitudes could have come to influence Americans' already racialized partisan attachments in the Age of Obama.

There are still reasons to suspect, however, that President Obama's presence in the White House further enhanced that significant pre-2008 relationship between racial attitudes and white Americans' partisan attachments. First, while racial attitudes were an undeniably important determinant of party identification in the pre-Obama era, their influence on mass partisanship was far from overwhelming. More blatant forms of prejudice like desire for intimate social distance between the black and white races, social dominance orientation, and antiblack affect and/or stereotypes were almost entirely unrelated to white Americans' pre-Obama partisan preferences (Sears et al. 1997; Sears, Henry, and Kosterman 2000; Valentino and Sears 2005; Tesler 2013b; chap. 5; also see new results below). Moreover, the significant relationships that were found between racial policy liberalism and Democratic Party identification were not equally present among all members of the population. Rather, the impact of racial attitudes on party identification was concentrated among politically informed Americans who were aware of the two parties' divergent positions on matters of race (Layman and Carsey 2002; also see new results below).

Racial symbolism may have also been losing some of its centrality in the two parties' public images during the decade preceding Obama's presidential victory. Chapter 1 discussed how racially charged issues that helped fuel the partisan divide about race (e.g., busing, affirmative action, welfare, and crime), had lost much of their political prominence since Bill Clinton's second term in office, as Democrats heeded their electoral temptation of racial silence. Those racialized issues were primarily displaced by moral and military matters in popular partisan discourse after President Clinton's Monica Lewinsky scandal and the 9/11 terrorist attacks. With racial issues largely receding from the political scene, there were some indicators of a declining significance of race in Americans' political preferences before Barack Obama became the Democratic nominee for president. Kinder and Drake (2009), for instance, argue that the increased focus on terrorism and national security after 9/11 reduced the impact of white racial prejudice on public opinion. And Hajnal and Lee (2011) show that "in the last few decades—at least until the successful candidacy of Barack Obama—African Americans have been slowly but surely moving away from an exclusive relationship with the Democratic Party." There could have still been some room left, then, for President Obama's presence to heighten the cognitive association between race and party, especially among low-information Americans who had not yet connected their racial attitudes to their partisan attachments.

That potentially heightened mental association between race and party could have led to some significant changes in PID despite Americans' stable partisan identities. As Green, Palmquist, and Schickler (2002, 141) argue, partisanship is not inherently stable; instead, "party attachments tend to be stable because the social group imagery associated with the parties tends to change slowly over time. Once a person's party attachments take root, they are seldom disrupted by new conceptions of the partisan groups and the social coalitions that they comprise." One way to alter this social group imagery is to change the composition of party leadership. The Republican Party, for instance, effectively altered its public persona by putting Southerners into top party positions throughout the 1980s and 1990s, paving the way for party realignment in the South (Green, Palmquist, and Schickler 2002, 13).

Even more relevant for our purposes, the religious and racial backgrounds of prior presidential candidates caused attitudes about those groups to immediately spill over into Americans' partisan attachments. Attitudes toward Catholic groups were a stronger predictor of ANES panelists' Democratic Party identifications in 1960 than they were before John F. Kennedy's presidential candidacy renewed the association between Democrats and Catholicism (see results in chap. 9). And even more important, Sears, Citrin, and Kosterman (1987) showed that the increased association between the Democratic Party and African Americans, which presumably resulted from Jesse Jackson's 1984 presidential campaign, immediately accelerated the growing polarization of Southern partisanship by both racial attitudes and race.

President Obama's position as the de facto figurehead of the Democratic Party could have similarly reinvigorated the party's longstanding association with African Americans in the minds of the electorate. If, as suspected, a black president from the Democratic Party who strongly evoked racial predispositions once again situated race at the forefront of the party's image, the logical upshot would be an increased influence of racial attitudes on white Americans' partisan attachments. All told, then, we would expect racial attitudes to have spilled over into white Americans' party identifications, albeit in a more limited fashion than we have seen with other political evaluations directly connected to Barack Obama.

* * *

The results presented in this chapter handsomely support that hypothesis. Party identification became more polarized by racial attitudes in the Obama era than it had been shortly prior to his ascendancy. Even after controlling for economic conservatism, moral traditionalism, religious beliefs and activity, and military support, racial attitudes became significantly stronger predictors of white partisanship in the Age of Obama. That growing racialization of Obama-era mass partisanship was found in three different repeated cross-sectional surveys and extended to both new and old-fashioned forms of racial prejudice, all the while the impact of nonracial factors remained mostly stagnant. In other words, the effect of racial attitudes on party identification increased relative to nonracial predispositions. Racial resentment also powerfully predicted changes in party identification among white panelists who were reinterviewed in the 2006–10 General Social Survey (GSS) and the 2007–11 Cooperative Campaign Analysis Project (CCAP) when no such changes were found in the 2000-2002-2004, and 2004–6 ANES panel studies. And as expected, the spill-over of racialization into white Americans' partisan attachments was most pronounced among low-information Americans who had not consistently connected their racial predispositions to their partisan attachments in the pre-Obama period. This chapter's concluding remarks go on to detail why these results are probably the most important findings in the entire book. For party identification is both the most influential and probably the most enduring of all political attitudes

Correlations between Racial Attitudes and Party Identification (1988–2012)

The first test of this chapter's main hypothesis that Barack Obama's presidency helped racialize white Americans' partisan attachments examines the bivariate correlations (meaning there are no other control variables included) between racial attitudes and PID in time-series surveys conducted by the ANES, the GSS, and Pew from 1988 to 2012. Correlations measure the association between two variables, with a correlation of 1.0 being perfect correspondence, and a correlation of 0.0 representing no linear relationship whatsoever. Political attitudes tend to correlate only modestly with one another is survey data. In fact, the correlation between party identification and ideological self-placement is considered quite strong at around only 0.5.

That being said, figure 7.1 graphs out the over-time correlations between racial attitudes and the party identifications of white respondents in the three surveys. The panels in that display reveal several interesting patterns. First, the correlation between Republican PID and racial conservatism generally increased during the 1980s and 1990s. Those findings are consistent with research showing that racial attitudes became more important in mass partisanship in the post–civil rights era as older citizens who came of age before the parties diverged so sharply on racial issues were gradually replaced by incoming partisans whose party attachments were formed after that new race-based schism between Democratic and Republican politicians (Carmines and Stimson 1989; Layman and Carsey 2002; Stimson 2004; Valentino and Sears 2005).

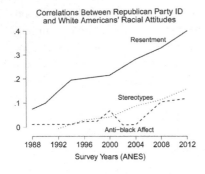

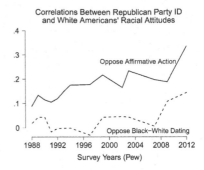

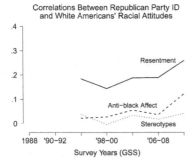

FIGURE 7.1. Correlations between Republican Party Identification and White Americans' Racial Attitudes
Source: American National Election Studies (ANES) cumulative file; 2012 ANES; Pew Values merged file; General Social Survey (GSS) cumulative file.

Second, these growing correlations between racial conservatism and Republican Party identification reached a plateau by the late 1990s in the Pew and GSS surveys. Moreover, the increased correlation between racial resentment and PID from 2000 to 2004 in the ANES was spurious, as this relationship actually weakened from 2000 to 2004 after other important factors were taken into account.[6] These results, therefore, support Stimson's (2004) contention that the evolution of race as a partisan issue had fully run its course by the year 2000.

Third, the strength of racial conservatism's relationship with Republican PID depended fundamentally on the measurement of antiblack attitudes. Racial resentment has always been a more powerful predictor of party identification than more blatant forms of prejudice like antiblack stereotypes and antiblack affect. Similarly, opposition to affirmative action, which as discussed in prior chapters is an excellent proxy variable for racial resentment,[7] was a consistently stronger correlate of white

Americans' partisan identifications than old-fashioned racist desires for intimate social distance between the races in the 1988–2012 Pew Values Surveys (PVS). These greater effects of racial resentment on party identification are likely a result of racial resentment's significant relationship with ideological conservatism (Sears et al. 1997; Hughes 1997; Sears and Henry 2005), as well as the more blatant measures' aforementioned inability to capture racial sympathy, and the changing political debate in the post–civil rights era from old-fashioned racist concerns about desegregation to an equality of outcomes agenda that evoked racially resentful anxieties about black deservingness and work ethic (Virtanen and Huddy 1998, 313).

Fourth, and most important for our purposes, nearly all the racial attitudes in the three panels of figure 7.1 show spikes in their correlations with party identification after Barack Obama's rise to prominence. The relationship between racial resentment and Republican PID, for instance, noticeably strengthened in the GSS and ANES surveys. The second panel of the display further shows that the jumps in pre- to post-2008 correlations between opposition to affirmative action and Republican identification were even starker in the PVS, as they increased from .19 in 2007 to .33 in 2012.

Some racial attitudes that were entirely unrelated to party identification in the pre-Obama era also became significant correlates of partisanship. The correlation between antiblack affect and partisanship in the GSS, for example, quadrupled from .03 in the pooled 1994–2008 surveys to .12 in the two surveys conducted after Obama was elected; and the first panel shows an analogous pre- to post-Obama enhanced relationship between antiblack affect and Republican PID among white respondents who were interviewed in the 2008 and 2012 ANES surveys. Finally, opposition to interracial dating, which was unrelated to party identification throughout the pre-Obama period, became a highly significant ($p < .001$) correlate of white partisanship in the 2009 and 2012 PVS.

The third panel of the display shows that antiblack stereotypes did not undergo the same pre- to post-Obama spike in correlations with Republican PID in the GSS that the other racial attitudes exhibited.[8] Yet, despite that curious result, the overall pattern in figure 7.1 is unmistakable. Party identification became more polarized by racial attitudes in the Obama era than it had been beforehand. The next sections of this chapter go on to show just how much more polarized PID was by racial attitudes in the Age of Obama, and how much of that polarization was actually about racial predispositions, as opposed to nonracial considerations.

Independent Effects of Racial Attitudes on Party Identification (2000–2012)

The bivariate correlations in figure 7.1 are certainly consistent with this chapter's main hypothesis that party identification became more heavily influenced by racial attitudes in the Age of Obama than it had been before. Yet, those same results remain silent about how much of the enhanced Obama-era relationships were actually about racial attitudes per se. It could be, for instance, that the growing correlations between racial predispositions and white partisanship in the Age of Obama were spuriously produced by other factors related to PID. In fact, moral traditionalism, religiosity, foreign policy hawkishness, authoritarianism, cultural conservatism, and ideological self-placement are among the many attitudes that have become more closely aligned with mass partisanship in recent years (Hetherington and Weiler 2009; Laymen and Carsey 2002; Levendusky 2009; Leege et al. 2002; Fiorina 2006; Gelman 2010; Abramowitz 2010; Putnam and Campbell 2010; Pew Research Center 2012b). It is therefore imperative to determine whether the *independent relationships* between racial conservatism and Republican PID also increased from before to after Obama's rise to prominence. Simply put, if racial attitudes became more important in white Americans' partisan attachments during Barack Obama's presidency, then they should be a stronger predictor of party identification after controlling for nonracial predispositions.

Table 7.1 tests that expectation with the GSS, ANES, and PVS's respective time series of repeated cross-sectional surveys. That model regresses Republican PID on racial conservatism, moral traditionalism, conservative economic attitudes, military support, and religious activity and beliefs. In other words, the coefficients disclose the impact of racial conservatism on party identification, while holding these nonracial predispositions constant. Racial resentment is used as our measure of racial conservatism in the ANES and GSS, while the PVS's opposition to interracial dating and affirmative action questions are combined into a two-item racial conservatism scale. Economic conservatism is an additive index based on opposition to government spending on such social programs as education, childcare, Social Security, and helping the needy; and moral traditionalism

TABLE 7.1. (OLS) Predictors of White Americans' Republican Party Identifications

	ANES			GSS			PVS		
	2000–2004	2008–12	Diff.	2000–2008	2010–12	Diff.	2002–7	2009–12	Diff.
Racial Conservatism	.169***	.291***	.122**	.118***	.196***	.077*	.096**	.243***	.148**
	(.037)	(.027)	(.046)	(.020)	(.030)	(.037)	(.032)	(.043)	(.054)
Economic Conservatism	.315***	.297***	−.018	.270***	.305***	.035	.362	.362	.000
	(.035)	(.021)	(.041)	(.022)	(.026)	(.041)	(.025)	(.030)	(.039)
Moral Traditionalism	.417***	.325***	−.092	.125***	.096**	−.029			
	(.043)	(.031)	(.053)	(.021)	(.036)	(.042)			
Military Support	.164***	.157***	−.007	.179***	.192***	.013	.225	.316	.090*
	(.040)	(.030)	(.001)	(.014)	(.022)	(.026)	(.027)	(.035)	(.044)
Bible Literalism	−.001	.017	.018	.020	.077*	.057			
	(.030)	(.019)	(.035)	(.016)	(.029)	(.033)			
Religious Attendance	.003	.084***	.080**	.088***	.072*	−.016	.190	.196	.007
	(.027)	(.017)	(.031)	(.017)	(.028)	(.032)	(.022)	(.028)	(.035)
Constant	−.033	−.106	−.073	.164***	.075*	−.088	.107***	−.017	−.124***
	(.032)	(.021)	(.038)	(.016)	(.024)	(.029)	(.020)	(.024)	(.031)
Observations	1,785	4,188	5,973	4,957	1,887	6,844	3,481	2,181	5,562

Source: American National Election Studies (ANES) cumulative file; 2012 ANES; General Social Survey (GSS) cumulative file; Pew Values (PVS) merged file.

Note: Dependent variables in the GSS and ANES are seven-point party identification, recoded from 0 (strong Democrat) to 1 (strong Republican); dependent variable in the PVS is five-point partisanship, recoded from 0 (Democrat) to 1 (Republican). All explanatory variables are coded from 0 to 1, with 1 being the highest value. Regression analyses use sample weights with robust standard errors that account for design characteristics.

*p < .05.
**p < .01.
***p < .001.

taps into aversion to newer or alternative lifestyles or premarital sex depending on the survey.[9] A full list of variables and coding can be found in the book's online appendix.[10]

With that model established, the coefficients in table 7.1 show that racial conservatism was a stronger determinant of Republican partisanship in the Age of Obama than it had been shortly before his presidential ascendancy. After controlling for several other notable predictors of PID, the polarization between the most racially conservative and the most racially liberal white Americans grew by more than ten points on a 0–100 Republican identification scale from before to after Barack Obama became his party's nominee for president. Moving from least to most racially resentful was associated with a twenty-nine–point increase in Republican identification among the ANES's 2008–12 white respondents, compared to only a seventeen-point increase in 2000–2004. The third column of table 7.1 further shows that this uptick in racial resentment's effect on Obama-era partisanship was statistically significant ($p < .01$).[11] The results in the next three columns also indicate that racial resentment was a significantly stronger predictor of party identification in the pooled 2010–12 GSS than it was in that time series from 2000 to 2008 ($p = .04$).[12] The biggest boost in racial conservatism's relationship with Republican PID was again found in the PVS, though. As can be seen in the final columns of the table, the Obama-era impact of racial attitudes on white Americans' partisanship grew by 150 percent in those surveys, from roughly ten points on a 0–100 scale in the pooled 2002–7 PVS to nearly twenty-five points in 2009 and 2012—another highly significant difference in over-time effects ($p < .01$).

The coefficients for the remaining variables in the table are also quite telling. In contrast with the significant increases in racial conservatism's impact on Republican identification uncovered in all three time-series surveys, the effects of economic conservatism, moral traditionalism, military support, and religious beliefs and behavior on white partisanship were mostly unchanged from before to after Obama became the Democratic nominee president.[13] Those static effects, to be sure, do not imply that nonracial factors were unimportant predictors of Obama-era partisanship, nor do they indicate that non-racial issues were displaced in the party alignment by the increased effects of racial resentment.[14] In fact, the nonracial variables in table 7.1 combined to explain much more of the variance in white partisanship than racial attitudes. It does, however, appear that Barack Obama's presidency made racial attitudes a more important ingredient of party identification *relative to nonracial determinants* of white partisanship—a finding, you may recall, that is similar to the spill-over of racialization into health care results presented in chapter 5.

* * *

Taking the ANES, GSS, and Pew results together, the most racially liberal and the most racially conservative white Americans' partisan attachments were polarized by about twelve points more on a 0–100 scale in the Age of Obama than they were shortly beforehand. That Obama-era polariza-tion of white partisanship by racial attitudes was nearly twice as large as it was in the years immediately preceding the 2008 election, and it occurred without corresponding increases in the effects of nonracial predisposi-tions. It is also important to note that this enhanced polarization of mass partisanship by racial attitudes was brought about by the two sides of ra-cialization. After controlling for the factors in table 7.1, the most racially liberal whites moved nine points more Democratic in the 2008–12 ANES study than they had in 2000–2004, whereas the most racially conservative whites became about three points more Republican.

Old-Fashioned Racial Attitudes and Party Identification (2000–2012)

The increased effects of racial attitudes on Obama-era party identifica-tion were unlikely limited to just racial resentment. We saw earlier in this chapter that more blatant racial prejudice measures like antiblack affect and desire for intimate social distance between the races were essentially uncorrelated with PID throughout the pre-Obama period. Yet, we have also repeatedly seen Obama's ascendancy activate those same outdated racial attitudes in white Americans' political preferences. Recall from the results and discussions in prior chapters that old-fashioned racism (OFR) and antiblack affect became significantly stronger determinants of Obama-era voting behavior for both president and Congress than they had been in prior decades' elections (see also Tesler 2013b).[15] It is not too surprising, then, that figure 7.1 suggested antiblack affect and opposition to interracial dating also spilled over into white Americans' partisan at-tachments in the Age of Obama.

There is a lingering question, though, of whether those enhanced effects would hold up in the presence of controls for other important predictors of party identification. It is possible, for instance, that the modest correlations shown in figure 7.1 between party identification and our overt measures of racial prejudice were subsumed by more powerful predictors of partisanship like economic conservatism, moral traditionalism, military support, and religiosity. Table 7.2 therefore tests the relationship between old-fashioned racial attitudes and Republican PID while holding these other factors constant.

The coefficients in the table show that the independent effects of OFR and antiblack affect on Obama-era partisanship were significantly larger than they had been in the years prior to his presidency. After controlling for economic, religious, and military attitudes, the numbers in the first column of the table suggest that opposition to interracial dating may not have even been positively associated with Republican PID from 2002 to 2007. The second column's coefficients, however, denote a modest, but statistically significant ($p = .04$), six-point impact of this OFR measure on party identification in the 2009–12 PVS. That strengthened pre- to post-Obama relationship was also statistically significant ($p = .03$).

The GSS columns in table 7.2 go on to show that OFR—measured in that survey by subtracting how white respondents would react to a close relative marrying an African American from how they would feel about him or her marrying someone of the same race[16]—also became a significant predictor of Republican party identification for the first time in their 2010–12 surveys ($p = .01$). All else being equal, white respondents who strongly preferred racial endogamy were about seven points more Republican on a 0–100 scale in those two Obama-era surveys than whites who did not object to their close relatives marrying black spouses—an effect on party identification that was also significantly stronger than the one uncovered in the 2000–2008 GSS ($p = .04$).

The remaining columns in table 7.2 disclose almost identical results for antiblack affect in the ANES and GSS surveys. In fact, all the OFR and antiblack affect results have the following three things in common: (1) Both of these blatant racial prejudice measures had no independent relationship whatsoever with party identification in the years immediately preceding Obama's presidential nomination; (2) old-fashioned racism and antiblack affect became statistically significant predictors of Republican PID for the first time in surveys conducted after Obama became the face of the Democratic Party; and (3) the greater effects of those racial attitudes on partisanship in the Age of Obama were significantly (or almost significantly) stronger than their pre-Obama effects.[17]

TABLE 7.2. (OLS) Predictors of White Americans' Republican Party Identifications

	PVS		GSS		ANES		GSS	
	2002–7	2009–12	2000–2008	2010–12	2000–2004	2008–12	2000–2008	2010–12
Intimate Social Distance (OFR)	−.020	.062*	.002	.068*				
	(.022)	(.030)	(.015)	(.027)				
Black Affect					−.035	−.130***	−.001	−.133*
					(.052)	(.034)	(.030)	(.053)
White Affect					−.060	−.039	.018	.065
					(.055)	(.034)	(.032)	(.057)
Economic Conservatism	.376***	.403***	.287***	.315***	.322***	.323***	.312***	.315***
	(.024)	(.029)	(.024)	(.035)	(.035)	(.021)	(.031)	(.053)
Moral Traditionalism			.136***	.094*	.458***	.399***	.079**	.109*
			(.023)	(.036)	(.042)	(.030)	(.029)	(.042)
Military Support	.252***	.345***	.210***	.200	.219***	.251***	.203***	.161***
	(.027)	(.035)	(.015)	(.022)	(.043)	(.030)	(.019)	(.032)
Bible Literalism			.040*	.098***	.016	.046*	.019	.109*
			(.018)	(.028)	(.029)	(.020)	(.023)	(.042)
Religious Attendance	.200***	.200***	.080***	.072**	−.008	.062***	.113***	.056
	(.022)	(.022)	(.018)	(.028)	(.026)	(.017)	(.023)	(.042)
Constant	.137***	.137***	.210***	.166***	.071	.065*	.223***	.236***
	(.019)	(.019)	(.014)	(.014)	(.041)	(.030)	(.033)	(.054)
Observations	3,481	2,181	4,323	1,918	1,800	4,182	2,502	915

Source: American National Election Studies (ANES) cumulative file; 2012 ANES; General Social Survey (GSS) cumulative file; Pew Values (PVS) Merged File.

Note: Dependent variables in the GSS and ANES are seven-point party identification, recoded from 0 (strong Democrat) to 1 (strong Republican); dependent variable in the PVS is five-point partisanship, recoded from 0 (Democrat) to 1 (Republican). All explanatory variables are coded from 0 to 1, with 1 being the highest value. Regression analyses use sample weights with robust standard errors that account for design characteristics. OFR, old-fashioned racism.

*p < .05.

**p < .01.

***p < .001.

To be sure, the relationships between Republican PID and these more overt racial prejudice measures were still not especially strong; and they obviously paled in comparison to the aforementioned effects of racial resentment on white Americans' partisan attachments. Nevertheless, the results suggest that the election of a black president from the Democratic Party—even one who was virtually silent about racial issues during the first term of his presidency (Coe and Schmidt 2012; Gillion 2012)—helped make OFR a significant determinant of white partisanship after long being a dormant factor in American politics. When taking that prolonged period of OFR's political quiescence into account, these results may be even more noteworthy than the larger effects of racial resentment on Republican PID in the Age of Obama.

Racial Resentment and Partisan Change in Panel Data (2000–2011)

Our repeated cross-sectional analyses, however, still cannot tell us whether the stronger relationships between racial attitudes and Obama-era PID were actually the result of white Americans' changing their partisan attachments in accordance with their underlying racial attitudes because of Obama's rise to prominence within the Democratic Party. It could be, for instance, that some individuals changed their racial attitudes to comport with their prior partisan preferences precisely because Barack Obama was now the face of his party. In other words, was racial resentment driving partisan changes or were prior partisan attachments causing white Americans to change their racial attitudes? Once again it is essential to augment our repeated cross-sectional results with panel surveys that reinterviewed the same respondents before and after Obama became the Democratic nominee for president in order to address such reverse causality concerns.

Fortunately, we can leverage a series of panel surveys conducted by the ANES and GSS between 2000 and 2010 to test whether racial resentment predicted partisan changes more powerfully in the Age of Obama era than had done beforehand. Those results are presented in table 7.3. The model employed here includes a lagged dependent variable for each respondent's party identification in the previous panel wave. You may recall from the district-level analyses of congressional election returns in the previous chapter that including this earlier measure of partisanship allows us to assess the remaining predictors' impact on the *change in PID*

TABLE 7.3. **(OLS) Predictors of White Americans' Republican Party Identifications**

	ANES			GSS	CCAP
	2000–2002	2000–4	2004–6	2006–10	2007–11
Lagged Racial Resentment	.049	−.002	.033	.123***	.100***
	(.044)	(.068)	(.064)	(.033)	(.024)
Lagged Social Spending Support	−.029	−.068	−.069	−.110*	−.004
	(.027)	(.055)	(.060)	(.042)	(.020)
Lagged Defense Support	.052	−.060	.077	.029	.052*
	(.050)	(.050)	(.095)	(.027)	(.020)
Lagged Moral Traditionalism	.009	.085	.040	.035	.072**
	(.060)	(.060)	(.059)	(.042)	(.023)
Lagged Bible Literalism	.002	.016	.038	−.035	
	(.060)	(.048)	(.059)	(.042)	
Lagged Religious Attendance	.075**	.048	.080*	.028	.002
	(.026)	(.032)	(.037)	(.036)	(.016)
Lagged Partisanship	.776***	.852***	.805***	.704***	.744***
	(.033)	(.030)	(.047)	(.034)	(.028)
Constant	.052	.102	−.058	.120*	.002
	(.048)	(.068)	(.068)	(.047)	(.011)
Observations	758	619	477	581	1,735

Source: 2000-2002-2004 American National Election Studies (ANES) panel; 2006 ANES pilot study; 2006-2008-2010 General Social Survey (GSS); 2007-2008-2011 Cooperative Campaign Analysis Project (CCAP).
Note: Dependent variable is seven-point party identification, recoded from 0 (strong Democrat) to 1 (strong Republican). All explanatory variables are coded from 0 to 1, with 1 being the highest value. Regression analyses use panel weights with robust standard errors that account for design characteristics.
*$p < .05$.
**$p < .01$.
***$p < .001$.

from one panel wave to the next. The coefficients in the first column, for instance, denote the impact of each variable's impact on partisan change from 2000 to 2002; the second columns tell how they affected partisan change from 2000 to 2004, and so forth.

The results from 2000-2002-2004 and 2004–6 ANES panels, therefore, indicate that racial resentment had little impact on partisan changes throughout the time period immediately preceding Obama's ascendancy. Averaging across those ANES survey results, the most racially resentful became only about three points on a 0–100 scale more Republican than their least-resentful counterparts over the course of those panel studies. The null effects of racial resentment on partisan changes from 2000 to 2006 make sense in light of our earlier discussion of the diminished salience of racial issues in the decade prior to Obama's presidential victory, as well as our discussion in this chapter about how racial resentment's impact on party identification had reached a plateau by 2000.

It would make perfect sense in light of results presented throughout the book, though, for racial resentment to have significantly predicted changes in PID from before to after Obama became the Democratic nominee for president. And that is precisely what happened. After controlling for economic, moral, military, and religious predispositions,[18] the coefficients in table 7.3 show that racial resentment, as measured in 2006, was a highly significant predictor of partisan changes in the 2006–10 GSS panel study ($p <. 001$). All else being equal, the most racially resentful grew about twelve points more Republican than their least racially resentful counterparts from before to after Obama's presidential nomination in those surveys—an effect four times greater than the impact of racial resentment on partisan changes from 2000 to 2006. Consistent with that finding, the final column of the table shows that racial resentment was also a significant and sizable predictor of partisan change among white panelists who were reinterviewed in the 2007–11 CCAP.[19]

In sum, Barack Obama's presidential candidacy and presidency appear to have made racial resentment a significantly stronger predictor of white partisan change than it had been in the years immediately preceding his rise to prominence.

Low-Information Racialization

The spillover of racialization into white Americans' partisan attachments might seem all the more remarkable because race was already so prominent in the pre-Obama party alignment. Yet, while many readers of this book will surely take it as a given that the Democratic Party for some time now has been more supportive of racial policies than the Republican Party, a substantial proportion of the population had a difficult time making that connection before Barack Obama ran for president. Less than one-third of pure Independents, for instance, rated the Democratic Party higher than the Republican Party on the ANES's aforementioned "aid to blacks scale" from 1972 to 2000 (Layman and Carsey 2002, 790); and figure 7.2 similarly shows that only 42 percent of whites without any college education rated Democratic presidential candidates higher on this measure than Republican nominees between 1988 and 2004.[20]

Those informational differences had important implications for the racialization of partisan attachments in the pre-Obama period. In fact, Layman and Carsey (2002, 799) argue "that mass response to recent elite-level developments [e.g., divergent issue positions between the parties]

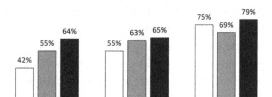

FIGURE 7.2. Percentage of White Respondents Who Rated the Democratic Presidential Candidate More Supportive on the ANES's "Aid to Blacks Scale" Than the Republican Candidate, by Education Level
Source: ANES cumulative file; 2012 ANES.

should be limited to party identifiers . . . who are aware of party polarization on each separate issue agenda." These authors call that pattern of high-information polarization "conflict extension." Conflict extension's expectations are further confirmed by the results below, which show that the significant pre-Obama relationships between racial conservatism and Republican PID were heavily concentrated among better-educated Americans who were disproportionately aware of the ongoing partisan cleavages over race-targeted policies.[21]

Barack Obama's presidency, however, almost certainly made it easier for low-information Americans to connect race to partisan politics. Indeed, even the most politically apathetic segments of the population should have still known that the president was a black Democrat. It is not too surprising, then, that figure 7.2 shows a large Obama-era increase in the percentage of poorly educated Americans who rated the Democratic presidential candidate as more supportive of federal aid to blacks than the Republican nominee. There was a twenty-two-percentage-point increase pre- to post-Obama in the likelihood of non-college-educated whites saying that the Democrat presidential nominee (in this case Obama) was more supportive than the Republican Party's candidate of government aid to African Americans. The display also shows that this knowledge of Democratic presidential nominees' greater support for race-targeted policies remained similarly high among white college graduates from before to after Barack Obama appeared on the national ballot. Simply put, Barack Obama's presidential candidacies noticeably shrunk the education gap in awareness of the two parties' differing positions on race.

We would, therefore, expect the spike in Obama-era correlations between racial attitudes and party identification to have been particularly pronounced among lower-information Americans. The results presented in figure 7.3 strongly support that expectation. The first panel of that display, for instance, shows a dramatic Obama-era increase in the correlation between white racial resentment and Republican PID among ANES respondents without any college education. As can be seen, this lower-education group's correlations, jumped from .06 in 2004 to .38 in 2012. At the same time, though, there was little pre- to post-Obama change in the relationship between racial resentment and partisanship among white respondents who attended at least some college.

The right panel of Figure 7.3 illustrates a strikingly similar pattern in the PVS. Like the ANES results, there was an enormous post-Obama increase in correlations between racial conservatism and Republican PID among poorly educated respondents in those surveys; and also like the

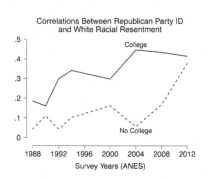
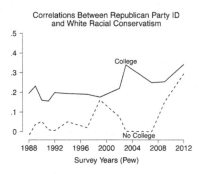

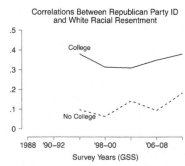

FIGURE 7.3. Correlations between Republican Party Identification and White Americans' Racial Attitudes, by Education
Source: American National Election Studies (ANES) cumulative file; 2012 ANES; Pew Values merged file; General Social Survey (GSS) cumulative file.

ANES, those enhanced relationships were accompanied by a much more limited spillover of racialization into partisanship among college-educated respondents. The upshot is that low-information whites linked their racial attitudes to their partisan attachments at nearly the same high rates as their better-educated counterparts did in these two 2012 surveys. The final panel of figure 7.3 shows a less pronounced pattern of low-information racialization among GSS respondents. Yet, the Obama-era correlation still doubled in those surveys among poorly educated whites, from .09 in the pooled 1994–2008 sample to .18 in the 2010–12 GSS.

It is important to note that these strengthened relationships between racial conservatism and Republican PID held among poorly educated respondents after controlling for the same measures of economic conservatism, moral traditionalism, religious beliefs and activity, and military support that we accounted for in our earlier analyses.

It is also worth mentioning that this pronounced, and independent, pattern of low-information racialization is distinct from well-established models of polarization. Indeed, the conventional wisdom is that politically informed respondents are most likely to polarize in response to new partisan developments because they are more likely to receive that information than their less engaged counterparts (Zaller 1992; Hetherington 2001; Laymen and Carsey 2002).[22] The connection among Obama, race, and party, however, was undoubtedly an easier signal for poorly educated Americans to receive than most other political messages. Consequently, the spillover of racialization into white partisanship was strongest among non-college-educated Americans (who typically have low levels of information about politics) who had not consistently linked their racial attitudes to their partisan attachments in the pre-Obama period.

Concluding Remarks

We now know that the spillover of racialization into American politics extended all the way into white Americans' relatively crystallized partisan attachments. Partisanship became more polarized by racial attitudes from before to after Obama's ascendancy in three different surveys, with that growing polarization of PID occurring over both old and newer forms of racial prejudice. Unlike the results in chapters 5 and 6, those increased effects of racial attitudes on partisan attachments were produced by the two sides of racialization. White racial liberals became increasingly

Democratic while white racial conservatives became increasingly Republican. Some of the chapter's results, you may have noticed, were not nearly as large in magnitude as many of the other racial spillover effects presented in the book. All things considered, though, they are still probably its most important findings.

It is hard to overstate PID's importance. Indeed, mass partisanship influences just about everything in contemporary American society. It not only powerfully shapes our vote choices and policy preferences but also often dictates whom we choose to date and to marry (Alford et al. 2011; Iyengar, Sood, and Lelkes 2012), which political rumors we accept and reject (Berinsky 2015), how we perceive objective national conditions like the unemployment rate and federal budget deficit (Shani 2006; Bartels 2002, 2012; Bullock et al. 2013; see also table 3.1), which neighborhoods we decide to live in (Bishop 2009; Atkinson 2013; Motyl et al. 2014; though see Nall and Mummolo 2013), and even how we feel about Big Bird and Godfather's Pizza (Republican presidential candidate Herman Cain's restaurant chain).[23] Simply put, the growing racialization of party identification is by itself *the* growing racialization of American politics and society.

The racialization of PID is also more likely to leave a lasting mark on American politics than some of the other racial spillover effects presented in the book. For, as mentioned earlier, partisan attachments persist rather stably throughout the lifecycle because the social group imagery associated with the parties tends to change slowly after it takes roots (Green, Palmquist, and Schickler 2002). The Party of Lincoln, perhaps most notably, retained overwhelming black support for decades after the Republicans abandoned their Reconstruction efforts to help freed slaves in the late nineteenth century (Weiss 1983). The enhanced polarization of white partisanship by racial attitudes in response to Democrats becoming the Party of Obama could therefore leave an imprint on the American political landscape that endures long after he leaves office.

The Expanding Political Divide between White and Nonwhite Americans

Because it's a changing country; the demographics are changing. It's not a traditional America anymore. And there are fifty percent of the voting public who want stuff, they want things. And who is going to give them things? President Obama. He knows it and he ran on it. And, whereby twenty years ago President Obama would have been roundly defeated by an establishment candidate like Mitt Romney, the white establishment is now the minority. — Bill O'Reilly, on why Barack Obama was reelected, election night 2012[1]

Bill O'Reilly's much-publicized election night proclamation that "the white establishment is now the minority" drew criticism for hastening the decline of white political influence in the United States.[2] White Americans, after all, were still the clear majority of the electorate in 2012 (72 percent in the exit polls; 73.7 percent in the census) and remained vastly overrepresented at every level of government in the United States (except, of course, president).[3] That was not the only controversial comment that O'Reilly made on Fox News's 2012 election night coverage, either. The top-rated cable news commentator was also criticized for suggesting that minority voters were takers who overwhelmingly supported Barack Obama because they "want stuff, they want things."[4] O'Reilly, however, made one outstanding point in the epigraph that introduced this chapter, which was simply unassailable: Barack Obama's electoral coalition would have been "roundly defeated" twenty years earlier by a candidate like Mitt Romney. As mentioned in the introductory chapter, President Obama performed slightly worse among white voters (39 percent) than Michael Dukakis did when he lost the 1988 election to George H. W. Bush by eight percentage points.

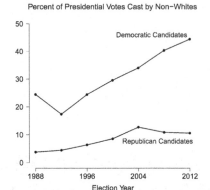

Percent of Presidential Votes Cast by Non−Whites

FIGURE 8.1. Percentage of Presidential Votes Cast by Nonwhites (Two-Party Vote Only), 1988–2012
Source: Exit polls, 1988–2012.

So, how exactly did Barack Obama manage to beat Mitt Romney by four percentage points in the 2012 presidential election with such a low share of white votes? Figure 8.1 helps answer this question, showing the percentage of the two parties' presidential vote tallies that came from nonwhite Americans in every election since 1988.[5] Michael Dukakis did not stand a chance of winning the 1988 presidential election with only 40 percent of the white vote because nonwhites accounted for less than 25 percent of his total electoral support. Bill Clinton also received more than 75 percent of his votes from white Americans in both the 1992 and 1996 presidential elections. Averaging pre-Obama-era elections, whites cast 74 percent of the Democratic Party's presidential votes between 1988 and 2004. Barack Obama relied on a much different electoral calculus, though. In fact, nonwhites cast 40 percent and 44 percent of Barack Obama's votes in 2008 and 2012, respectively.

Perhaps equally important, figure 8.1 also shows that the Republican Party depended almost exclusively on the support of white voters in the 2008 and 2012 presidential elections. Only about 10 percent of all votes for John McCain and Mitt Romney came from nonwhite Americans. Thus, the Democratic Party's expanding nonwhite coalition, and the Republican Party's inability to broaden their base of support beyond white America, made it possible for Barack Obama to easily win reelection with a lower share of the two-party white vote than any presidential candidate had received since 1984.[6]

Three factors helped the Democratic Party expand their nonwhite coalition so rapidly from 24 percent in 1996—the last time the Democrats won the presidency in the pre-Obama era—to 44 percent in 2012. First, the changing US demographics altered the composition of the voting-age population. In 1996, 79.2 percent of the voting-eligible population (VEP) was white. That percentage, however, dropped down to 71.2 percent in 2012. The decrease in white eligible voters was primarily filled by Latinos, whose VEP increased from 4.7 percent in 1996 to 8.4 percent in 2012. But the percentage of eligible Asian American voters also increased significantly from 1.7 percent in 1996 to 2.9 percent in 2012.[7]

Not only were there more eligible nonwhite voters than there had been in recent election years but racial and ethnic minorities also turned out to vote at higher rates in 2012 than they had in the past. African Americans, in particular, were eager to show up at the ballot booth to vote for Barack Obama. In the twenty years prior to Obama's first presidential contest, only about 57 percent of African Americans voted in presidential elections. That percentage jumped up to 65 percent and 66 percent in 2008 and 2012, respectively, with black Americans more likely to vote than whites for the first time ever in 2012.[8] While Latino and Asian American turnout did not increase nearly as dramatically as these record-high rates of black voting, both groups' turnout was up a couple of percentage points in 2012 from their 1996–2004 averages.[9] The upshot of the changing demographics and this increased minority turnout was that the white electorate declined from 82.5 percent in 1996 to 73.7 percent in 2012 (File 2013).

Finally, Barack Obama expanded the Democrats' nonwhite base of support because he was more popular among racial and ethnic minorities than recent Democratic presidential candidates had been.[10] President Obama performed particularly poorly in 2012 among white voters; his share of the two-party white vote was nearly five percentage points below the mean level of white support for Democratic candidates between 1988 and 2004 (39.8 percent to 44.7 percent). Yet, he was five percentage points more popular with African Americans in 2012 than his 1988–2004 Democratic predecessors (94 percent to 89 percent).[11] He also performed five percentage points better among Latinos in 2012 than Democratic presidential candidates did, on average, from 1988 to 2004 (72 percent to 67 percent). And Barack Obama received a whopping 74 percent of the two-party Asian American vote in 2012, despite the fact that Democrats, such as Bill Clinton, Al Gore, and John Kerry, received only a combined 49 percent of this group's votes from 1992 to 2004.[12]

Simply put, then, white and nonwhite Americans' 2012 vote preferences were more divided than they had been in the pre-Obama era. Much like the unusually strong effects of racial attitudes on mass assessments of Barack Obama documented earlier, these results naturally raise the question of whether the expanding divide in presidential voting between white and nonwhite Americans also reproduced itself in additional areas of mass politics. In other words, did the spillover of racialization extend to a growing partisan divide between white and nonwhite Americans in the Age of Obama?

* * *

This chapter answers the question of whether spillover extended to a growing partisan divide by exploring the political divide between white and nonwhite Americans before and after Barack Obama became president. Like white racial liberals and white racial conservatives, black and white Americans were much more divided in their assessments of Barack Obama's job performance than their evaluations of other recent presidents. That racial divide was especially pronounced between racially resentful whites and racially conscious blacks, too. Moreover, and much like the spillover of racial attitudes into white Americans' political preferences, Barack Obama's presence in the White House helped enhance the already substantial black-white racial divide in a number of political opinions. The racial divide in health care opinions increased substantially from before to after Barack Obama's ascendancy and party identification grew significantly more divided by color in the Obama era. As we will also see in this chapter, Latinos were even more likely to have moved to the Democratic Party than blacks were in the Obama era. Yet unlike African Americans, whose growing Democratic identification was most pronounced among blacks who rated their own group most favorably, the spike in Latinos' affiliation with the Democratic Party was most heavily concentrated among Hispanics who felt colder toward whites. With the Republican Party increasingly viewed as a party of and for white Americans in the Obama Era, attitudes about whites were also strong predictors of Asian Americans' and Native Americans' 2012 partisan attachments. In sum, this chapter shows that mass politics was more divided by and over race in the Age of Obama than it had been in modern times.

Black-White Racial Divide in Obama Approval

As just mentioned, the black-white racial divide in 2012 presidential voting was about ten percentage points larger in 2012 than it was from 1988 to

2004. Merely looking at presidential voting understates the unique nature of the racial divide in public opinion about President Obama. Democratic presidential candidates received nearly 90 percent of the black vote in pre-Obama presidential elections from 1988 to 2004. That overwhelming black support created a ceiling effect, which made it impossible for any Democratic presidential candidate to perform much better among this group. African Americans, however, have not been nearly as uniform in their approval of Democratic presidents' job performances. President Clinton, whose popularity among African Americans was considered at the time to be "exceptionally strong" (Tate 1994, 207), had an approval rating near 70 percent in three national surveys of black Americans commissioned during the first two years of his presidency.[13] Consequently, the black-white racial divide in President Clinton's pooled approval ratings from the 1994–2000 ANES surveys (thirty percentage points) was considerably smaller than the forty-five-percentage-point divide in black and white Americans' support for Democratic presidential candidates between 1988 and 2004.

Barack Obama's approval ratings, however, were more divided by color than Bill Clinton's. Black Americans were about fifty percentage points more likely to approve of Barack Obama than whites in Gallup polls conducted throughout most of his presidency (see fig. 8.2). The black-white racial divide in presidential approval was also more than fifty percentage points in the 2012 American National Election Study (ANES), with 92 percent of African Americans approving of Barack Obama's job performance in that survey compared to 40 percent of whites. Moreover, President Clinton's approval rating among blacks often increased and decreased in accordance with his white support. That is, when whites' opinions of Bill Clinton changed, so did those of blacks.[14] President Obama's black approval rating, by contrast, was much more stable. Figure 8.2, which plots Obama's weekly Gallup approval rating by race, shows that President Obama's support from African Americans held pretty steady at around 90 percent approval throughout most of his first term in office.[15] Meanwhile, white Americans fit the more usual pattern of presidential approval (Mueller 1973; Brody 1991; Green, Palmquist, and Schickler 2002; Sides and Vavreck 2013), whereby their support for Obama waned over time. With President Obama's white approval gradually declining during the course of his presidency, and his black support holding relatively constant, the racial divide in presidential approval increased from forty-two percentage points in 2009 to fifty points in 2010 and fifty-three points in 2014.

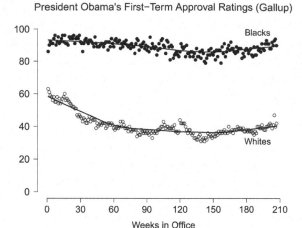

FIGURE 8.2. President Obama's First-Term Weekly Approval Rating, by Race
Source: Gallup's weekly tracking polls.

Kinder and Dale-Riddle (2012, 152) suggested that Barack Obama's unwavering support from African Americans was rooted in racial group consciousness: "Support for the president among African Americans," they wrote, "is perhaps, an affirmation of group solidarity; standing with the president an expression of racial pride." That contention seems hard to argue with, too. After all, group consciousness is one of the most important determinants of black public opinion and political behavior (Gurin, Hatchett, and Jackson 1989; Dawson 1994, 2001; Tate 1994; Kinder and Sanders 1996; Kinder and Winter 2001; Sears and Savalei 2006; Sniderman and Piazza 2002; Harris-Lacewell 2004; Kinder and Dale-Riddle 2012). Racial group identification was also a significant predictor of black support for presidential candidates like Jesse Jackson and Barack Obama (Dawson 1994; Tate 1994; Tesler and Sears 2010; Kinder and Dale-Riddle 2012). And, perhaps most important for our purposes, in-group consciousness shaped prior presidents' black approval ratings. As Michael Dawson (1994, 162) noted, "Historically, African Americans' perceptions of the relationship between racial group interests and the current administration have helped determine African American presidential approval."

We can also leverage the oversample of African Americans in the 2012 ANES survey to more directly determine whether Barack Obama's unusually strong black support was a byproduct of in-group solidarity. Racial group thermometers are one of many indicators of in-group favoritism (Sears and Savalei 2009), and Kinder and Dale-Riddle (2012, 188–89) used thermometer ratings of blacks to test the effects of "racial group solidarity" on African Americans' support for Jesse Jackson in 1988 and Barack Obama in 2008.[16] Figure 8.3 similarly uses black-thermometer ratings to test the chapter's first major hypothesis that differences in African Americans' strong support for Bill Clinton's and Barack Obama's respective presidencies were most pronounced among racially conscious blacks who rated their own group most favorably. The display plots the probability of African Americans strongly approving of Barack Obama's and Bill Clinton's job performances as a function of their black-thermometer ratings. The analysis here uses "strongly approve" as its dependent variable of interest because nearly all the African American respondents in the 2012 ANES approved of Barack Obama's job performance, leaving little variation left for the black thermometer to explain.

That being said, the results in figure 8.3 suggest that Barack Obama's atypically strong support from African Americans was rooted in racial group consciousness. As can be seen, the black thermometer was weakly related to African Americans' strong approval of Bill Clinton's job performance in pooled 1994–2000 ANES surveys.[17] In the 2012 ANES, however, the black thermometer was a highly significant ($p < .001$) predictor of African Americans' strong support for Barack Obama.[18] As a result, the display shows that Obama's greater popularity among African Americans

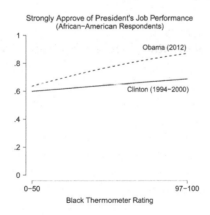

FIGURE 8.3. African Americans' Strong Approval of President Clinton and President Obama as a Function of Black-Thermometer Ratings
Note: Probabilities based on logistic regression coefficients in the online appendix. Predicted probabilities were calculated by setting the white thermometer to its sample mean.
Source: American National Election Studies (ANES) cumulative file; 2012 ANES.

(80 percent strongly approving compared to 66 percent strongly approving of Clinton) was most pronounced among racially conscious African Americans. Indeed, African Americans who rated their own group most favorably were about twenty percentage points more likely to strongly approve of President Obama than President Clinton. Consistent with that finding, there was a very similar pattern with black respondents' thermometer ratings of Bill Clinton and Barack Obama. That is, African Americans' warmer feelings toward President Obama than President Clinton were also most pronounced among blacks who rated their own group most favorably.[19]

* * *

All told, then, presidential assessments were increasingly divided by and over race during Barack Obama's presidency. The racial divide in Barack Obama's presidential approval ratings was about twenty to twenty-five percentage points greater than it had been for Bill Clinton.[20] Moreover, this divide in support for President Obama was especially prominent between racially resentful whites, who, as shown in prior chapters and elsewhere (Tesler and Sears 2010), were more opposed to Obama than high-profile white Democrats and racially conscious blacks who had a stronger affinity for President Obama than they had for white Democrats like Bill Clinton.

Black Support and the Racial Divide in Health Care Opinions

Like the spillover of racial attitudes from Barack Obama into related political evaluations documented throughout the book, the unusually large racial divide in public support for the first African American president should have reproduced itself in a number of Obama-era political preferences. As Kinder and Winter (2001, 452) put it, "Issues can be formulated and framed in such a way as to light up or downplay racial identity, and therefore, in such a way as to expand or contract the racial divide in opinion." Attributing policies to black sources, such as Barack Obama, seems likely to "light up" racial identity, and therefore expand the racial divide in public opinion. In fact, prior experimental research shows that ascribing positions to such black elites as Jesse Jackson and Colin Powell expanded the black-white racial divide in public opinion, with African

Americans increasingly likely to adopt those viewpoints (Peffley and Hurwitz 2010; Kuklinski and Hurly 1994).

We should expect a similar result for Barack Obama's policy positions, especially given his aforementioned popularity among African Americans and the expanding racial divide in public support for Barack Obama over the course of his presidency. The chapter's second major hypothesis, then, is that health care opinions should have been more divided by race after Barack Obama became so closely aligned with this policy than they were before his presidency.

That expectation is borne out in figure 8.4. This display shows that in March 2008, 41 percent of our white 2008–9 Cooperative Campaign Analysis Project (CCAP) panelists said that health care should be voluntarily left up to individuals compared to 18 percent of our black respondents. When these same panel respondents were surveyed in November 2009, though, the prior twenty-three point racial divide had widened to thirty-three percentage points. As can be seen, 46 percent of whites now preferred privately administered health care compared to just 13 percent of our black panelists.

Just like the enhanced polarization of white Americans' health care opinions by racial attitudes during Barack Obama's presidency discussed in chapter 5, though, the president's party affiliation rather than his race could have easily been responsible for that suspected increase in black support for health care reform. Indeed, African Americans are the

Percentage Saying Health Care Should be Voluntarily Left Up to Individuals

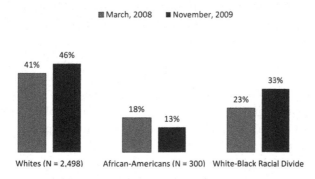

FIGURE 8.4. Health Care Opinions in March 2008 and November 2009 by Race
Source: 2008–9 Cooperative Campaign Analysis Project panelists interviewed in both March 2008 and November 2009.

Democratic Party's most loyal constituency. Any Democratic president's health care reform efforts may have therefore galvanized black support. That alternative explanation seems unlikely since prior experiments suggested that African Americans are more supportive of black Republicans' positions than they are of white Democrats' endorsements (Kuklinski and Hurly 1994). More importantly, though, we can further interrogate this partisan possibility because several polling firms repeatedly asked about "President Clinton's health care plan" in 1993–94 and used similarly worded questions to gauge support for President Obama's proposals in 2009–10.[21] If the racial divide in 2009–10 is simply a party-specific phenomenon, then we should see a similar gap between blacks and whites in their approval of both Democratic presidents' health care plans.

The evidence presented in figure 8.5, however, suggests that President Obama possessed a unique potential to polarize Americans' issue opinions by race. Four survey firms continuously monitored public support for President Clinton's health care reform plan in 1993 and 1994.[22] Because of the small number of African Americans in the typical media poll, the surveys are aggregated to create a pooled sample for each of the four firms. From these four pooled samples, the results in figure 8.5 show that the differences between black and white Americans in support for President Clinton's health care plan ranged from a low of twenty percentage points in the *LA Times* sample to a high of thirty percentage points in the Gallup surveys.

These large differences in the health care opinions of black and white Americans in 1993 and 1994 grew noticeably larger in 2009 and 2010.[23] As the 2009–10 results in figure 8.5 show, the black-white racial divide in support for President Obama's proposals ranged from a low of forty percentage points in the pooled *Economist* sample to a high of fifty-two percentage points in the *Rasmussen* surveys. Averaging across the four pooled 1993–94 and 2009–10 samples in the display, 69 percent of African Americans, compared to 43 percent of whites, favored Bill Clinton's health care plan. That twenty-six–point racial division in 1993–94 expanded into a forty-five-point gulf in 2009–10, with 83 percent of blacks supporting President Obama's health care proposals and only 38 percent of whites doing the same.

The deep divide in black and white Americans' support for a number of policies ranging from affirmative action to governmental health care was well established long before Barack Obama became president (Tate 1994; Bobo and Kluegel 1993; Kinder and Sanders 1996; Schuman et al.

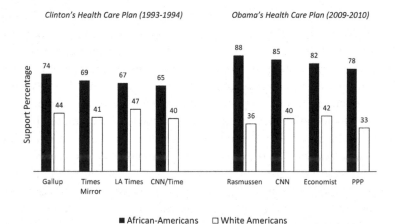

FIGURE 8.5. Support for Health Care Proposals by Presidential Sponsor and Respondents' Race
Source (left to right): (1) Gallup: fourteen surveys from September 1993 to July 1994, pooled black sample, N = 1,019; (2) *Times Mirror*: four surveys from September 1993 to June 1994, pooled black sample, N = 420; (3) *LA Times*: four surveys from September 1993 to April 1994, pooled black sample, N = 492; (4) CNN/*Time*: thirteen surveys from September 1993 to August 1994, pooled black sample, N = 1,337; (5) Rasmussen: twenty-seven surveys from June 2009 to March 2010, pooled black sample, $N \approx$ 2,700; (6) CNN: six surveys from June to November 2009, pooled black sample, N = 516; (7) YouGov/*Economist*: twenty-four surveys from August 2009 to March 2010, pooled black sample, N = 2,803; (8) PPP: nine surveys from August 2009 to March 2010, pooled black sample, $N \approx$ 850.
Note: All survey questions are similarly worded, asking respondents whether they favored or opposed Bill Clinton's health care reform plan and whether they favored or opposed Barack Obama's health care reform plan.

1997; Kinder and Winter 2001). That profound divide in health care opinions, however, appears to have grown even wider during his presidency.

The Growing Black-White Racial Divide in Obama-Era Macropartisanship

Barack Obama's presidency marked a potential turning point in the well-documented black-white racial divide in party identification. As discussed in chapter 1, the percentage of African Americans who identified with the Democratic Party gradually declined by roughly twenty percentage points from 1968 to 2004 (Hajnal and Lee 2011; Luks and Elms 2005). Luks and Elms (2005, 737) further argue that the increased willingness of young African Americans to identify as Republicans and Independents from 1973 to 1994 stemmed in part from the reluctance of recent Democratic administrations to intervene on behalf of racial progress the way that their presidential predecessors did during the civil rights era. This conclusion suggests that the ongoing generational replacement of older African Americans, who came of age when the party leadership was more active in support of racial equality, with younger blacks who came of age under a Democratic Party that generally heeded its electoral temptation of racial silence, would have further accelerated the black exodus from the Democratic Party in the years prior to Barack Obama's election.

Hajnal and Lee (2011, 141), however, wisely concluded their trend analysis of black partisanship by posing the question, "Does a black president mean the end of the decline in African American attachment to the Democratic Party"? There are reasons to believe that it might have. For starters, the health care results presented both earlier in this chapter and in chapter 5 indicate that Barack Obama's strong connection to the issue polarized public opinion by both racial attitudes *and* race. Moreover, chapter 4 discussed how the changing effects of racial attitudes on white support for Hillary Clinton from 2008 to 2012 were very similar to the dynamic effects of race. We might, therefore, expect the spillover of racialization into partisan attachments, as shown with racial attitudes in chapter 7, to have also taken the form of a growing black-white racial divide in Obama-era party identification. Indeed, prior research showed that Jesse Jackson's 1984 primary campaign for the Democratic presidential nomination immediately polarized southern partisanship by both racial attitudes and race (Sears, Citrin, and Kosterman 1987).

We also saw earlier in this chapter that racial group consciousness undergirded African Americans' extraordinarily strong support for Barack Obama (see also Kinder and Dale-Riddle 2012). African Americans, especially those with high levels of in-group consciousness, may therefore have been increasingly drawn to the Democratic Party because a black president whom they overwhelmingly supported led it. That suspected movement of racially conscious African Americans to the Democratic Party in the Obama era would have inevitably caused a growing black-white racial divide in macropartisanship. The chapter's third major hypothesis, then, is that the large pre-Obama black-white racial divide in party identification grew even wider in the Age of Obama.

The huge pre-Obama racial divide in Democratic Party identification did, in fact, grow significantly wider during after Barack Obama's rise to prominence. Figure 8.6 leverages the oversamples of African Americans

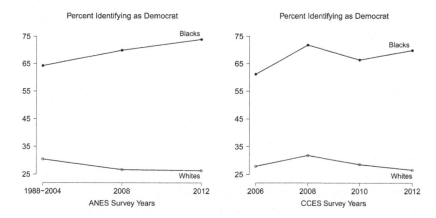

FIGURE 8.6. Democratic Party Identification by Race
Note: Democratic-leaning Independents are not included in the figures.
Source: American National Election Studies (ANES) cumulative file; 2012 ANES; Cooperative Congressional Election Study (CCES) 2006; CCES 2008; and CCES 2012.

in the 2008 and 2012 ANES surveys to show how the black-white divide in party identification changed in those two Obama-era surveys from its 1988–2004 baseline percentage. African Americans' identification with the Democratic Party was ten percentage points higher in 2012 than it was in the pooled pre-Obama ANES surveys.[24] Meanwhile, white identification with the Democratic Party decreased by about four percentage points over that time period. As a result of those divergent trends, the black-white divide in macropartisanship expanded significantly in the Age of Obama.

Aside from the ANES results, a number of other commercial and academic surveys confirm that the black-white divide in party identification increased substantially during the Obama era. Figure 8.6 also uses Cooperative Congressional Election Study (CCES) data, which included at least two thousand black respondents in every one of its biennial election year surveys, to show that black identification with the Democratic Party increased by about nine percentage points from 2006 to 2012. At the same time, though, the percentage of white Democrats decreased by one to two percentage points from 2006 to 2012 in the CCES. Thus, the black-white divide in macropartisanship increased by double digit in CCES surveys. Survey data collected by Pew and Gallup throughout Barack Obama's presidency also suggested that the black-white divide in Democratic Party identification increased by as much as ten percentage points from before to after Barack Obama ran for president (Pew Research Center 2011, 2012b; Newport 2013; Jones 2014; Hajnal and Lee 2011; see also results in the online appendix).

One likely reason African Americans became significantly more Democratic during this time period was that Barack Obama's rise to prominence signaled his party might become more supportive of African American interests. Consistent with that expectation, African Americans saw a much larger divide between Barack Obama and Mitt Romney in their support for "aid to blacks" than they saw between prior Democratic and Republican presidential candidates.[25] That increase in perceived Democratic support for black interests could have been especially important for our purposes of explaining the increase in black partisanship because racial identity measures liked linked fate—the notion that one's personal well-being is directly affected by the well-being of the larger black community—were only "relatively small" predictors of Democratic partisanship in the National Black Election Studies conducted during the 1980s and 1990s (Hajnal and Lee 2011, 134). In other words, having an African American president from the Democratic Party in the White House, who was perceived as more supportive of black interests than his predecessors, could have made group consciousness a more important determinant of African Americans' party identifications than it had been in the pre-Obama era.

Table 8.1 tests that expectation with ANES data. The coefficients in the table disclose the impact of African Americans' racial group thermometer ratings on their seven-category Democratic Party identifications after controlling for the same nonracial control variables used to predict white partisanship in the previous chapter. As can be seen, the black-thermometer rating was the one variable in the table whose impact on African American partisanship changed significantly from before to after Barack Obama's rise to prominence. After controlling for economic conservatism, moral traditionalism, military support, Bible literalism, and white-thermometer ratings, African Americans' thermometer ratings of blacks were essentially unrelated to their party identifications from 1988 to 2004. In both the 2008 and 2012 ANES surveys, though, the black-thermometer rating was a highly significant predictor of African American partisanship. That change in the black-thermometer rating's impact on African American party identification from 1988–2004 to 2008–12 was statistically significant, too.

It appears, then, that African Americans grew increasingly Democratic

TABLE 8.1. **(OLS) Predictors of African Americans' Identification with the Democratic Party**

	1988–2004	2008	2012
Black Thermometer	.061	.236***	.246***
	(.053)	(.061)	(.046)
White Thermometer	−.067	−.129*	−.100**
	(.050)	(.055)	(.055)
Moral Traditionalism	−.031	−.001	−.034
	(.049)	(.055)	(.040)
Economic Conservatism	−.191**	−.069	−.210***
	(.066)	(.069)	(.051)
Military Support	.026	.105*	.064
	(.044)	(.049)	(.037)
Bible Literalism	.023	.013	.078**
	(.029)	(.032)	(.022)
Constant	.899***	.667***	.713***
	(.065)	(.065)	(.053)
Observations	722	497	898

Source: American National Election Studies (ANES) cumulative file; 2012 ANES.
Note: Dependent variable is seven-point party identification, recoded from 0 (strong Republican) to 1 (strong Democrat). All explanatory variables are coded from 0 to 1, with 1 being the highest value. Regression analyses use poststratification weights with robust standard errors that account for design characteristics.
$*p < .05.$
$**p < .01.$
$***p < .001.$

during the Obama era in large part because of racial group solidarity. That is, African Americans who rated blacks most favorably were most likely to migrate to Barack Obama's Democratic Party. Those results, when combined with the white partisanship findings in prior chapter, also suggest that attitudes about African Americans drove the growing black-white divide in Obama-era party identification: White Americans who harbored out-group resentment toward blacks became increasingly Republican, whereas African Americans who rated their own racial group most favorably became more Democratic. The upshot was a growing polarization of mass partisanship by and over race.

The Growing White-Latino Divide in Obama-Era Party Identification

This growing Obama-era divide in party identification by and over race was not too surprising. After all, the racial divide in approval of Barack Obama's presidency was exceptionally large, with that chasm greatest between racially conscious blacks and racially resentful whites. It makes perfect sense, according to the spillover of racialization hypothesis, for those same patterns to have reproduced themselves in the Obama-era partisan attachments of black and white Americans.

The growing partisan divide between whites and Latinos in the Age of Obama was more unexpected, though. As can be seen in figure 8.7, the percentage of respondents who identified as Democrats in the Pew Hispanic Center's National Surveys of Latinos increased from 31 percent in both 2003 and 2007 all the way to 48 percent in 2012. In other words, Latinos were even more likely than African Americans to move to the Democratic Party in the Age of Obama. Given the trends in white partisanship shown in figure 8.6, which revealed a slight decline in white Americans' Democratic Party identifications, the divide between whites and Latinos in macropartisanship increased by as much as twenty percentage points during Barack Obama's presidency.

Unlike African Americans' greater Democratic identification in the Obama era, it is difficult to make the case that Barack Obama, and the spillover of racialization from mass assessments of his presidency into related political opinions, was directly responsible for this growing white-Latino partisan divide. To be sure, Barack Obama was very popular with Latinos throughout most of his presidency. Yet, that popularity was not nearly as strong or stable as his black support. President Obama's Hispanic approval ratings in weekly Gallup polls eroded over the first three years of his presidency and dipped slightly below 50 percent in several 2011 surveys. Moreover, the exit polls suggest that Bill Clinton won an

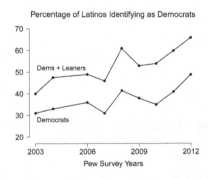

FIGURE 8.7. Percentage of Latinos Identifying as Democrats, 2003–12
Source: Pew Hispanic Center National Surveys; percentages accessed from Roper Center's iPOLL databank.

even larger share of the two-party Latino vote in his presidential elections than Barack Obama did in his victories. And Bill Clinton's longstanding support from Latinos was cited as a major reason why Hillary Clinton decisively won the Hispanic vote against Barack Obama in the 2008 presidential primaries (Barreto et al. 2008; Tesler and Sears 2010).

Rather than their affinity for President Obama, Latinos' growing identification with the Democratic Party was more likely rooted in the Republican Party's increasingly hostile rhetoric and policy positions toward minorities during Obama's presidency. Or as Stanford political scientist Gary Segura said in a 2012 PBS interview, "The president has widely disappointed Latino voters through the failure to pursue immigration reform through unprecedented deportations. But he can credibly claim to be better than the alternative when the alternative is saying horrible things."[26] These "horrible things," perhaps most notably, included Republicans' and Tea Partiers' frequent portrayals of Latino immigrants and immigration as a threat to Americans and American culture (Parker and Barreto 2013, 166; Skocpol and Williamson 2012, 76).

Such sentiments were also prevalent in Republican-sponsored state and national policies. Arizona's SB 1070, which the Obama administration challenged in court because it allowed for the racial profiling of Latinos based on the suspicion that they could be undocumented immigrants, was passed into law in 2010 almost entirely with Republican votes. Barack Obama and the Republican Party also clashed over the DREAM Act—a policy supported by the president in 2011 and prevented from passing by House Republicans in 2012—which was to grant legal status to young undocumented immigrants if they attended college or enlisted in the armed force. Finally, Republican presidential candidates surely alienated Latinos even further with their rhetoric and policy positions in the 2011 and 2012 primary debates. Collingwood, Barreto, and Garcia-Rios (2014, 4) aptly described these presidential candidates' strategy to appeal to the GOP's "racially resentful base" in 2012: "In an effort to attract a perceived anti-immigrant voting bloc in the conservative primary elections, the leading Republican candidates took very hardline stances against undocumented immigrants, bilingual education, and bilingual voting materials."

Those hardline policy positions and the anti-Latino rhetoric that accompanied them were likely to alter Hispanics' partisan attachments. In fact, prior research shows that Republicans' strong support for California's Proposition 187—a 1994 ballot initiative that rendered undocumented immigrants ineligible for such public services as health care and education—helped shift the partisan attachments of Latinos in the Golden State toward the Democrats (Bowler, Nicholson, and Segura 2006; Barreto and Ramirez 2013).

Polling data suggests that Latinos were paying attention to these partisan developments. Hispanics increasingly thought that the Democratic Party cared more about Latinos than Republicans did during Barack Obama's presidency. Figure 8.8, for example, shows that 55 percent of the Latino respondents surveyed by the Pew Hispanic Center in 2012 thought that the Democratic Party had more concern for Latinos than the Republican Party—an increase of more than twenty percentage points since 2007. Likewise, only 33 percent of respondents in a 2012 national survey of Latinos commissioned by CNN said that the Republican Party "is generally doing a good job these days of reaching out to blacks, Hispanics, and other minorities."[27] That figure was down eighteen percentage points from the 51 percent of Latinos who thought Republicans were doing a good job of reaching out to minorities in a 2000 CNN Poll.[28] Meanwhile, the percentage of Latinos who thought the Democratic Party was doing a good job with minorities slightly increased from 75 percent in 2000 to 77 percent in 2012. National surveys conducted in 2012 by the polling firm Latino Decisions, also showed that Latinos were at least forty percentage points more likely to say that the Democratic Party was doing "a good job" in its outreach to Hispanic voters than they were to say the Republican Party was doing a good job of reaching out to their ethnic group.[29]

With the Democratic Party increasingly viewed as the party more supportive of Latino interests in the Age of Obama, we might expect the

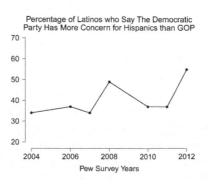

FIGURE 8.8. Percentage of Latinos Who Say the Democratic Party Has More Concern for Hispanics Than the Republican Party, 2004–12
Source: Pew Hispanic Center National Surveys; percentages accessed from Roper Center's iPOLL databank.

relationship between Hispanic in-group consciousness and Democratic Party identification to have increased over time. After all, table 7.1 showed that the effect of black-thermometer ratings on African Americans' partisan attachments increased significantly after Barack Obama's ascendancy signaled that his party may be more supportive of "aid to blacks." Moreover, and also like African Americans, in-group consciousness has long been an important predictor of Latinos' political attitudes and behavior (DeSipio 1996; Sanchez 2006; Barreto 2010; Hajnal and Lee 2011; Masuoka and Junn 2013). The chapter's fifth hypothesis, then, is that Latinos' in-group identifications may have been activated by the perceived growing distance between the parties in their concern for Hispanics.

Table 8.2 once again tests that expectation with ANES data. The coefficients in the table disclose the impact of Latinos' thermometer ratings of racial and ethnic groups on their seven-category Democratic Party identifications after controlling for several factors. The results, therefore, provide some support for the hypothesis that Latinos' increased identification with the Democratic Party was concentrated among ethnically conscious group members. After controlling for the other variables in table 8.2, thermometer ratings of other Hispanics were a non-significant determinant of Latinos' partisanship from 1988 through 2004. That baseline effect, however, nearly tripled in 2008 and 2012, with the Hispanic-thermometer rating now a statistically significant predictor of Latinos' identification with the Democratic Party in those two Obama-era surveys.

Table 8.2, however, shows that the impact of attitudes about whites on Latino partisanship changed even more dramatically over time. In the pre-Obama era, from 1988 to 2004, higher thermometer ratings of whites were actually associated with greater Latino support for the Democratic Party. In 2012, however, the white thermometer was a strong and highly significant predictor of Latinos' identification with the Republican Party. So much so, that moving from a white-thermometer rating of 0 to a rating of 100 decreased Democratic Party identification by 28 percent of the seven-point scale's range. That changing effect from 1988–2004 to 2012 of Latinos' white-thermometer ratings was statistically significant, too. The results, therefore, suggest that Latino's growing identification with the Democratic Party in 2012 was most pronounced among Hispanics who felt colder toward whites.

Although these results were not quite as expected, they make sense in light of the findings from a 2010 Latino Decisions survey. That poll found that most Latinos viewed the Republican Party as the party for white people. The survey showed that 59 percent of Latinos thought that

TABLE 8.2. **(OLS) Predictors of Latinos' Identification with the Democratic Party**

	1988–2004	2008	2012
White Thermometer	.184	−.021	−.277***
	(.124)	(.098)	(.059)
Black Thermometer	−.089	.175	.154**
	(.124)	(.103)	(.056)
Hispanic Thermometer	.081	.223*	.213**
	(.112)	(.101)	(.065)
Moral Traditionalism	−.158	−.188*	−.302***
	(.090)	(.090)	(.054)
Economic Conservatism	−.372**	−.500***	−.555***
	(.137)	(.112)	(.062)
Military Support	−.100	−.173*	.007
	(.100)	(.079)	(.043)
Bible Literalism	.040	.027	−.010
	(.137)	(.045)	(.029)
Constant	.810***	.820***	1.01***
	(.104)	(.107)	(.062)
Observations	351	396	869

Source: American National Election Studies (ANES) cumulative file; 2012 ANES.
Note: Dependent variable is seven-point party identification, recoded from 0 (strong Republican) to 1 (strong Democrat). All explanatory variables are coded from 0 to 1, with 1 being the highest value. Regression analyses use poststratification weights with robust standard errors that account for design characteristics.
*$p < .05$.
**$p < .01$.
**$p < .001$.

the Republican Party "strongly welcomes" white Americans, compared to just 10 percent who said the GOP strongly welcomes Latinos.[30] Unfortunately, we cannot compare how that percentage may have changed over time. Yet the above-referenced survey data, which showed that a growing number of Latinos thought that the Republican Party was doing a bad job of reaching out to minorities and had less concern for Latinos than the Democratic Party, suggests that Latinos increasingly viewed Republicans as a party of and for white Americans. As a likely result of that hardening partisan image of Republicans as the "Party of White People," attitudes about whites became an increasingly important determinant of Latino partisanship.

Asian Americans and Republicans as the Party of White People

Asian Americans' support for the Democratic Party, as alluded to at the beginning of this chapter, has increased dramatically in the past two decades. In 1992, when the exit polls first reported Asian Americans' vote choices, this group decisively preferred George H. W. Bush to Bill Clinton (55 percent to 31 percent, respectively). Asian American support for Democratic presidential candidates, however, has increased in every subsequent election. So much so, that Barack Obama won 74 percent of the two-party Asian American vote in 2012. That growing Democratic support extended to party identification, as well. National surveys of Asian Americans conducted by the Pew Research Center in 2012 and 2013 found that 50 percent and 64 percent of Asians identified as Democrats or leaned Democratic in those respective polls (Pew Research Center 2013c). By contrast, well under half the respondents in the 2000–2001 National Asian American Political Survey identified or leaned Democratic (Bowler and Segura 2012; Lien, Conway, and Wong 2004).

Asian Americans' strong and growing identification with the Democratic Party is somewhat peculiar. Higher income Americans tend to support Republicans (Gelman 2010; Bartels 2008; McCarty, Poole, and Rosenthal 2006), and Asian Americans are the highest-earning racial/ethnic group in the United States. This paradox prompted political scientists Alexander Kuo, Neil Malhotra, and Cecilia Mo to conduct an important study, fittingly titled "Why Do Asian Americans Identify as Democrats?" The answer to their question, according to these authors, is social exclusion and intergroup solidarity. That is, "Asian Americans view the contemporary Republican Party as excluding them from society and perceiving them as foreign. . . . The second explanation [intergroup solidarity], which is not mutually exclusive, is that Asian Americans believe they have common interests with other ethnic minority groups that have been longstanding constituencies within the Democratic Party, and thus align themselves with these groups rather than whites" (Kuo, Malhotra, and Mo 2014, 3–4). Kuo, Malhotra, and Mo (2014) support those hypotheses with some ingenious experiments. Most notably, they found that priming social exclusion with the use of insensitive white lab administrators who questioned their participants' citizenship before entering the laboratory shifted Asian Americans' partisan preferences thirteen percentage points more Democratic.

Like our analyses of Latino partisanship above, those social exclusion findings suggest that Asian Americans largely viewed the contemporary Republican Party as the party of whites. We might, therefore, expect attitudes about white Americans to have also been important determinants of Asians Americans' partisan attachments. Unfortunately, the data for testing that hypothesis is not nearly as good as the data used to assess the changing impact on racial group thermometer ratings on the partisan attachments of whites, African Americans, and Latinos. The ANES, for example, includes only a tiny number of Asian Americans in their election-year surveys. Nevertheless, we can still glean some insights into how Asian Americans' thermometer ratings of various racial and ethnic groups impacted their partisan attachments in the 2011–12 CCAP survey because this massive survey of forty-four thousand respondents included more than eight hundred Asian Americans. At the same time, though, the CCAP's nationally representative Internet survey may not be representative of minority populations. Indeed, minority panelists who volunteer to take Internet surveys administered in English, such as the CCAP, are unlikely to reflect the full variation in these groups' political opinions. So, some caution is required in interpreting the results.

With that said, table 8.3 shows the effect of racial and ethnic thermometer ratings on minority groups' party identifications in the CCAP. There are several noteworthy numbers in that table. Beginning with the first two columns, we see that warmer feelings towards African Americans were very strong determinants of black and mixed-race Americans' Democratic Party identifications in the CCAP. After controlling for the other variables in table 8.3, moving from lowest to highest on the black thermometer increased African American and mixed-race respondents' Democratic Party identifications by 39 percent and 23 percent of the scale's range, respectively. These results are consistent with our earlier finding that racial group solidarity became an increasingly important determinant of black partisanship in the Age of Obama (table 8.1). At the same time, though, attitudes about whites were almost entirely unrelated to those two groups' partisan attachments—a finding also consistent with prior research showing that in-group solidarity is a stronger predictor of African Americans' political opinions than out-group resentment of whites (e.g., Kinder and Winter 2001).

The remaining columns of the table, however, tell a much different story for Latinos, Asian Americans, and Native Americans. More specifically, those coefficients show that attitudes about whites were strong and highly significant determinants of each groups' identification with the Republican Party. All else being equal, moving from the coldest to the warmest rating of whites decreased Democratic Party identification by 19 percent of the scale's range for Latinos, 24 percent for Asian Americans, and 32 percent for Native Americans. The Latino results, you may recall, are

TABLE 8.3. **(OLS) Predictors of Democratic Party Identification by Race/Ethnicity**

	African Americans	Mixed Race	Latinos	Asian Americans	Native Americans
White Thermometer	−.042	−.058	−.191***	−.237***	−.315**
	(.023)	(.057)	(.037)	(.064)	(.113)
Black Thermometer	.392***	.229***	.186***	.212*	.164
	(.030)	(.060)	(.039)	(.087)	(.137)
Hispanic Thermometer	−.100***	.045	.178***	.001	.133
	(.028)	(.061)	(.050)	(.071)	(.113)
Asian Thermometer	−.110***	.037	−.121**	.087	−.085
	(.030)	(.039)	(.039)	(.061)	(.109)
Economic Conservatism	−.290***	−.288***	−.341***	−.244***	−.319***
	(.020)	(.032)	(.027)	(.033)	(.067)
Moral Conservatism	−.140***	−.169***	−.201***	−.215***	−.403***
	(.018)	(.042)	(.028)	(.042)	(.084)
Religious Service Attendance	−.077***	−.015	.048	−.017	−.026
	(.016)	(.035)	(.028)	(.034)	(.056)
Constant	.840***	.617***	.766***	.731***	.967***
	(.029)	(.070)	(.048)	(.065)	(.082)
Observations	4,630	929	3,558	814	288

Source: 2011–12 Cooperative Campaign Analysis Project (CCAP).
Note: Dependent variable is seven-point party identification, recoded from 0 (strong Republican) to 1 (strong Democrat). All explanatory variables are coded from 0 to 1, with 1 being the highest value. Regression analyses use poststratification weights with robust standard errors that account for design characteristics.
*$p < .05$.
**$p < .01$.
***$p < .001$.

consistent with our earlier findings that warmer ratings of whites changed from being positively associated with Democratic partisanship in the pre–Obama era to a strong negative relationship in the Age of Obama, presumably because Latinos increasingly viewed Republicans as the party of white people (table 8.2).

The large effects of antiwhite attitudes on Asian Americans' support for the Democratic Party seem to fit into that "party of whites" paradigm as well. Moreover, those strong effects of antiwhite affect are consistent with the contention by Kuo, Malhotra, and Mo (2014) that social exclusion of Asian Americans by whites drives support for the Democratic Party. Table 8.3 also supports their second hypothesis that intergroup solidarity leads Asian American to identify with the Democratic Party. For, as can be seen, warmer thermometer ratings of blacks were also strongly linked to Asian Americans' identification with the Democratic Party. Finally, Asian Americans' thermometer ratings of their own group were not significantly related to their partisan attachments—a result similar to Hajnal and Lee's (2011) contention that racial identity has a weaker effect on Asian American partisanship than it does for Latinos.

There, unfortunately, has been very little work on the partisan attachments of Native Americans. So, we cannot similarly place the large effects of the white thermometer on their party identifications into a broader context. However, given the results for Asian Americans and Latinos, these findings suggest that Native Americans may have also viewed the modern Republican Party as the party of whites.

Concluding Remarks

The results in this chapter, in combination with the earlier findings presented throughout the book, suggest that the growing black-white divide in Obama-era political opinions was in large part about President Obama and attitudes toward African Americans. The exceptionally large black-white divide in Barack Obama's presidential approval ratings was most pronounced among racially resentful whites and racially conscious blacks. So, too, was the expanding racial divide in macropartisanship, as attitudes about African Americans became an increasingly important determinant of both black and white Americans' partisan identifications in the Age of Obama.

The growing number of Latinos and Asian Americans who identified as Democrats in the Obama era, however, seems to have been more about social exclusion and attitudes toward whites than it was about President Obama and feelings toward blacks. To be sure, Barack Obama's Democratic presidency and the hostile reaction to it from his partisan opponents likely contributed to minority groups' enhanced image of Republicans as the party of white people. A clear majority of Latinos, for example, thought that race was a factor in opposition to his presidency in a 2009 Pew poll (63 percent);[31] and most of the Latinos (61 percent) in a 2010 ABC survey thought that the Tea Party Movement was based to some degree on racial prejudice toward the president.[32] Barack Obama's ascendancy also helped give rise to the more ethnocentric elements of the Republican Party, such as the Tea Party (Parker and Barreto 2013), who were most opposed to immigration. Yet, unlike the growing black-white racial divide in Obama-era party identification, the partisan preferences of Latinos and Asian Americans would have most likely moved further away from white Americans even if Barack Obama had not been elected president in 2008. For, as mentioned earlier, Latinos preferred Hillary Clinton by a large margin to Barack Obama in the 2008 presidential primaries.

Minority voters' overwhelming support for Democrats could, therefore, continue into the foreseeable future. In fact, political commentators argued long before Barack Obama's presidential candidacy that the growing nonwhite electorate will inevitably lead to a longstanding Democratic majority in national politics (e.g., Judis and Teixeira 2004). Some astute academic commentators, however, have pushed back on this common "demographics as destiny" argument (Vavreck 2014; Bartels 2014; Piston 2014). Asian American and Latino voters, they point out, may not be as solidly Democratic as is often assumed. In keeping with that contention, Hajnal and Lee (2011) showed that these groups' party attachments are less crystallized than black and white partisanship. We witnessed this point firsthand in figures 8.6 and 8.7, too, where we saw that Latino macropartisanship fluctuated much more between 2006 and 2012 than did the percentage of whites and blacks who identified as Democrats. That instability was again on display a 2013 Pew Hispanic Center survey, in which the percentage of Latinos who identified or leaned Democratic was down thirteen percentage points from its record high of 66 percent in 2012. With Asian American and Latino partisan attachments not yet crystallized, a concerted effort by Republicans to reach out to minorities could help reverse the trend of growing Latino and Asian American support for the Democratic Party. Indeed, polling by Latino Decisions suggests that Republicans could make serious inroads with Hispanics if they supported comprehensive immigration reform.[33]

Conversely, Republicans could also stave off electoral defeat in the years ahead by turning out more whites and/or winning a larger share of their votes. Republican elites, in fact, regularly debated during Barack Obama's second term in office whether the party's best bet to retake the White House was to reach out to minorities or to pursue this white voter strategy (Edsall 2013; Trende 2013; Brownstein 2013). Republican strategist, Sean Trende (2013), summarized the latter approach's potential: "It's entirely possible that as our nation becomes more diverse, our political coalitions will increasingly fracture along racial/ethnic lines rather than ideological ones. . . . I don't see any compelling reason why these trends can't continue, and why a Republican couldn't begin to approach Ronald Reagan's 30-point win with whites from 1984 in a more neutral environment than Reagan enjoyed."

There's some social scientific evidence to support that argument, too.

Just drawing attention to the country's changing demographics in a survey experiment significantly increased the percentage of white Independents who expressed prejudiced attitudes, took conservative policy positions, and identified as Republicans (Craig and Richeson 2014a, 2014b). Ryan Enos's (2014, 2015) innovative work on racial threat similarly shows that increased contact with racial and ethnic minorities in Chicago and Boston, respectively led whites to express more ethnocentric attitudes, turn out to vote in higher numbers, and support Republican candidates at greater rates. As a result of such studies, Larry Bartels (2014) concluded: "The changing American polity may come to look more like [Republican] Texas than like the multicultural Democratic stronghold of California. In an increasingly diverse America, identity politics will continue to cut both ways."

Finally, the results presented throughout the book suggest that Republicans could be quite constrained in their minority outreach after Barack Obama leaves office. Chapters 6 and 7, for example, showed that rank-and-file Republicans were more racially conservative during his presidency than they had been in modern times. Consequently, it may be increasingly difficult for a Republican candidate to reach out to minorities and still win his or her party's presidential nomination. Mitt Romney, after all, had to take a very hard-line on immigration during the presidential primaries to curry favor with his party's base (Collingwood, Barreto, and Garcia-Rios 2014). We also saw in chapter 6 that the internal divisions between congressional Republicans in the Obama era came down in large part to how racially resentful their constituents were (see fig. 6.7). A majority of Republicans in the House of Representatives could, therefore, fear that reaching out to minorities will cost them their jobs. Indeed, House Majority Leader Eric Cantor's (R-VA) tepid support for immigration reform was widely cited, rightly or wrongly, as a major reason why he lost his district's 2014 primary to a fervently anti-immigrant opponent.[34] Given these constraints, the Republicans' most viable option going forward might be to try to mobilize and win more white votes. If so, then mass politics might grow even more divided by color in the post–Obama era.

Conclusion

Racial Politics in the Obama and Post-Obama Eras

We cannot ignore the inequities that persist in our justice system.... Imagine what we would feel, and what we would do, if white drivers were three times as likely to be searched by police during a traffic stop as black drivers instead of the other way around. If white offenders received prison sentences ten percent longer than black offenders for the same crimes. If a third of all white men—just look at this room and take one-third—went to prison during their lifetime. Imagine that. That is the reality in the lives of so many of our fellow Americans in so many of the communities in which they live. — Hillary Clinton, on the racial unrest in Ferguson, Missouri, August 2014[1]

For the second consecutive summer of Barack Obama's second term in the White House, the country's precarious racial fault line ruptured over the fatal shooting of an unarmed black teenager. The book, as you will recall, began with President Obama's rare comments on race after the July 2013 acquittal of George Zimmerman brought the country's simmering racial tensions to the surface. One year later, the deadly shooting of an African American teenager, Michael Brown, by a white police officer, Darren Wilson, caused an even stronger uproar in Ferguson, Missouri. Brown's death led to a series of race-based protests—some violent, most peaceful—against both the long history of police misconduct toward the African American community in Ferguson and the city's lack of racial representation in local government.[2] These protests were met by a militarized police response, which many criticized for exacerbating the racial unrest that went on for nearly two weeks.[3]

After a few months of détente, race relations eroded even further. Protests erupted in 170 cities across the United States following a St. Louis County grand jury's failure to indict of Officer Wilson on November 24, 2014.[4] Many of these rallies intensified shortly thereafter when a grand jury in Staten Island, New York City, analogously failed to indict a white police officer, Daniel Pantaleo, who was videotaped putting an unarmed black man, Eric Garner, in a chokehold that caused his subsequent death. While most of the demonstrations around the protestors' rallying cry "Black Lives Matter" were peaceful, two New York City police officers were killed in the line of duty on December 20, 2014, as ostensible revenge for the deaths of Michael Brown and Eric Garner.

These events left Americans more pessimistic about race relations than they had been in decades. Aside from the immediate aftermath of the 1992 Los Angeles race riots, significantly more Americans (13 percent) mentioned racism and race relations as the most important problem facing the country in a December 2014 Gallup poll than they had in any other poll conducted by the firm since the late 1960s.[5] More respondents also said that American race relations were bad (57 percent) in a December 2014 NBC News/*Wall Street Journal* survey than they had in any other NBC/*Wall Street Journal* poll since the 1990s.[6] And the percentage of Americans who thought that race relations had deteriorated during Barack Obama's presidency (53 percent in a Bloomberg News poll and 62 percent in a Fox News poll) reached an all-time high by the end of 2014.[7]

Like the introductory chapter's discussion of the George Zimmerman and O. J. Simpson murder trials, Americans' reactions to the events in Ferguson and Staten Island were once again sharply divided by race. African Americans were roughly fifty percentage points more likely than whites to disagree with the nonindictments of both police officers involved in the respective deaths of Michael Brown and Eric Garner (Pew Research Center 2014b). Unlike the aftermath of George Zimmerman's 2013 acquittal, though, President Obama did not speak at length about the racial dynamics motivating the American public's divergent reactions to these 2014 incidents. For, as Ezra Klein reported in August 2014, "The problem [with such a statement on race] is the White House no longer believes Obama can bridge divides. They believe—with good reason—that he widens them."[8]

There were certainly good reasons why the White House held that belief. After all, we have seen throughout the book that Barack Obama consistently widened racial divides, despite his best efforts to neutralize the political impact of race. More specifically, the book has shown that the election of President Obama helped usher in a *most-racial political era* where racially liberal and racially conservative Americans were more divided over a whole host of political positions than they had been in modern times. A natural consequence of that growing racialization of mass politics, as argued in the introduction, was that Democrats and Republicans should have increasingly viewed racial controversies like the shooting deaths of Trayvon Martin and Michael Brown through very different lenses. And indeed they did.

The top panel of figure 9.1, in fact, shows enormous partisan differences in public opinion about a wide array of race-evoking issues during Barack Obama's presidency. These race-infused issues, which powerfully separated Democrats from Republicans, included the following: (1) the Zimmerman verdict, (2) the forced sale of the NBA's Los Angeles Clippers after the team's owner Donald Sterling was recorded making racist statements; (3) the 2013 Academy Award for best picture going to *12 Years a Slave*; (4) the authorities' militarized response to protestors in Ferguson; (5) the nonindictment of Officer Darren Wilson for the shooting death of Michael Brown; and (6) the nonindictment of Officer Daniel Pantaleo for the death of Eric Garner. Taken together, Democrats and Republicans were divided by forty-three percentage points in their opinions about George Zimmerman, Donald Sterling, *12 Years a Slave*, the Ferguson protestors, Michael Brown, and Eric Garner.[9] Partisans were also deeply divided over whether the shooting deaths of Trayvon Martin and Michael Brown were even about race. Democrats were again more than forty percentage points more likely than Republicans to have said that the premature deaths of both Brown and Martin raised important racial issues (Pew Research Center 2014c).[10]

As mentioned at the beginning of this book, Democrats and Republicans have not always seen racial controversies so differently. The bottom panel of figure 9.1, in fact, shows relatively modest partisan divisions in response to earlier race-related incidents, such as (1) a racially charged 1984 New York City subway shooting, when Bernhard Goetz shot four African American youths whom he claimed were going to mug him;[11] (2) the aforementioned O. J. Simpson verdict; and (3) the 1992 acquittal of four white Los Angeles police offers who were videotaped beating an African American motorist, Rodney King.

Even more importantly, three high-profile race-related incidents that occurred shortly before Barack Obama's first presidential election failed to generate the same partisan divisions as the Obama-era issues shown in

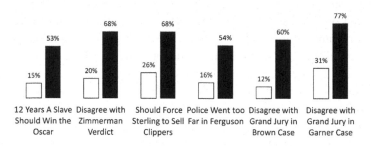

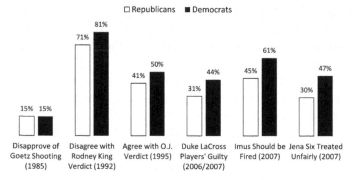

FIGURE 9.1. Opinions about Race-Related Incidents by Party Identification
Source (left to right): (1) PPP poll, March 2014; (2) Pew poll, July 2013; (3) *HuffPost/*You-Gov poll, April 2014; (4) Averages of Pew poll, August 2014, and YouGov poll, August 2014; (5) Pew poll, December 2014; (6) Pew poll, December 2014; (7) Gallup/*Newsweek* poll, February–March 1985; (8) CBS News poll, May 1992; (9) Gallup/CNN/*USA Today* poll, October 1995; (10) Averages of *Gallup* poll, April 2006, and *CNN* poll, January 2007; (11) ABC/*Washington Post* poll, April 2007; and (12) *CNN* poll, October 2007. All data used in bottom panel were obtained from the Roper Center's data archive.

the top panel of figure 9.1. Despite the fact that African Americans were fifty percentage points more likely than whites to have thought that charging six black teenagers (the Jena Six) with attempted murder for beating a white classmate was unjust,[12] Democrats as a whole were merely seventeen percentage points more likely than Republicans to think that these black students were treated unfairly.[13] Democrats were also just thirteen percentage points more likely to say that the white Duke University lacrosse players who were charged with sexually assaulting a black woman were guilty.[14] And in the case most analogous to the Donald Sterling episode, when radio personality Don Imus made insensitive racial comments,

Democrats were only sixteen percentage points more likely than Republicans to want him fired from his talk show.

To be sure, many of these prior partisan divisions were substantively significant and reflected the importance of race and racial attitudes in the pre-Obama party alignment. The pre- to post-Obama comparisons in figure 9.1 are also complicated by the fact that no two incidents were exactly alike. Yet the overall patterns in the two panels of that display are unmistakable; and taken together, the results in figure 9.1 speak rather eloquently to the consequences of racial attitudes or race and party identification becoming more closely aligned during Barack Obama's presidency. Indeed, the findings suggest that Democrats and Republicans had increasingly *separate realities* about race in the Age of Obama—a logical upshot of the spillover of racialization into mass politics documented throughout the book.

Qualifying the Results

Given those increasingly separate racial realities, some might naturally suspect that just about everything in American politics was about race during Barack Obama's presidency.[15] As discussed in chapter 2, though, there should have been important limitations on the reach of the spillover of racialization. Consistent with those theoretical expectations, a number of results presented in both the previous chapters and elsewhere offer some important qualifications of the book's key findings.

Not All of President Obama's Issue Positions Racialized Public Opinion

Several of our racial spillover results have shown that Barack Obama's positions activated race-based attitudes in public opinion rather than nonracial considerations. Survey experiments that connected President Obama to government health insurance, the 2009 stimulus package, Sonia Sotomayor's Supreme Court nomination, 2010 Democratic congressional candidates, and tax increases, all activated racial attitudes without increasing the already large baseline effects of partisanship and ideology (chaps. 4–5; Tesler and Sears 2010; Tesler 2013b). Moreover, the enhanced pre- to post-Obama racialization of health care opinions, mass assessments of Hillary Clinton, support for same-sex marriage, perceptions of the election-year unemployment rate, partisan attachments, and aggregate election returns for the House of Representatives, all occurred without further activating the large pre-Obama effects of nonracial considerations (chaps. 3–8).

As first suggested in chapter 2, however, Barack Obama's positions were unlikely to have increased the effects of racial attitudes on political evaluations that were already highly racialized. Instead, we might expect Obama's positions to further increase the effects of partisanship and ideology on public opinion about those issues. This is precisely what we saw with public support for the assault weapons ban in chapter 5, too. Figure 5.4 showed that experimentally highlighting Barack Obama's gun control position was more likely to activate partisan and ideological considerations than racial resentment in public opinion about this rare issue where the pre-Obama effects of racial attitudes rivaled the baseline impact of party and ideology. John Sides's (2013a) survey experiments similarly found that the spillover of racialization was less pronounced from President Obama into issues that were already influenced by racial attitudes (e.g., aid to the urban poor) than into issues that were not previously racialized (e.g., closing Guantanamo Bay); and Obama's presidency did not increase the effects of racial attitudes on policies like federal aid to blacks that were already highly racialized (Kinder and Chudy 2014). Finally, the welfare advertisement experiment described in chapter 4, which explicitly connected Barack Obama to welfare spending, failed to enhance the large baseline effects of racial attitudes on this well-established race-evoking issue.[16]

These results thus appear to add an important caveat to the book's spillover of racialization findings, which showed that Barack Obama's visible positions tended to activate racial attitudes in mass politics relative to nonracial considerations. If racial attitudes had a stronger pre-Obama effect on public opinion than party identification, then racial attitudes were unlikely to further spillover into public opinion. Instead, President Obama was more likely to activate party and ideology in those infrequent instances.

Racial Considerations Were One of Many Important Factors in the Obama Era

It is also worth repeating chapter 2's statement that, even if every single one of Barack Obama's positions had produced strong and lasting racial spillover effects, it still would not imply that race-based attitudes were the most important determinant of political preferences in the Age of Obama.

Racial considerations were one of many factors that shaped public opinion about Barack Obama's party and policies during his presidency. The results in table 5.1, for example, showed that party identification, ideological self-placement, limited government preferences, and self-interested concerns about out-of-pocket medical expenses were all significant predictors of mass health care opinions after President Obama became the face of the policy in the fall of 2009. Moreover, these nonracial factors combined to explain much more of the variation in white Americans' feelings toward governmental health insurance than racial attitudes did. Much like those health care findings, the chapter 7 analyses also found that the combined effects of such nonracial factors as economic conservatism, moral traditionalism, military support, and religious considerations had a larger influence on white Americans' partisan attachments than racial attitudes had on party identification in the Obama era.

To be sure, the dynamic effects of racial attitudes on mass politics tended to outweigh the changing impact of nonracial considerations during Barack Obama's presidency. That is, the effects of racial attitudes on mass political evaluations often increased in importance relative to nonracial predispositions. Moreover, those increased effects of racial attitudes should have been particularly consequential. Since, as discussed multiple times, recent research shows that attitudes like racial resentment are emotionally charged in ways that race-neutral values like ideological conservatism are not. The spillover of racialization, therefore, almost surely contributed to the growing affective polarization of the electorate, whereby Democrats and Republicans had increasing disdain for one another during Barack Obama's presidency. Yet, as significant as those results may be, they are a far cry from saying that race was the only, or even the most noteworthy, determinant of Americans' political preferences in the Age of Obama.

Not Every Spillover of Racialization Effect Persisted

Perhaps the most important qualification of the book's results, as the theoretical expectations outlined in chapter 2 suggested, is that not all our racial spillover effects should have persisted over time. Instead, political evaluations constantly linked to Barack Obama had the greatest potential to leave lasting racial spillover effects on mass politics. The obvious example here is Obamacare. Chapter 5 showed that the increased effects of racial resentment on Cooperative Campaign Analysis Project (CCAP) panelists' health care opinions from December 2007 to November 2009 persisted when these exact same individuals were reinterviewed in 2012. Additional results from the 2010–12 Cooperative Congressional Election Study (CCES) panel study of nearly twenty thousand respondents also showed that racial resentment had the same very large effect on white panelists' opposition to the Affordable Care Act (ACA) in both 2010 and 2012;[17] and new analyses from the 2014 CCES survey of fifty-six thousand respondents further indicate that the relationship between racial resentment and opposition to Obamacare was as strong as ever more than five years after the president's proposals were first debated in Congress.[18] It appears, then, that the persistent link between President Obama and this legislation that ultimately took his name helped make racial attitudes a chronic determinant of public opinion about the ACA.

Many of President Obama's visible policy positions, however, did not receive the same prolonged media scrutiny. We would not expect the spillover of racialization into those political evaluations to have been as permanent, then, as the spillover of racialization into health care. In fact, we saw in chapter 5 that Barack Obama's historic announcement that he supported same-sex marriage further racialized public opinion about this policy for only one week in May 2012. The effects of racial resentment on same-sex marriage opinions, as shown in figure 5.6, returned to their pre-announcement levels soon after news of the president's much-publicized endorsement of marriage equality faded from the national headlines.

Some of the political evaluations that have become more heavily influenced by racial attitudes and race during Barack Obama's presidency, then, will surely become less racialized after he leaves office. We would not expect subjective evaluations of objective economic conditions, for instance, to remain racialized once those assessments are no longer a strong rationale for either supporting or opposing Barack Obama's presidency. Nor would we expect public opinion about Mitt Romney to remain racialized now that his presidential campaign against Barack Obama is an increasingly distant political memory. Indeed, the large effects of racial resentment on John McCain's favorability ratings in fall 2008 quickly returned to their pre-Obama levels soon after his electoral defeat (Tesler and Sears 2010, fig. 4.5).

At the same time, though, I have made the case throughout the book that some spillover of racialization findings will more than likely continue influencing American politics even after Barack Obama leaves office. So, let's turn our attention away from these qualifications to a few of the book's potential implications.

Spillover Effects beyond Race and Obama

Regardless of how long the spillover of racialization from Barack Obama into mass politics may last, one of the book's most important implications is that source cues provided by the background characteristics of elite issue advocates offer another avenue to activating group-based considerations in political evaluations. In fact, this path to racialization might be even more effective in polarizing public opinion by racial predispositions than the well-documented effects of subtle race-coded communications in previous racial-priming research. Implicit racial appeals have to walk a fine line to avoid violating strong societal norms of racial equality, and even then they can lose their effectiveness if criticized for playing the race card (Mendelberg 2001, 2008). Moreover, the priming effects from such subtle race appeals are thought to be short lived, losing much of their impact when communications make new considerations salient (Kinder and Sanders 1996). In contrast, there is nothing necessarily untoward about communications that point out a racialized public figure's policy positions. The spillover of racialization should be longer lasting than campaign appeals that prime race, as well, if the media persistently highlight the racialized source's position (i.e., Obamacare).

The studies referenced back in chapter 2, which showed that the races, religions, and genders of prominent elite sources can all activate group-based considerations in mass opinion formation, also indicate that social background spillover effects are not simply unique to our first African American president. Figure 9.2, in fact, presents new evidence showing that attitudes about Catholics spilled over into Americans' 1960 partisan attachments after John F. Kennedy's presidential candidacy heightened the association between the Democratic Party and Catholicism. As can be seen in that graph, both Catholics and respondents who trusted Catholic groups in the 1956 wave of the 1956–60 American National Election Studies (ANES) panel study were upward of fifteen percentage points more likely to identify as Democrats in 1960 than they had been four years earlier. Meanwhile, the partisan identifications of non-Catholics and panelists who did not explicitly trust Catholic groups were virtually unchanged over that same time period. Much like the growing racialization of party identification in the Age of Obama, then, partisan attachments became more polarized by religious considerations in 1960 because of Kennedy's bid to become the first Catholic president.

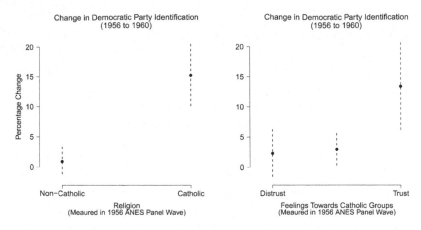

FIGURE 9.2. Change in Democratic Party Identification from 1956 to 1960, by Religion and Attitudes toward Catholic Groups
Note: Dashed lines are 95 percent confidence intervals.
Source: 1956–60 American National Election Studies (ANES).

The common thread linking the book's Obama-era racialization findings together with other research on spillover effects from politicians into mass politics is that each public figure's social background (e.g., JFK's religion, Hillary Clinton's gender, and Jesse Jackson's race) factored prominently into how Americans evaluated them. Gender attitudes, for instance, were a strong determinant of public opinion about Hillary Clinton when her association with health care helped gender Americans' issue positions (Winter 2008); attitudes about Catholics had an unusually large effect on opinions about JFK in 1960 when his candidacy caused religious considerations to spill over into Americans' partisan attachments (Converse et al. 1961; Kinder and Dale-Riddle 2012; Tesler 2015b); mass assessments of Jesse Jackson were much more racialized than public opinion about white Democrats were when his 1984 candidacy polarized Southern partisanship by racial attitudes and race (Sears, Citrin, and Kosterman 1987; Sears et al. 1997); and, of course, Barack Obama was viewed by many Americans through an especially powerful racial lens when his presidency further racialized mass politics.

Group membership, however, does not guarantee that group-specific attitudes will be implicated in public opinion (Kinder and Dale-Riddle 2012). Aside from just membership, a politician's perceived solidarity with his or her social group may be even more relevant (Kinder 2013; Kinder and Dale-Riddle 2012). Barack Obama's Democratic partisanship and his rootedness in African American life as a community organizer in Chicago, for example, were sure signs to many that he was not only black but also *for* African Americans. Indeed, we have seen that Barack Obama was perceived as being more supportive of black interests by both black and white Americans than prior Democratic presidents and presidential candidates. African American, Latino, and female presidential nominees from the Republican Party almost certainly would not evoke racial, ethnocentric, or gender predispositions as powerfully as Barack Obama's presidency activated racial attitudes, though. Rather, those Republican candidates' affiliation with the political party that is perceived as less supportive of women and minority group interests would inevitably cross-pressure voters about where their group-based loyalties lay.

Consistent with that contention, racial attitudes were not significant predictors of public opinion about Colin Powell when he considered running for the Republican Party's presidential nomination in the 1990s (Kinder and Dale-Riddle 2012; Kinder and McConnaughy 2006). Nor did modern sexism independently influence public opinion about the former Republican Secretary of State, Condoleezza Rice, despite the fact that these gender attitudes were very powerful predictors of holding unfavorable opinions toward Democratic women like Hillary Clinton and Michelle Obama (McThomas and Tesler forthcoming). Likewise, attitudes about Latinos had a stronger impact on public opinion about a prominent Hispanic Democratic, Sonia Sotomayor, than they had about Marco Rubio as a potential 2012 Republican vice presidential candidate.[19] The results thus suggest that the visible positions of black, female, and Latino Republicans would not produce strong racial, gender, and ethnic spillover effects. The spillover of group-based attitudes into public opinion, instead, should necessarily be smaller when politicians' social backgrounds and party identifications create cross-pressures about their solidarity with specific groups (e.g., black Republicans, Evangelical Democrats).

The applicability of the book's findings for other potential spillover effects beyond race and Obama, however, still needs to be tested more directly. Although previous research, the results in figure 9.2, and our theoretical expectations all suggest that group-based spillover effects are not simply restricted to Obama's race, a black president might be especially likely to polarize public opinion by group-based attitudes. The president, after all, is the center of the political universe and race has historically been more salient in American political life than other social identities (e.g., Citrin and Sears 2014; Sears and Savalei 2006; Kinder and Dale-

Riddle 2012). To be sure, this does not mean that a future black president from the Democratic Party, such as Senator Corey Booker (D-NJ) or
Governor Deval Patrick (D-MA), would have the same racializing effect
on mass politics that Barack Obama had. The next black president not
only would lack Obama's historic position as *the first* but also might pre-
side over a political environment with less room to racialize mass politics,
because racial liberals and racial conservatives are better sorted into the
Democratic and Republican camps than they were before Barack Obama
became president (see discussion below). Nevertheless, it is unlikely that
group-based spillover effects, including the spillover of racialization, are
unique to Barack Obama.

This book will, therefore, hopefully spark new inquiries into the effects
of other politicians' salient social background characteristics on public
opinion. Such findings would have especially important implications for
American politics as the demographic composition of elected officials inevitably changes in the decades ahead. That is, we may see a number of
group-based attitudes become more important in mass politics because of
the diversifying social background characteristics of prominent political
figures. Take the growing number of women in elected office, for example.
With the independent effects of gender attitudes on public support for
Hillary Clinton in 2011 and 2012 approaching the impact of racial resentment on mass assessments of Barack Obama (McThomas and Tesler
forthcoming), we might even expect her 2016 presidential candidacy to
activate gender predispositions in public opinion the way that racial attitudes spilled over from Barack Obama into relevant political evaluations
during his presidency.

A Lasting Racialization of Mass Politics?

As mentioned above, some of the book's racial spillover findings will inevitably dissipate in the immediate future. Most of the chapters' concluding remarks, however, offered reasons to believe that at least some of the
spillover of racialization from Barack Obama into mass opinion will continue influencing American politics after he leaves the White House. Beginning in chapter 4, the concluding remarks argued that the spillover of
racialization into mass assessments of public figures will probably make
racial attitudes a more powerful determinant of Americans' 2016 vote
choices than they were in pre-Obama presidential elections. Public opin-

ion about the outgoing president is an important cause of voting behavior in open-seat contests like the 2016 presidential election (Abramowitz 1988, 2008; Hillygus and Jackman 2003; Tesler and Sears 2010; Johnston, Hagen, and Jamieson 2004). Moreover, the legacies of Jimmy Carter, Bill Clinton, and George W. Bush loomed large in public opinion about their presidential successors (Sides and Vavreck 2013, 25–26). Obama's race may, therefore, continue to influence mass assessments of presidential candidates and presidents in both 2016 and beyond.

The results in chapter 5 are even more likely to affect American politics after Barack Obama leaves office. We have discussed how race-based and race-evoking issues like busing, affirmative action, welfare, and crime lost much of their political prominence as the Democratic Party heeded its electoral temptation of racial silence in the decade or more prior to Barack Obama's presidency. Health care, however, is now one of those race-evoking issues. As Kinder and Chudy (2014, 21) observed about the increased Obama-era effects of racial resentment on health care opinions, "The effect of prejudice after Obama approximates the effect due to prejudice on explicitly racial policies [like affirmative action]." These strong effects show no signs of abating. With the ACA and its implementation figuring to remain a major political issue into the foreseeable future, this racialized policy could help maintain some of the Obama-era racialization of mass politics. Indeed, we saw in chapter 6 that the ACA vote in the House of Representatives led to more racialized voting patterns in the 2010 midterms than prior congressional elections, and the ACA even appeared to racialize roll call voting in the House of Representatives to end the government shutdown in October 2013.

Aside from those results, the racialization of voting for Congress documented in chapter 6 could also have some lasting effects. Typically, 90 percent of the incumbents in the House of Representatives run for reelection and 90 percent of them win (Jacobson 2004). With the same candidates running election after election, the racialized voting patterns uncovered in the 2010, 2012, and 2014 congressional elections could reproduce themselves long after Obama leaves office. As discussed in chapter 6, familiar voting patterns are one likely reason why racial attitudes did not strongly influence white Americans' votes for the House of Representatives in the pre-Obama era, despite the fact that roll call voting on racial issues in Congress was well sorted along party lines by the 1980s.

The results discussed in chapters 7 and 8, however, are probably the most likely to leave a lasting mark on the American political landscape.

Party identification, as mentioned multiple times, is both the most influential and most enduring of all political attitudes. A look back at the coefficients in table 7.1 helps prove this point that, once a particular attitude is associated with party identification, its influence is difficult to displace. George W. Bush's identity as a devout born-again Christian was a major factor in the strong polarization of public opinion about his presidency (Jacobson 2007). Religiosity, however, was a less salient feature of Barack Obama's presidential persona, leading to a sharp increase in the percentage of Americans who thought religion as a whole was losing its influence in American life since George W. Bush left office (Pew Research Center 2014a). Despite that perceived waning influence, the effect of religious service attendance on party identification did not decline during Barack Obama's presidency. Nor did the impact of military support on party identification recede even though the partisan conflict over the Iraq and Afghanistan wars had been more salient during George W. Bush's presidency than it was during Barack Obama's first term in office. In fact, table 7.1 showed that the pre- to post-Obama effect of military support on Republican Party identification actually increased in Pew Values surveys conducted in 2009 and 2012—a likely upshot of prior research showing that the partisan attachments of young Americans who came of age in the aftermath of 9/11 were more heavily influenced by support for the military than the party identifications of older Americans and prior youth cohorts (Sears and Tesler 2009).

These results, along with the voluminous political science literature on the enduring nature of partisan attachments, suggest that the enhanced effects of racial attitudes on Obama-era party identification might persist past his presidency. The "Party of Lincoln," most relevantly, retained overwhelming black support for decades after the Republicans abandoned their Reconstruction efforts to help freed slaves in the late nineteenth century (Weiss 1983). The growing polarization of white partisanship by racial attitudes in response to Democrats becoming the "Party of Obama" could similarly leave an imprint on the American political landscape that endures long after he leaves office. That lasting imprint would be especially consequential, too. With party identification exerting influence over a wide array of political and social behaviors, the growing racialization of partisan attachments is by itself the growing racialization of American politics and society.

Chapter 8's discussion of the Republicans' hardening persona as the "Party of White People" during Barack Obama's presidency also has potentially lasting and significant implications for American politics and society. To be sure, previous research suggests that the partisan attachments of Asian Americans and Latinos are not as crystallized as white and black Americans' party identifications (Hajnal and Lee 2011). As such, the strong effects of attitudes toward whites on Latinos' and Asian Americans' partisan attachments might not be as enduring as the increased Obama-era influence of attitudes toward African Americans on both white and black Americans' party identifications. At the same time, though, the book's results, which showed that rank-and-file Republicans were more racially conservative during Obama's presidency than they had been in modern times, suggest that the Republican Party could be increasingly constrained in their efforts to reach out to minorities. Such constraints would most likely solidify the Republicans' image as the party of whites and extend the growing Obama-era political divide between white and nonwhite Americans into the post-Obama era.

That expanding divide may also require the Democratic Party to increasingly eschew their pre-Obama electoral temptation of racial silence in order to mobilize minority and racially liberal white voters. White Democrats by and large heeded that temptation of racial evasion during the 1990s and 2000s in an effort to retain racially conservative Reagan Democrats (see discussion in chap. 1). With the expanding nonwhite electorate changing the electoral calculus to such a degree that Barack Obama won reelection rather easily in 2012 with only 39 percent of the white vote, though, it may soon be in Democrats' national interests to appeal more directly to minorities and their racially sympathetic white allies. Indeed, it's hard to imagine Bill Clinton making as strong of a statement about racial inequality in the 1990s as Hillary Clinton made in the epigraph that introduced this chapter when whites comprised over three-quarters of his electoral coalition. One of Hillary Clinton's first major policy statements as a 2016 presidential candidate, in fact, repudiated her husband's crime policies for having a discriminatory impact on African Americans.[20] Such a turn toward explicit racial appeals by the Democrats would also help maintain, or even expand, the growing racialization of Obama-era mass politics into the post-Obama era.

Concluding Remarks

Of course, it is impossible to know how the events and results documented throughout the book will affect the American political landscape in the post-Obama era. It could be that Barack Obama was such a singular political figure that the influence of racial attitudes and race on mass political decision making quickly returns to its pre-Obama levels. Or, more likely, the growing racialization of mass politics documented in this book could have electoral consequences that reverberate long after Barack Obama leaves the White House.

Either way, it is abundantly clear from the evidence presented that Barack Obama presided over a most-racial political era in which racially liberal and racially conservative Americans were more divided over a whole host of issues than they had been in modern times. This polarization of mass politics by and over race almost surely contributed to the especially rancorous political environment surrounding Obama's presidency. It led Democrats and Republicans to perceive events in the realm of race much more differently than they had in the past; and it left Americans increasingly pessimistic about race relations going forward. Far from ushering in the onset of a post-racial society, then, Obama's presidency should stand out as yet another profound and sobering reminder of the ongoing importance of race in America.

Notes

Introduction

1. For a complete transcript of Obama's comments about the Trayvon Martin incident and the George Zimmerman verdict, see http://www.whitehouse.gov/the-press-office/2013/07/19/remarks-president-trayvon-martin.

2. For more on the White House Press Corps' surprised reaction to Barack Obama's statement, see http://www.huffingtonpost.com/2013/07/19/press-obama-trayvon-martin-remarks_n_3624957.html?utm_hp_ref=media.

3. For more on the racial divide in reactions to the Zimmerman verdict, see http://www.people-press.org/2013/07/22/big-racial-divide-over-zimmerman-verdict/; and http://www.washingtonpost.com/blogs/post-politics/wp/2013/07/22/zimmerman-verdict-86-percent-of-african-americans-disapprove/.

4. For more on this mounting pressure on Obama to make a statement about race and the Trayvon Martin incident, see http://www.huffingtonpost.com/2013/07/21/tavis-smiley-obama-trayvon-martin-pushed-podium_n_3631739.html.

5. Obama said at the beginning of his speech that he thought it might be useful to expand on his initial thoughts about the ruling after watching the debate about race and the Trayvon Martin incident play out over the course of the last week.

6. Quoted in http://www.washingtonpost.com/politics/obama-from-rev-wright-to-trayvon-martin/2013/07/20/709ad8b8-f151-11e2-9008-61e94a7ea20d_story.html.

7. Quoted in http://www.rushlimbaugh.com/daily/2013/07/22/obama_s_trayvon_speech_shows_ he_s_no_different_than_jesse_jackson_or_al_sharpton.

8. Quoted in http://www.foxnews.com/on-air/oreilly/2013/07/23/bill-oreilly-president-obama-and-race-problem.

9. See, e.g., http://www.breitbart.com/InstaBlog/2013/07/19/Obama-s-race-baiting; and http://www.nationalreview.com/article/353970/obama-administrations-race-baiting-campaign-andrew-c-mccarthy; and https://www.teaparty.org/obama-race-baits-the-trayvon-martin-case-26589/.

10. According to a March 24–27, 2012, YouGov/*Economist* poll, blacks were forty-three percentage points more likely than whites to think George Zimmerman should definitely be arrested, whereas Democrats were thirty percentage points more likely than Republicans to say he should definitely be arrested. See http://cdn.yougov.com/cumulus_uploads/document/5ntutkvq0d/econTab Report.pdf.

11. For more on the huge racial divide in responses to the O. J. Simpson case, see http://www.nytimes.com/1995/10/02/us/trial-leaves-public-split-on-racial-lines .html.

12. There was also little difference in how white Democrats and white Republicans responded to a racially charged 1984 New York City subway shooting, where Bernhard Goetz shot four African American youths whom he claimed were about to mug him. According to a February 28 to March 1, 1985, Gallup/*Newsweek* poll (accessed from the Roper Center's data archive), 63.6 percent of white Republicans "approved" of the shooting compared to 57.2 percent of white Democrats. See fig. 9.1, too.

13. For a full transcript of McCain's speech, see http://www.cnn.com/2008 /POLITICS/11/04/mccain.transcript/index.html?iref=newssearch.

14. See also figures AI.1, AI.2, and AI.3 in the online appendix to view the sharp increase in both black and white Americans' post-Obama perceptions of black progress across several different polling firms' surveys.

15. According to a July 27–28, 2010, Fox News poll, 37 percent of registered voters said relations between the races have gotten worse since Barack Obama became president, compared to 30 percent who said they had gotten better. A March 2–7, 2011, CBS/*New York Times* poll reported that 26 percent of respondents said race relations have gotten worse since Barack Obama became president compared to just 12 percent who thought they had gotten better. And 19 percent of respondents in a November 2–5, 2011, NBC News survey thought that race relations had gotten worse since Obama has been president, compared to 16 percent who said they had gotten better. All results accessed from iPOLL. In an August 2011 YouGov/*Economist* poll, 30 percent said race relations had gotten worse since Obama has been president, compared to 11 percent who said they had gotten better. Results reported in http://today.yougov.com/news/2013/07/16/race-relations-obama -era-low/.

16. According to an August 2013 Rasmussen poll, 43 percent of Americans thought that race relations had gotten worse since Barack Obama became president compared to just 10 percent who thought they had gotten better. An August 2014 CBS/*New York Times* poll similarly showed that 35 percent of Americans thought that race relations were worse since Obama became president compared to 10 percent who thought they had improved (accessed from iPOLL). And a July 2013 YouGov/*Economist* poll found that 43 percent of Americans thought that race relations had gotten worse compared to 9 percent who thought they had got-

ten better. See http://today.yougov.com/news/2013/07/16/race-relations-obama
-era-low/. As discussed in chap. 9, that ratio of respondents who thought race relations were worse than better since Barack Obama became president grew to as
much as 6:1 in polling conducted in December 2014.

17. George H. W. Bush defeated Michael Dukakis by a popular vote margin
of 53.4 percent to 45.7 percent and an electoral college vote margin of 426 to 111.

18. Bill O'Reilly even famously proclaimed on election night 2012 that "the
white establishment is now the minority"—a claim discussed more in later chapters. For more media analyses of racial polarization in the 2012 election, see http://
articles.latimes.com/2012/nov/01/news/la-pn-race-polarized-electorate-20121031;
http://www.msnbc.com/msnbc/race-polarizes-2012-electorate; and http://www
.thedailybeast.com/articles/2012/11/07/a-racially-polarized-election-augurs-ill-for
-barack-obama-s-second-term.html.

Chapter 1

1. Barack Obama made that statement in an interview with the *New Yorker*'s David Remnick. Quoted in http://www.newyorker.com/magazine/2014/01/27
/going-the-distance-2.

2. It is also important to note that African Americans had been gaining influence within the Democratic Party for several decades prior to the civil rights
movement and helped push the Democratic Party to become more supportive of
civil rights legislation (Tate 1994; Lee 2002).

3. In fact, Matthew Atkinson (2012) shows that the correlation between legislatures' positions on civil rights and their left-right ideologies on economic issues,
as measured by first-dimension DW NOMINATE scores, increased from less than
.50 in the pre–civil rights era to .90 by 1990.

4. Quoted in http://www.thenation.com/article/170841/exclusive-lee-atwaters-
infamous-1981-interview-southern-strategy.

5. Ian Hanley Lopez (2014, 4), for example, described Reagan's welfare queen
anecdote as follows: "Campaigning for president, Ronald Reagan liked to tell
stories of Cadillac-driving 'welfare queens' and 'strapping young bucks' buying
T-bone steaks with food stamps. In flogging these tales about the perils of welfare
run amok, Reagan always denied any racism and emphasized that he never mentioned race. He didn't need to because he was blowing a dog whistle."

6. Along with generational replacement, some Americans also changed their
partisan preferences to comport with their racial attitudes (e.g., Sears and Funk
1999). In fact, Green, Palmquist, and Schickler (2002, 141) estimate that about half
of southern realignment was caused by cohort replacement.

7. Klinkner and Smith's (2002) discussion of Reagan Democrats' defection is
based in large part on Stanley Greenberg's classic 1985 study of Democratic defec-

tion in Macomb County, Michigan, where he found that whites had come to view both the Democratic Party and the federal government as tools of black interests.

8. Several scholars have noted this turn toward racial silence by the Democratic Party, including Kinder and Sanders (1996); Frymer (1999); Dawson (1993); Klinkner and Smith (1999); King and Smith (2011); and Hajnal and Lee (2011).

9. The Supreme Court's 1974 ruling in *Milken v. Bradley* that school systems were not responsible for desegregation across district lines severely limited the impact of busing. The Supreme Court also restricted the use of racial preferences in the 1970s, as they outlawed racial quotas from being used in college admissions in *Regents of the University of California v. Bakke* (1978). A number of states went even further, outlawing the use of race-based preferences in state-run universities.

10. We referred to this generation as "the post-retrenchment cohort" because they came of voting age after the retrenchment efforts to roll back racially liberal policies had largely run their course. See also Luks and Elms (2005) for an analysis of the declining role of race in pre-Obama youth partisanship.

11. See also Tesler and Sears (2010; fig 7.1) for results showing that attitudes about Muslims were also an unusually strong predictor of Obama's favorability ratings in August 2007, months before the first primary votes were cast.

12. As Schuman et al. (1997) and others have pointed out, though, some opposition to intimate interracial relationships remained (see also Tesler 2013a; and Huddy and Feldman 2009 for measurements showing some white subscription to old-fashioned racist attitudes).

13. Because of these similarities, I use symbolic racism and racial resentment more or less interchangeably in this volume to describe the central racial attitude used in the empirical analyses.

14. For a full transcript of O'Reilly's remarks, see http://www.foxnews.com/on -air/oreilly/2014/08/27/bill-oreilly-truth-about-white-privilege.

15. Quoted in http://thinkprogress.org/economy/2014/03/12/3394871/ryan -poverty-inner-city/. While Paul Ryan did not explicitly refer to African Americans in this context, "inner city" has been shown to be a racialized code word associated with blacks (Peffley and Hurwitz 2005; White 2007).

16. The high-scale reliability of these items ($\alpha \approx .75$ across all surveys) also suggests that symbolic racism, as measured with Kinder and Sanders's (1996) racial resentment battery, reflects an internally consistent construct rather than the four multiple and diverse themes with which it is operationalized. Simply put, the seemingly diverse sentiments expressed in the racial resentment questions are answered by survey respondents as if they had one thing primarily in mind. Presumably the reason for this consistency is that racial resentment is a substantively meaningful package of beliefs about blacks to most Americans, wherever they stand.

17. The .50 midpoint is, indeed, a rather arbitrary dividing line between racial liberals and racial conservatives. For example, if we only used the "blacks should work their way up with no special favors" racial-resentment item, then nearly

70 percent of Americans would be classified as racial conservatives because they agree with this statement. On the other hand, if we only employed the "past discrimination has made it difficult for blacks" racial-resentment item, then only about 40 percent of the public would be classified as racially resentful. References to the .50 midpoint are an interpretative tool, then, and not an authoritative demarcation line between racial liberals and racial conservatives.

18. This refers to Obama's net effect on racial prejudice. There is some evidence, however, that individuals who disliked Barack Obama became more racially conservative and individuals who liked him became more racially liberal during his presidency, canceling each other out in the aggregate (Tesler 2013b).

19. In fact, according to the 2008–9 ANES panel study, Americans actually saw Barack Obama as more typical of most men (mean = .39 on a 0–1 exemplar scale) than most blacks (.34 on the same 0–1 exemplar scale).

Chapter 2

1. Quoted in http://www.huffingtonpost.com/2009/02/18/new-york-post-chimp -carto_n_167841.html.

2. See, e.g., http://www.theguardian.com/world/2009/feb/18/new-york-post -cartoon-race; http://cityroom.blogs.nytimes.com/2009/02/18/chimp-stimulus -cartoon-raises-racism-concerns/?_php=true&_type=blogs&_r=0; and http://www .nbcnews.com/id/29263781/ns/politics/t/cartoon-said-link-obama-dead-chimp/.

3. Quoted in http://www.huffingtonpost.com/2009/02/18/ny-post-cartoon -controver_n_167928.html.

4. See http://www.huffingtonpost.com/2009/02/19/new-york-post-employees -u_n_168267.html.

5. Quoted in http://cityroom.blogs.nytimes.com/2009/02/19/new-york-post -apologizes-for-chimp-cartoon/.

6. This was not unique to Barack Obama, as legislation often becomes synonymous with its presidential sponsor (e.g., "Bush Tax Cuts")

7. This isn't to say that no other president's policies have become racialized. These prior presidents, however, did not have to worry about their policies becoming racialized just because of their racial background.

8. Racial priming builds off of general theories of priming, which argue and show that sustained information flows about a particular subject can make that factor a more important ingredient of subsequent political evaluations (e.g., Iyengar and Kinder 1987; see Kinder 2003 for a review).

9. Consistent with that argument, racial resentment is more strongly linked to support for limited government when the recipients of government spending are black as opposed to white (DeSante 2013).

10. Kinder and Chudy (2014), in fact, show that racial attitudes were not a

stronger determinant of public opinion about abortion during the Obama presidency than they were beforehand.

11. Indeed, an experiment embedded in an August 2009 Pew Religion and Public Life survey suggested that the effects of ethnocentric attitudes on public opinion about abortion significantly changed after respondents were told Barack Obama's position.

12. A sizable proportion (27 percent), however, thought that blacks would benefit more from health care reform legislation than whites. These results are from an original survey of 3,147 registered voters conducted by the polling firm YouGov in November 2009.

13. Survey by Associated Press, Stanford University. Methodology conducted by Knowledge Networks, August 31 to September 7, 2010, and based on 1,251 online interviews (sample: national adult). The poll was fielded by Knowledge Networks using its national panel, which is randomly selected from the entire national population and subsequently provided Internet access, if needed. Results accessed from iPOLL databank.

14. Given these similarities, attitude strength and crystallization are used interchangeably.

15. For the growing ideological polarization of Democrats and Republicans in Congress, see especially McCarty, Poole, and Rosenthal (2006, 2013) and Mann and Ornstein (2012).

16. In fact, including more controls generally helps the spillover of racialization because Obama tended to activate racial attitudes relative to nonracial predispositions.

17. The other benchmark survey in the social sciences is the Panel Study of Income Dynamics, conducted by the Survey Research Center at the University of Michigan.

18. More specifically, every panelist participated in the March 2008 wave of the original 2007–8 CCAP, the first panel wave that included Kinder and Sanders's (1996) racial resentment battery. The original 2007–8 CCAP included twenty thousand respondents. YouGov then invited a nationally representative subsample of these respondents to take the respective reinterview surveys and constructed our final sample of at least three thousand panelists to ensure the data would be representative of the general registered voter population. Because the 2007–8 CCAP and the subsequent reinterviews were constructed to be representative of the registered voter population, there were virtually no differences between the two samples in March 2008 measures of such key variables as party identification, ideology, education, and racial resentment. Like other surveys conducted by YouGov/Polimetrix, the CCAP used a matching algorithm to produce an Internet sample that closely approximates the demographic makeup of the high-quality random sample carried out by the US Census Bureau in the American Community Study (Rivers 2006; Vavreck and Rivers 2008). Previous YouGov surveys perform well

in predicting public opinion and vote choice (Vavreck and Rivers 2008; Ansolabehere and Rivers 2013), and all the analyses are weighted to the general population to foster comparability between different sampling designs.

Chapter 3

1. Barack Obama made that statement in response to the following comments by Attorney General Eric Holder: "Though this nation has proudly thought of itself as an ethnic melting pot, in things racial, we have always been and we, I believe, continue to be in too many ways essentially a nation of cowards." For more on both Obama's and Holder's comments, see http://www.nytimes.com/2009/03/08/us/politics/08race.html?_r=0.

2. This refers to the individual-level effects of racial attitudes on vote choice. There is some evidence, however, that Bradley underperformed his polls because white voters were reluctant to tell pollsters that they did not support his candidacy (Hopkins 2009).

3. Barack Obama, for instance, jokingly answered David Letterman's question about racist opposition to his presidency and health reform proposals in September 2009, saying, "I think it's important to realize that I was actually black before the election." For more on this exchange, see http://www.cbsnews.com/news/obama-tells-letterman-i-was-black-before-the-election/. See also chap. 5 for a discussion of how Obama downplayed the role of race-based opposition to his health care plan. At the same time, though, Obama seemed more comfortable acknowledging the significant race-based opposition to his presidency during his second term, as he stated in an interview with the *New Yorker*: "There's no doubt that there's some folks who just really dislike me because they don't like the idea of a black President." Quoted in http://www.newyorker.com/magazine/2014/01/27/going-the-distance-2.

4. As mentioned in this chapter's first note, Obama was quick to distance himself from comments about race made early on in his term by his attorney general Eric Holder. And the White House encouraged its African American "green jobs czar," Van Jones, to resign after several of his controversial statements surfaced. For more on Jones, see http://www.huffingtonpost.com/2009/09/06/glenn-beck-gets-first-sca_n_278281.html.

5. Quoted in http://www.cnn.com/2010/POLITICS/07/23/sherrod.firestorm/index.html.

6. Quoted in Desmond King and Rogers Smith's *New York Times* op-ed, "On Race, the Silence is Bipartisan," September 2, 2013, http://www.nytimes.com/2011/09/03/opinion/on-race-the-silence-is-bipartisan.html?_r=0.

7. For more on Maxine Waters's statement, see http://www.politico.com/news/stories/0811/61628.html.

8. Quoted in http://www.boston.com/news/politics/politicalintelligence/2011 /05/west_obama_a_bl.html.

9. See, e.g., http://www.newrepublic.com/blog/jonathan-chait/obamas -moderate-health-care-plan; and http://krugman.blogs.nytimes.com/2012/02/05 /obama-the-moderate/.

10. For examples of that media coverage, see http://krugman.blogs.nytimes .com/2012/02/05/obama-the-moderate/?_r=0; and http://www.washingtonpost.com /blogs/wonkblog/post/obama-the-most-polarizing-moderate-ever/2011/08/25 /gIQArzcRwQ_blog.html.

11. Poole and his colleagues' make all their data available at the website http:// www.voteview.com.

12. This revised figure from 2013, of 0.75 percent is considerably better than estimates from 2012. Even still, Bartels's (2013) model, which used the earlier growth estimate of 0.3 percent, predicted that Obama would win by 4.6 percentage points.

13. See, e.g., Pew Research Center, "Demographic & Economic Data by Race," August 22, 2013, http://www.pewsocialtrends.org/2013/08/22/kings-dream -remains-an-elusive-goal-many-americans-see-racial-disparities/4/.

14. There is some evidence, in fact, suggesting that the economy is less important in open-seat elections like 2008 than it is when the president is running (Holbrook 2008; Nadeau and Lewis-Beck 2001).

15. For more on Limbaugh's statement, see http://thinkprogress.org/politics /2009/01/20/35012/limbaugh-obama-fail/.

16. Quoted in Jonathan Chait's *New York Magazine* column "Anarchists of the House," July 21, 2013, http://nymag.com/news/features/republican-congress-2013-7/.

17. OLS is used here to ease interpretation. The statistical and substantive implications are the exact same when using ordered logit instead.

18. Both presidents could also point to factors beyond their control for this increased unemployment—Bush inheriting a recession and then dealing with the aftermath of 9/11; and Obama inheriting the worst economy since the Great Depression.

19. The 2008 results are less informative since the economy was so bad at the time of the 2008 ANES survey that even the most ardent conservative Republicans would have had a hard time altering reality to make recent unemployment figures consistent with their support for John McCain.

20. Census projections, for instance, suggest that by 2043 whites will no longer be the majority in the United States.

21. Consistent with those findings, Enos (2014) shows that experimentally introducing only two native Spanish speakers into the daily routines of white Bostonians who rarely encountered Latinos made them significantly less supportive of immigration.

22. See chap. 8 epigraph and introduction for more on O'Reilly's statement.

23. While McCain did not make appeals to Obama's race, the McCain campaign in general, and Sarah Palin in particular, seemed much more comfortable trafficking in "Obama as other" appeals (Tesler and Sears 2010, chap. 7).

24. For more on the criticism of Santorum's comment, see http://www.cbsnews .com/8301-503544_162-57352570-503544/naacp-blasts-santorum-for-targeting -blacks-in-entitlement-reform/; and http://thinkprogress.org/economy/2012/01 /03/396428/santorums-racist-welfare-rant/.

25. For more on this comment and the racial controversy it stirred, see http:// www.cbsnews.com/8301-503544_162-57353438-503544/gingrich-singles-out -blacks-in-food-stamp-remark/; and http://www.foxnews.com/politics/2012/01/06 /gingrich-african-american-community-should-demand-paychecks-not-food -stamps/.

26. For more on this racially charged debate exchange, see http://campaignstops .blogs.nytimes.com/2012/01/17/newt-gingrich-and-the-art-of-racial-politics/; http:// www.salon.com/2012/01/17/juan_williams_stands_in_for_obama_at_fox_debate/.

27. Jesse Jackson, for instance, wrote in the *Huffington Post*, "Gingrich's campaign limped into South Carolina on life support. His revival came from his cunning peddling of a poisonous potion of race-bait politics to a virtually all-white electorate"; see http://www.huffingtonpost.com/rev-jesse-jackson/gingrich-plays -old-south_b_1227879.html.

28. Such leading fact checkers as PolitiFact, the *Washington Post*'s fact checker, and FactChecker.org all gave the ad their most dishonest rating. For more, see http://www.npr.org/blogs/itsallpolitics/2012/08/22/159791065/despite-fact-checks -romney-escalates-welfare-work-requirement-charge.

29. Quoted in Thomas Edsall's *New York Times* column "Making the Election about Race," August 27, 2012, http://campaignstops.blogs.nytimes.com/2012/08/27 /making-the-election-about-race/.

30. For more on Biden's racially controversial comment, see http://www.politico .com/news/stories/0812/79717.html; and http://articles.latimes.com/2012/aug/15 /news/la-pn-biden-chains-romney-welfare-sloths-20120814.

31. These analyses use vote intention to keep continuity with both the CCAP panel results from July 2012 presented later in the chapter, and our prior analyses in *Obama's Race*, which also used vote intention. The substantive implications remain the same regardless of whether vote intention or vote choice is used as the dependent variable.

32. One likely explanation for why the thermometer ratings were not activated in 2008 voting behavior was that antiblack affect was a considerably stronger predictor of party identification in the 2008 ANES (see results in chap. 7), which could have mediated any enhanced influence of the thermometers on vote choice.

33. There is some evidence, in fact, that ideology, party identification, and racial resentment all changed in accordance with prior opinions of Barack Obama (Tesler 2013a, 2015b; Lenz 2012).

34. Pasek et al. (2014), for instance, report a reduced role of racial prejudice on 2012 voting. At the same time, though, they report an increased association between racial resentment and party identification. It is likely, then, that the effects of racial attitudes on 2012 may be working through their increased relationship with party identification (see Weisberg 2014 for a similar conclusion).

35. The 2012 ANES included an online component, conducted by Knowledge Networks/GFK, along with its familiar face-to-face survey. Moreover, the face-to-face survey administered the stereotype and thermometer items on a laptop to help mitigate social desirability pressures to rate all groups equally.

36. Survey was commissioned with Lynn Vavreck and David Sears.

37. See especially Martin Parlett's 2014 book on this topic, *Demonizing a President: The "Foreignization" of Barack Obama*. Such "Obama as other" statements by prominent Republicans again made headlines in 2015, when Rudy Giuliani suggested that Barack Obama did not love America, and when Republican presidential candidate Scott Walker responded to those comments by saying he did not know whether Obama loved America or whether he was a Christian. In response to those statements, a February 2015 *HuffPost/*YouGov poll asked respondents, "Do you think Barack Obama loves America?" Only 11 percent of Republicans said yes, whereas 69 percent said no. For more, see http://www.huffingtonpost.com/2015/02/24/obama-loves-america-poll_n_6745082.html.

38. With Donald Trump making very public allegations that the president was not born in the United States, and only 38 percent of Americans saying President Obama was "definitely" born in the United States in a *USA Today* poll (see http://usatoday30.usatoday.com/news/washington/2011-04-27-obama-birth-certificate_n.htm), Barack Obama released his "long form" birth certificate on April 27, 2011, which proved he was born in Hawaii. While that release temporarily reduced the numbers of birthers in opinion polls, the percentage of Americans soon returned to their preannouncement levels (Berinsky 2012).

39. Meanwhile, the percentage of CCAP panelists who thought that Obama was a Christian declined by five percentage points. These panel results are consistent with Obama-era surveys conducted by Pew and the Associated Press, which also indicate that that percentage of Americans who thought Barack Obama was Muslim increased from before to after he became president.

40. We asked a representative sample of one thousand Americans in an October 2012 survey whether a number of factors, such as Barack Obama's race, religion, education, and family, made them more likely, less likely, or neither more nor less likely to vote for him.

41. In addition to these analyses, Sides and Vavreck (2013) found racial resentment was a strong predictor of 2012 vote choice, though slightly weaker than its influence in 2008. And Stephens-Davidowitz (2013) found that racist Google searches had the same effect on aggregate election in both 2008 and 2012. In fact, while racist Google searches explained 24 percent of the variation in media mar-

kets' presidential votes from 2004 to 2008, they did not explain any of the change in Obama's fortunes from 2008 to 2012. Finally, Bafumi and Geer (2014) show that the effects of racial threat on presidential voting intensified from 2008 to 2012, "as racial issues have increasingly come to the forefront of national political discourse."

Chapter 4

1. For the full video of this interview between Stephen Colbert and Charlie Crist, see http://thecolbertreport.cc.com/videos/8yt2ar/charlie-crist. For the media's coverage of Crist's racial comments on the *Colbert Report*, see http://miamiherald .typepad.com/nakedpolitics/2014/02/charlie-crist-plays-the-obama-race-card-but -says-hes-not-on-colbert.html; and http://www.newsmax.com/Politics/Charlie -Crist-politics-race-Stephen-Colbert/2014/02/12/id/552296/.

2. Excerpt from Crist's book quoted at http://www.newsmax.com/Politics /Charlie-Crist-politics-race-Stephen-Colbert/2014/02/12/id/552296/.

3. Crist made that statement in a May 2014 interview with Fusion's Jorge Ramos, host of *America*. For video of the interview, see http://fusion.net/video /embed?id=657267. For media coverage of the interview, see http://www.upi.com /Top_News/US/2014/05/06/Charlie-Crist-left-the-GOP-over-partys-racism /7471399412031/; http://www.politico.com/story/2014/05/charlie-crist-racism-drove -me-from-gop-106442.html; and http://theweek.com/speedreads/index/261151 /speedreads-charlie-crist-gops-intolerable-views-turned-me-into-a-democrat.

4. The other members of the team were John Geer (Vanderbilt), Brendan Nyhan (Dartmouth), John Sides (George Washington), and Lynn Vavreck (UCLA).

5. The follow-up questions after the ad asked whether Obama's and Romney's policies would be good or bad for the following groups: the rich, the poor, the middle class, blacks, and whites. I then used those items to construct an instrument for Romney and Obama favorability based on their relationships with pretreatment Romney and Obama favorability ratings in the control group (Franklin 1989; Zaller 1992). More specifically, the instruments were constructed from the following predicted favorability equations (all variables coded 0–1):

> Romney favorability = .266 + .158 (help blacks) − .039 (help whites) + .483 (help poor) − .187 (help rich) + .262 (help middle class)
>
> Obama favorability = .016 − .204 (help blacks) + .291 (help whites) + .096 (help poor) + .033 (help rich) + .801 (help middle class).

These five variables make for reliable instruments, as they explain 62 percent and 63 percent of the respective variation in Romney and Obama's favorability ratings. The racial priming results are also similar when using only Americans' responses to the policy questions (Tesler 2012b)

6. That 2 percent difference was far from statistically significant, though ($p = .43$).

7. The Romney camp, however, was probably better at targeting the ad to racial conservatives who were more receptive to this message than our national sample. And if they were able to specifically target those individuals, then the ad could have made him more popular.

8. Kinder and Sanders (1996) and Mendelberg (2001) persuasively argue that the Bush campaign intentionally used the Willie Horton issue to appeal to racial conservative voters.

9. The alpha reliability of this two-item scale was .81.

10. It is important to note that, like the welfare ad experiment, all our explanatory variables were measured *before* the "explicit prompt" and the presidential-approval dependent variable. These results are, therefore, not subject to Lenz's (2009, 2012) valid concerns about reverse causality induced by posttreatment measures of explanatory variables in priming experiments (see also Tesler 2015b).

11. Racial resentment and OFR were strongly correlated among these panelists ($r = .46$). Nevertheless, many respondents gave very different answers to these questions. The modal score on the racial resentment scale, for instance, was the most resentful while the modal score on this OFR measure was the least racist position.

12. The "us" here refers to conversations David Sears and I had with the 2008 Election Lunch Group at UCLA.

13. That change in racial resentment's impact on mass assessments of Hillary Clinton was also highly significant ($p < .001$).

14. Among the 324 African Americans who were interviewed in both the March 2008 and July 2012 CCAP panel waves, 50 percent rated Hillary Clinton favorably in March 2008. When these exact same panelists were reinterviewed in July 2012, though, 80 percent rated her favorably.

15. This proved to be quite important, as the baseline effects of racial resentment on evaluations of Buddy Clinton were different across the two experimental conditions.

16. This also makes it a conservative test of the spillover of racialization, since some respondents may have recognized the picture in the "Splash condition" as Bo Obama.

17. These results are very similar regardless of whether we are using five-category favorability ratings of both dogs or a dichotomous variable for rating one dog higher than the other ($p = .04$ and $p = .02$, respectively). See online appendix for both sets of results. Those significantly different effects of racial resentment also occurred without significantly enhancing the effects of party and ideology.

18. This result is also somewhat surprising in light of the theoretical expecta-

tion put forth in chap. 2 that the spillover of racialization should be especially pronounced into political evaluations where Americans do not already have crystallized opinions. Indeed, I suspected that this experiment would not work because most Americans surely have much stronger opinions about dogs than they do about policy issues.

19. Ansolabehere and Fraga's (2014) CCES analyses also attest to the viability of opposition to affirmative action as a measure of racial conservatism. They found that opposition to affirmative action was a significantly strong predictor of evaluating white Democratic members of the House of Representatives more favorably than black Democrats in the House of Representatives.

20. At the same time, though, the spillover of racialization into mass evaluations of Charlie Crist may have been mitigated by the fact that he was running against an African American Democratic candidate for Senate, Kendrick Meeks, in 2010, since, as fig. 4.1 showed, racial resentment was a strong predictor of evaluating Barack Obama's political opponents favorably.

Chapter 5

1. Quoted in Mark Silva, "In Media Blitz, Obama says Vitriol Isn't Racism-Based." *LA Times*, September 19, 2009.

2. This is based on the Project for Excellence in Journalism's weekly content analyses in their series of News Coverage Indexes. See http://www.journalism.org /news_index/99.

3. This is based on a LexisNexis search of broadcast news stories with "health care" in the headline and "angry" or "anger" in the body of the story.

4. Some of these plausible reasons include anxiety over government spending at a time of record deficits during the Great Recession and the growing polarization of both political elites and the mass public in the years leading up to Obama's election.

5. Quoted in http://www.nytimes.com/2009/08/07/opinion/07krugman.html.

6. This article can be found at http://www.huffingtonpost.com/ray-hanania /opposition-to-obama-healt_b_242938.html.

7. Carter made this statement in an NBC News interview with Brian Williams. For more on Carter's quotation, see http://voices.washingtonpost.com/44/2009/09 /15/carter_cites_racism_inclinatio.html; and http://www.theguardian.com/world /2009/sep/16/jimmy-carter-racism-barack-obama.

8. This is based on a LexisNexis search of broadcast news stories with "health care" in the headline and "racism," "racist," or "prejudice" in the body of the story.

9. For more on this incident, see Paul Kane, "Tea Party Protestor Accused of Spitting on Law Makers, Using Slurs," *Washington Post*, March 20, 2010.

10. There were a few stories about health care in 1993–94 that contained the

words "racist," "racism," or "prejudice" in the body of the story, but none were about opposition to the Clinton's health care plan.

11. To reproduce this graph, go to http://www.google.com/trends/explore#q =health%20care%20racism.

12. Mark Silva, "In Media Blitz, Obama Says Vitriol Isn't Racism-Based." *LA Times*, September 19, 2009.

13. For more on this comment, see http://www.cbsnews.com/news/obama-tells -letterman-i-was-black-before-the-election/.

14. Quoted in http://www.politico.com/story/2014/05/jay-rockefeller-john -johnson-race-106983.html. For more media coverage of the Senators' exchange, see http://www.cbsnews.com/news/dont-call-me-a-racist-republican-senator-ron -johnson-tells-democrat-jay-rockefeller/; http://www.kaiserhealthnews.org/Daily -Reports/2014/May/23/Rockefeller-on-racism-and-health-law.aspx; and http:// www.politico.com/story/2014/05/jay-rockefeller-john-johnson-race-106983.html.

15. This was based on the Project for Excellence in Journalism's weekly content analyses in their series of News Coverage Indexes. See http://www.journalism .org/news_index/99.

16. The online appendix is available at http://www.press.uchicago.edu/books /tesler.

17. As first reported in Tesler (2012c) and elaborated further in the online appendix of this book, the results were similar when using OLS regression on the full seven-point scale. The coefficients in table A5.1 of the online appendix, for example, show that racial resentment had a substantively small and nonsignificant independent influence on white respondents' seven-point health care placements in every previous ANES survey except for 1994. With ideological self-placement and party identification held constant, changing from least to most racially resentful decreased white support for governmental insurance by just 6 percent of this scale's range in the twenty years preceding Obama's presidency. That same change in white racial resentment decreased support for governmental health insurance by nearly 20 percent of the scale's range in both the 2012 ANES and in the September 2009 off-panel wave of the 2008-2009-2010 ANES panel study.

18. The ANES time series sample is typically constructed by area probability sampling and is conducted via face-to-face interviews. It is important to note that the effect of racial resentment (though not stereotypes) on health care opinions in the 2012 ANES was bigger for the Internet sample than it was for the face-to-face respondents. At the same time, though, this effect for the web-based panelists was more than twice as large as the effect of racial resentment on opposition to governmental health insurance on similar web-based panelists in the March 2009 ANES off-panel wave. So just looking at survey data collected by the web-based polling firm Knowledge Networks/GFK for the ANES also leads to the conclusion that racial attitudes became a significantly stronger predictor of health care opinions *after* Barack Obama became the face of the policy.

19. The March and September 2009 surveys both included the ANES's stan-

dard seven-point health care item and an additional seven-point scale, which asked how much more or less the federal government should spend on health insurance for adults. The two items form a reliable, fourteen-category government insurance scale (Cronbach's $\alpha \approx .65$ in both waves). The 2008–9 ANES panel study is merged with an off-panel file, whose content was not controlled by the ANES. The dependent variable of interest was asked in the March and September 2009 off-panel waves fortuitously fielded by Mark Schlesinger of Yale University.

20. This three-category variable is dichotomized into voluntary health care or not because respondents were unclear whether Obama favored a single-payer or a subsidized system.

21. The effect of racial resentment on health care opinions also increased significantly from March 2008 to July 2012 among the full sample of white panelists in the 2012 CCAP reinterviews (Tesler 2015b).

22. The logistic regression coefficient for party and ideology in December 2007 were 1.51 and 2.03, respectively. In November 2009 those coefficients were 1.61 and 2.11, respectively. Meanwhile, the effect of March 2008 tax-policy preferences decreased over time. See online appendix for full results.

23. As discussed in the concluding chapter, though, Barack Obama's activation of racial resentment in health care opinions relative to party and ideology likely stemmed from the fact that party and ideology were much more powerful combined predictors of health care opinions than racial attitudes prior to Obama's presidency. As indicated in fig. 5.5, issues in which the pre-Obama impact of racial attitudes rivaled the baseline effects of partisanship/ideology (e.g., gun control) Obama activated party more powerfully than racial resentment.

24. Those panel results in the online appendix, in fact, suggest a much bigger racializing effect of the 2009–10 debate over Obama's health care reform plan than any other results presented. The appendix is available at http://www.press.uchicago .edu/books/tesler/.

25. Kinder and Chudy (2014) also found that the effect of racial resentment on opposition to governmental spending for health increased significantly from 2006 to 2010 in the GSS panel study. For the online appendix, see http://www.press .uchicago.edu/books/tesler/.

26. The survey contained four forms, three of which were used for this experimental test.

27. The exact set up of the experiment was as follows:

> *Stripped/Neutral Condition:*
> We would like to get your opinion about two current health care proposals being debated.
>
> As you may know, some people have proposed a plan that would guarantee health insurance for all Americans. What do you think? Do you Favor or Oppose the federal government guaranteeing health insurance for all Americans?

Many of these same people have also proposed a government-administered health insurance plan, often called the "public option," to compete with private insurance. What do you think? Do you Favor or Oppose a government-administered health insurance option?

Clinton Condition:
We would like to get your opinion about two health care plans previously proposed by President Bill Clinton in 1993 that are still being debated today.

As you may recall, President Clinton proposed a plan that would have guaranteed health insurance for all Americans. What do you think? Do you Favor or Oppose the federal government guaranteeing health insurance for all Americans?

President Clinton also proposed a government-administered health insurance plan, often called the "public option," to compete with private insurance. What do you think? Do you Favor or Oppose a government-administered health insurance option?

Obama Condition:
We would like to get your opinion about two of President Barack Obama's current health care proposals.

As you may know, President Obama proposed a plan that would guarantee health insurance for all Americans. What do you think? Do you Favor or Oppose the federal government guaranteeing health insurance for all Americans

President Obama also proposed a government-administered health insurance plan, often called the "public option," to compete with private insurance. What do you think? Do you Favor or Oppose a government-administered health insurance option?

28. Cronbach's α = .90

29. Consistent with this claim, the Obama treatment had a much larger racializing effect among low-information respondents, who lacked both crystallized issue positions and the real-world contextual information needed to connect their predispositions to policy preferences (Converse 1964; Zaller 1992; Price and Zaller 1993; Tesler 2015a). The YouGov registered voter reinterview sample may therefore introduce a conservative bias into the results. Registered voters are more politically knowledgeable than nonvoters, as are respondents in volunteer Internet samples (Malhotra and Krosnick 2007; Hill et al. 2007). As such, the effects likely would have been greater in a lower information sample of the general public.

30. The mean health care support score for white respondents in the Clinton condition was .363 compared to .333 in the Obama condition (p = .10)

31. As was the case with Henderson and Hillygus's (2011) finding that racial resentment became a more important determinant of pre- to post-Obama health care opinions in panel data, related research also found racial attitudes had a stronger relationship with health care opinions when they were framed as Barack Obama's policies. Knowles, Lowery, and Schaumberg (2010), for instance, found that implicit racial prejudice was a stronger predictor of opposition health care reform when it was framed as Barack Obama's plan rather than when it had been framed as Bill Clinton's plan.

32. In fact, Filindra and Kaplan (2014) show that racial attitudes have long been a very strong predictor of public opinion about gun control.

33. That difference in the effects of racial resentment across conditions was marginally significant ($p < .10$).

34. Party/ideology had a significantly stronger effect on support for the assault weapons ban in the Obama-framed condition than in the neutral condition ($p = .01$)

35. Indeed, Google's News Reference Volume Trends shows that there was a huge spike in news coverage of "gay marriage" around President Obama's announcement that he supports same-sex marriage, which plummeted very shortly thereafter. See the graphic of these trends in news coverage in the online appendix.

36. These are based on searches of the iPOLL databank. The searches uncovered four questions, which contained the words "angry" and "Clinton" under the heading "health." However, unlike 2009–10 questions, which primarily gauged anger toward Obama's plan, those four items asked whether respondents would be angry if health care reform legislation *did not* pass.

37. The test, retest correlation between support for governmental health care in the 2006–8 GSS panel study was only .35.

38. Contrary to expectations, though, our survey respondents were not more likely to think that health care proposals disproportionately benefited blacks over whites in the Obama-framed experimental condition. See discussion in chap. 2 for more on the perceived racial beneficiaries of health care reform legislation.

39. Aside from the results presented in this chapter, the 2010–12 CCES panel study shows that racial resentment had almost identically strong effects on opposition to the ACA in both of those massive surveys ($N = 15,360$ white panelists in the analysis). After controlling for party and ideology, moving from least to most racially resentful (as measured in 2010) increased white panelists' probability of opposing the ACA by .60 in both the 2010 and 2012 panel waves.

Chapter 6

1. For a full transcript of President Obama's postelection remarks, see http://www.whitehouse.gov/the-press-office/2010/11/03/press-conference-president.

2. See http://www.huffingtonpost.com/news/tea-party-racism.

3. The peak in searches for "Tea Party Racism" on Google trends coincided with the release of this report in July 2010.

4. Survey by Pew Research Center for the People & the Press, July 15–18, 2010, and based on 1,003 telephone interviews. Results accessed from the Roper Center's iPOLL databank.

5. For full polling results from this survey, see http://www.nytimes.com/interactive /2010/04/14/us/politics/20100414-tea-party-poll-graphic.html#tab=5.

6. These results were featured by John Sides in *Monkey Cage* on December 12, 2011. For more, see http://themonkeycage.org/2011/12/12/tea-party-racism-some -experimental-evidence/.

7. To be exact, 49 percent said that at least some support for the Tea Party Movement was based on racial prejudice against President Obama. Survey by ABC News/*Washington Post*, April 22–25, 2010, and based on 1,001 telephone interviews. Results accessed from Roper's iPOLL.

8. Antiblack stereotypes, however, had a similarly large effect on opinions about both the Republican Party and the Tea Party Movement.

9. These two pooled ANES surveys were conducted in July 2010 and October 2010.

10. These measures were not available in the pooled 2010 surveys, which is why the analysis is limited only to 2012.

11. The 2010 preelection surveys were conducted by the Internet polling firm Knowledge Networks over the Internet, as was more than half of the 2012 ANES.

12. The results from the 2008 ANES are consistent with that contention, as the effect of racial resentment on white respondents' support for Republican candidates was three times great in that survey than it was in the pooled 1986–2004 pre-Obama baseline.

13. Party and ideology were also measured in the March 2008 CCAP in this model.

14. Party and ideology were also measured in the September 2008 CCAP in this model.

15. Unfortunately, the newly drawn congressional boundaries following the 2010 decennial census prohibit a similar pre- to post-Obama analysis of racial conservatism and district level returns in the 2012 elections for the House of Representatives.

16. For more on the CCES, and/or to download the data, see http://projects.iq .harvard.edu/cces.

17. More specifically, each survey years' opposition to affirmative action score was given equal weight in constructing this measurement, so that the 2010 CCES, which contains almost as many respondents as the combined 2006 and 2008 CCES, did not have a disproportionate impact on the results. This strategy of giving each survey year equal weight was also employed because affirmative action opposition

was measured on a seven-category scale in 2006 and a four-category scale in 2008 and 2010. These district-level measures were then squared to help account for the strong skew toward opposition to affirmative action, and recoded to range from 0 (the most racially liberal district, MI-14) to 1 (the most racially conservative district, ID-1).

18. Kerry vote proportion is used here instead of 2008 vote because, as fig. 5.4 shows, Obama evaluations mediated the enhanced effects of racial conservatism on Obama-era vote choices.

19. That would seem unlikely, though, since Democrats who voted against Obamacare came disproportionately from the South, and white Americans in the South disproportionately use racial attitudes in their partisan preferences (Valentino and Sears 2005).

20. Opposition to affirmative action is used here again as a proxy for racial resentment since our preferred measure of racial conservatism, racial resentment, was not included in the CCES prior to 2010.

21. The fiftieth House vote to repeal the ACA occurred in March 2014.

22. For a transcript of Obama's full statement, see http://www.whitehouse .gov/the-press-office/2013/10/01/remarks-president-affordable-care-act-and -government-shutdown.

23. See, e.g., http://www.salon.com/2013/10/01/the_real_story_of_the_shutdown _50_years_of_gop_race_baiting/; http://www.patheos.com/blogs/wwjtd/2013/10/ maddow-on-tea-party-racism-and-the-gops-story-on-the-shutdown/; http://www .huffingtonpost.com/walker-bragman/the-shutdown-is-about-mor_b_4067941 .html; http://www.mediaite.com/tv/serious-racism-here-ed-schultz-insists-gops -shutdown-showdown-motivated-by-hate/; and http://www.forbes.com/sites /robwaters/2013/10/14/shutdown-power-play-stoking-racism-fear-of-culture -change-to-push-anti-government-agenda/.

24. For more on Redford's statement that the shutdown was motivated by racism, see http://www.huffingtonpost.com/2013/10/16/robert-redford-shutdown _n_4109245.html. For more on Noth's comments, see http://www.mediaite.com /tv/actor-chris-noth-accuses-tea-party-of-racism-against-obama-recommends-they -be-horsewhipped/.

25. Quoted in http://www.thedailybeast.com/articles/2013/10/08/the-shutdown -isn-t-racist.html.

26. House members' ideological voting records in this analysis were measured by Stanford political scientist Simon Jackman's October 17 updated ideal points, retrieved from http://jackman.stanford.edu/blog/.

27. See also Tesler (2013b) for similar results showing that opposition to interracial dating significantly predicted white Americans' support for House Republicans for the first time in 2010.

28. Like the results in the 2010–12 CCES, moving from least to most racially resentful was associated with about a fifty-percentage-point increase in white vote

share for Republican House candidates in the 2014 CCES after controlling for party and ideology.

Chapter 7

1. For more on this statement, see http://www.huffingtonpost.com/2013/01/13/colin-powell-gop_n_2467768.html.

2. See, among others, http://tv.msnbc.com/2013/01/13/powell-slams-gop-for-dark-vein-of-intolerance/; and http://www.cbsnews.com/8301-34222_162-57563708-10391739/powell-blasts-gops-dark-vein-of-intolerance/.

3. For a look at these trends in searches for Republican racism, see http://www.google.com/trends/explore?q=republican+racism#q=republican%20racism&cmpt=q.

4. The 2010 CNN survey was conducted by Opinion Research Corporation, July 16–21, 2010, and based on 1,018 telephone interviews. The 2000 survey was commissioned by CNN/*USA Today* and was conducted by the Gallup Organization, August 4–5, 2000, with 1,051 telephone interviews. Both of these survey results were accessed from the Roper Center's iPOLL databank.

5. For over-time trends in support for presidential candidates from 1936 to 2012, see also http://www.gallup.com/poll/154559/us-presidential-election-center.aspx.

6. After controlling for the variables in table 7.1, the relationship between racial resentment and party identification was actually larger in 2000 ($b = .20$) than 2004 ($b = .11$).

7. The opposition to affirmative action item in the Pew Values Survey is an especially good proxy for racial resentment since that question's wording, "We should make every effort to improve the position of blacks and minorities even if it means giving them special treatment," closely approximates the "blacks should work their way up without any special favors" item in the racial resentment battery.

8. There was, however, a modest spike in pre- to post-Obama GSS correlations when using just the black stereotypes, as opposed to the difference between black and white stereotype measures, which was used in the display. The correlation between just the black stereotypes and Republican Party identification increased from –.01 in the pooled 2000–2008 GSS to .05 in the 2010–12 surveys.

9. The choices of control variables were dictated in large part by which items appear on the same survey forms as the racial conservatism questions in the GSS and the PVS. The GSS, for instance, administers its surveys on three question forms, only two of which asked the racial resentment questions. Some items that I would have liked to use as controls for moral traditionalism, then, like attitudes about abortion or homosexuality were not included because they were asked on different survey forms. The PVS now uses only two survey forms and has not asked

its religious fundamentalism or moral traditionalism questions on the same form as their race items in recent years.

10. The appendix is available at http://www.press.uchicago.edu/books/tesler/.

11. The results in that column are from a fully interactive model that interacted all the predictors with dummy variables for post-Obama surveys.

12. The 2008 GSS is included in the pre-Obama era because most of the GSS interviews in 2008 occurred before Obama secured the nomination, and nearly all of them occurred before he was officially nominated as the Democratic Party nominee.

13. There were, however, significant decreases in the constant term from before to after Obama. That change reflects the notable decline in Republican party identification that occurred during George W. Bush's second term in office, especially among racial liberals whose growing identification with the Democratic Party in the Age of Obama would be shown in the constant term. For trends in macro partisanship, see http://www.pewresearch.org/data-trend/political-attitudes/party-identification/.

14. In fact, no variable across these three surveys was a significantly weaker predictor of Obama-era partisanship than it was beforehand, though the diminished influence of moral traditionalism on ANES partisanship was marginally significant ($p = .09$).

15. See also Tesler (2013b) for old-fashioned racism's greater influence on presidential and congressional voting in 2008 and 2010, respectively.

16. The few white respondents who felt more favorably about their close relatives marrying a black spouse than a white spouse are coded the same as respondents who had no preference as to which race their close relative marries.

17. The p value on the interaction between black affect and 2008–12 was .14 in the ANES, though there are several other model specifications that achieve statistical significance. The p value on the interaction between black affect and 2010–12 was .03 in the GSS. However, the GSS sample was reduced by half its size in this model because moral traditionalism and black affect are asked on only one of the GSS's three survey forms. When the model omitted moral traditionalism to boost the sample size the p value diminished to $<.01$.

18. The control variables changed a bit in this model from the one used in tables 7.2 and 7.3 to make sure that the comparison between the pre-Obama ANES and post-Obama GSS results would be as comparable as possible.

19. Moving from lowest to highest in racial resentment, as measured in October 2008, was also associated with about a thirteen-point change on a 0-100 scale in Republican -Democratic favorability among CCAP panelists reinterviewed in both October 2008 and spring 2011. See Tesler (2013b) for results showing that old-fashioned racism was also a significant predictor of partisan change in these GSS and CCAP surveys.

20. Unfortunately, respondents were not asked to rank the two major parties

on "aid to blacks" in the 2008 and 2012 ANES. So, the results report perceptions of the two major party nominees on this scale.

21. Party identification was not the only pre-Obama political attitude to exhibit such high-information racialization, either. Several studies show that the effects of racial attitudes on social welfare policy preferences were strongest among politically informed individuals who could make the link between those governmental programs and African American recipients (Federico 2004; Huber and Lapinsky 2006; Goren 2013).

22. Zaller's (1992) model, however, also presupposes that low-information individuals who do not pay much attention to politics would be more likely to respond to partisan developments in the rare circumstance when they are especially likely to receive that new information. This appears to be the case for the easy connection between race and party during Obama's presidency.

23. The number of citations showing party's profound influence over voting and public policy preferences is much too vast to list. But see, among others, Campbell et al. 1960; Miller and Shanks 1996; Bartels 2000; Green, Palmquist, and Schickler 2002; Cohen 2003; Berinsky 2009; and Lenz 2012. For the Godfather's Pizza polarization, see http://themonkeycage.org/2011/11/17/partisanship-in -everything-views-of-godfathers-pizza/. For the Big Bird polarization, see http:// themonkeycage.org/2012/10/12/yellow-may-be-the-new-blue-what-voters-think -of-the-big-bird-ad/.

Chapter 8

1. For the full video and transcript of O'Reilly's statement, see http://nation .foxnews.com/bill-oreilly/2012/11/07/bill-o-reilly-white-establishment-now -minority.

2. See, e.g., http://www.huffingtonpost.com/brittney-bullock/bill-oreilly-white -establishment_b_2174200.html.

3. Despite making up 74 percent of the electorate and 72 percent of the voting-eligible population, whites were 95 percent of governors and lieutenant governors, 94 percent of United States senators, 84 percent of the House of Representatives, and 88 percent of state legislatures. For more on the racial composition of elected officials, see http://www.gmcl.org/maps/national/gender.htm.

4. Stephen Colbert, for instance, poked fun at Bill O'Reilly's statement, saying, "Traditional white people, of any race, we don't want things. We have things. We know what to do with things; we keep it with our stuff." For a video clip of Colbert's comments, see http://thecolbertreport.cc.com/videos/hbkurh/nontraditional -non-white-america. For more critiques of O'Reilly's statement, see http://www .washingtonpost.com/opinions/mitt-romneys-parting-gifts-to-the-country/2012/11 /15/9be1166a-2f62-11e2-a30e-5ca76eeec857_story.html; and http://thedailyshow.cc .com/videos/q7gcyp/it-was-the-best-of-times—it-was-the-best-of-times.

5. This is just based on the two-party vote to help keep continuity between years where the third-party candidate received a substantial proportion of the vote (e.g., 1992 and 1996) and years that did not have a viable third-party candidate.

6. Walter Mondale received only 34 percent of the white vote, and 41 percent of the total vote, in his 1984 landslide loss to Ronald Reagan.

7. All the figures in this paragraph are based on the following census report: Thom File (2013), "The Diversifying Electorate—Voting Rates by Race and Hispanic Origin in 2012 (and Other Recent Elections)," http://www.census.gov/prod /2013pubs/p20-568.pdf.

8. File (2013); Taylor (2013).

9. File (2013); Taylor (2013).

10. Some caution is required in interpreting these figures, however, because the exit polls have historically been inaccurate in estimating presidential vote shared by race and ethnicity.

11. Barack Obama's unusually strong black support was further magnified after accounting for record black turnout in the 2012 election. Indeed, 62 percent of the voting eligible black population voted for Obama in 2012 compared to 51 percent who voted for Democrats in 1988–2004 presidential election. These figures were calculated by multiplying the Democratic proportion of the two-party black turnout by the proportion of African Americans who voted.

12. Unlike other racial and ethnic group, the exit polls first reported Asian American vote shares in 1992.

13. President Clinton registered a 74 percent approval rating in the 1993–94 National Black Politics Study of 1,206 African Americans fielded from December 4, 1993, to February 13, 1994; he registered a 70 percent approval rating in *Time*/CNN's national survey of 503 African Americans fielded on February 16–17, 1994, and obtained a 71 percent approval rating in Gallup/CNN/*USA Today*'s national survey of 400 African Americans fielded on August 23–24, 1994.

14. These observations are based on Gallup polls conducted during the first two years of Bill Clinton's term in office, which can also be found in figure A8.1 of this book's online appendix.

15. That figure is based on a spreadsheet that Gallup had previously made publically available at http://www.gallup.com/strategicconsulting/172292/obama -weekly-job-approval.aspx. Those data, however, now require a subscription to Gallup Analytics to access.

16. Racial group thermometer ratings are an imperfect measure of racial group identification, and it would be preferable to test this hypothesis with other measures such as linked fate or racial identity items. However, this analysis derives its power by comparing measures over time in pooled ANES studies, which included a sufficient number of African Americans in the 1994–2000 analysis ($N \approx 700$). And the black thermometer is the only measure of racial group identification that allows for such over-time comparisons.

17. The scale was truncated in the display to begin at 0–50 because so few

African Americans rate their own group unfavorably. The results are even more pronounced when using the full scale.

18. The effect of the black thermometer was significantly stronger ($p < .05$) in 2012, too.

19. The coefficient for the black thermometer rating on African Americans' thermometer ratings of Bill Clinton from 1992–2000 ANES was .03, with a standard error of .047. The coefficient for the black-thermometer rating on African Americans' thermometer ratings of Barack Obama in the 2012 ANES was .264, with a standard error of .068—a significant difference in effects.

20. This is based on both ANES and Gallup surveys. Gallup surveys were accessed from the Roper Center. For more on Clinton's Gallup approval rating by race, see fig. A8.1 in the online appendix.

21. The small number of African American respondents in each experimental condition did not produce significant differences in black support between groups in the CCAP reinterviews.

22. These surveys were found by searching the iPOLL databank under the topic of health for "Clinton" and "support" of "favor." All datasets were then accessed from the Roper Center's data archive.

23. The CNN results are based on analyses of datasets accessed from the Roper Center's data archive. The *Economist* and *Public Policy Poling* publish all their results by race and *Rasmussen* does so for their premium members. These results were accessed from Pollster.com's link to every survey on health care reform since 2009: http://www.pollster.com/polls/us/healthplan.php.

24. Following Hajnal and Lee's (2011) analysis of black partisanship, fig. 8.6 excludes Democratic-leaning Independents from the analysis.

25. African Americans placed the Democratic presidential nominee about 1.5 points higher, on average, than his Republican opponent on this seven-category measure between 1988 and 2004. In the 2012 ANES, though, African American respondents rated Barack Obama 2.6 points higher than Mitt Romney on the aid to blacks scale.

26. Quoted in http://www.pbs.org/newshour/rundown/pollster-democrats -should-bait-gop-on-latino-issues/.

27. Survey by Cable News Network. Survey conducted by Opinion Research Corporation (ORC) International, September 25 to October 1, 2012, and based on 601 telephone interviews. Sample was national adult Hispanics. Results accessed from the iPOLL databank.

28. That percentage, however, is based on only sixty-seven Latino respondents in the following survey: Cable News Network, *USA Today*. Methodology conducted by Gallup Organization, August 4–5, 2000, and based on 1,051 telephone interviews. Raw data accessed from the Roper Center's data archive.

29. For these polling results, see http://www.latinodecisions.com/blog/2012/10 /08/republicans-fail-to-increase-their-image-among-latinos-but-have-opportunity -on-education/.

30. For more on this poll result, see http://www.latinodecisions.com/blog/2010/02/22/latinos-are-less-welcomed/.

31. This percentage is based on 376 Latinos in the following survey: Pew Research Center, National Public Radio. Survey conducted by Princeton Survey Research Associates International, October 28 to November 30, 2009, and based on 2,884 telephone interviews. Raw data accessed from the Roper Center's data archive.

32. This percentage is based on forty-three Latinos in the survey from ABC News/*Washington Post*, April 22–25, 2010, and is based on 1,001 telephone interviews. Raw data accessed from the Roper Center's data archive.

33. For more on this polling, see http://www.latinodecisions.com/blog/2014/06/04/new-poll-gop-actions-on-immigration-reform-key-to-their-futur/.

34. Aaron Blake further suggested in his *Washington Post* column that Cantor's loss would make Republicans even more reticent to move on immigration: "Expect Cantor's loss to sufficiently scare other Republicans away from taking any similar risks in their own careers." For more speculation that Eric Cantor's position on immigration hurt him in his primary loss, see http://www.washingtonpost.com/blogs/the-fix/wp/2014/06/11/yes-immigration-reform-hurt-eric-cantor/; http://blogs.rollcall.com/218/eric-cantor-defeat-immigration-reform-2014/?dcz=; http://www.nbcnews.com/politics/first-read/eric-cantor-casualty-immigration-reform-n128006; and http://www.nationalreview.com/corner/380089/illegal-immigration-and-eric-cantor-victor-davis-hanson. For an alternative perspective, see http://www.latinodecisions.com/blog/2014/06/12/why-eric-cantor-really-lost-and-what-it-means-for-gop-outreach-to-latinos/.

Chapter 9

1. Hillary Clinton made these comments in response to the unrest in Ferguson, Missouri, after an unarmed African American teenager, Michael Brown, was shot and killed by the police. For video of Clinton's statement, see http://abcnews.go.com/US/video/hillary-clinton-breaks-silences-ferguson-shooting-25168634.

2. In March 2015, the Justice Department issued a scathing report documenting how the Ferguson Police Department and municipal courts routinely discriminated against African Americans, burdening them with excessive use of force, jail terms, traffic stops, and fines. They also presented evidence suggesting that the police department's leadership perpetuated a culture of "explicit racial bias." For the full report, see http://www.justice.gov/sites/default/files/opa/press-releases/attachments/2015/03/04/ferguson_police_department_report.pdf.

3. See, e.g., http://www.politico.com/story/2014/08/ferguson-critics-police-militarization-110017.html; http://www.cnn.com/2014/08/14/us/missouri-ferguson-police-tactics/; and http://www.usnews.com/news/articles/2014/08/14/ferguson-and-the-shocking-nature-of-us-police-militarization.

4. For more on these protests, see http://www.economist.com/news/united-states/21635007-rioting-one-run-down-suburb-st-louis-shows-enduring-rift-between-blacks-and.

5. For the full trend in the percentage of Gallup respondents mentioning racism/race relations as the country's most important problem from 1948 through the end of 2014, see http://www.gallup.com/poll/180257/major-problem-race-relations-sharply-rises.aspx.

6. For trends in this NBC/*Wall Street Journal* poll item since the 1990s, see http://blogs.wsj.com/washwire/2014/12/17/poll-views-of-race-relations-worse-than-before-obama-took-office/.

7. For more on the Fox News poll, see http://video.foxnews.com/v/3964331797001/fox-news-poll—voters-say-race-relations-worse-under-obama/?#sp=show-clips. For more on the Bloomberg News poll, see http://www.bloomberg.com/politics/articles/2014-12-07/bloomberg-politics-poll-finds-most-americans-see-race-relations-worsening-since-obamas-election.

8. Quoted in Ezra Klein, "Why Obama Won't Give the Ferguson Speech His Supporters Want," August 18, 2014, http://www.vox.com/2014/8/18/6031197/obama-ferguson-race-speech.

9. Unlike the partisan reactions to the George Zimmerman and O. J. Simpson acquittals shown back in fig. I.1, this display uses all partisans rather than just white partisans because the Sterling results and the *12 Years a Slave* percentages were reported only by party. The Zimmerman and Ferguson stats, which were reported by both race and party, show that white Democrats and white Republicans were similarly divided in their responses to these two incidents.

10. There was a similarly large divide between Democrats and Republicans in their responses to Freddie Gray's death while in custody of the Baltimore Police Department. That racially charged incident, which occurred in April 2015 after the final version of this manuscript was submitted for publication, sparked prolonged racial unrest in Baltimore's streets. For results showing the large partisan differences in reaction to these events, see http://cdn.yougov.com/cumulus_uploads/document/6rg3753g54/tabs_OPI_freddie_gray_20150430.pdf.

11. Based on analyses of the following survey. CBS News/*New York Times*, May 6–8, 1992, national adult survey with 1,253 telephone interviews. The sample included an oversample of blacks weighted to reflect their actual percentage of the population. Data accessed from the Roper Center's data archive.

12. Of the 303 African Americans in the survey by Cable News Network, 84 percent said the Jena Six were treated unfairly compared to 34 percent of whites. Survey conducted by Opinion Research Corporation, October 12–14, 2007, and based on 1,212 telephone interviews. Sample was national adult, including an oversample of blacks.

13. According to these data, white Democrats were only twelve percentage points more likely than white Republicans to say that the Jena Six were treated unfairly.

14. This figure averages the results of similarly worded poll questions in the following surveys: (1) Cable News Network: survey was conducted by the Opinion Research Corporation on January 11, 2007, and based on 1,093 telephone interviews; and (2) *USA Today*: survey conducted by the Gallup Organization, April 28–30, 2006, and based on 1,011 telephone interviews. Both surveys were accessed from the Roper Center's data archive.

15. In fact, comedian Bill Maher even coined his own colorful term to describe the ubiquity of this phenomenon: "Blacktrack (verb): The act of changing one's mind because President Obama has agreed with you." For more on this term, see http://www.mediaite.com/tv/bill-maher-coins-new-term-to-describe-gopers-who -switch-positions-to-oppose-obama/.

16. After controlling for party and ideology, moving from least to most racially resentful increased white opposition to welfare spending by nearly seventy percentage points for both those who were randomly assigned to view the ad and for those who were assigned to the control group. See online appendix for full results.

17. The 2010–12 CCES panel study shows that racial resentment had almost identically strong effects on opposition to the ACA in both of those massive surveys (N = 15,360 white panelists in the analysis). After controlling for party and ideology, moving from least to most racially resentful (as measured in 2010) increased white panelists' probability of opposing the ACA by sixty percentage points in both the 2010 and 2012 panel waves.

18. Like the results referenced in the previous note, moving from least to most racially resentful increased white respondents' probability of voting against the ACA (if they were in Congress in 2010) by nearly sixty percentage points after controlling for party and ideology in the 2014 CCES.

19. That conclusion is based on results from the 2012 CCES, Brown University module. This survey included an experiment in which half the respondents were randomly told that Marco Rubio was considered as a vice presidential nominee for the Republican Party. Consistent with expectations the marginally significant effect of Hispanic favorability ratings ($p < .10$) on rating Rubio favorably in the baseline condition was reduced down to zero when respondents were told that he was a prominent Republican.

20. Bill Clinton concurred with his wife's 2015 comments and criticized his own crime policies for putting too many African Americans in prison. For more on Hillary and Bill Clinton's statements about the discriminatory impact of crime policies, see http://www.cnn.com/2015/05/06/politics/bill-clinton-crime-prisons -hillary-clinton/index.html; http://www.politico.com/story/2015/04/hillary-clintons -criminal-justice-plan-reverse-bills-policies-117488.html; and http://nypost.com /2015/04/29/hillary-criticizes-policies-enacted-during-bills-presidency/.

References

Abelson, Robert P. 1968. *Theories of Cognitive Consistency: A Sourcebook*. Skokie, IL: Rand McNally.

Abramowitz, Alan I. 1988. "An Improved Model for Predicting Presidential Election Outcomes." *PS: Political Science & Politics* 21 (4): 843–47.

———. 2010. *The Disappearing Center: Engaged Citizens, Polarization, and American Democracy*. New Haven: Yale University Press.

———. 2011. "The Race Factor: White Racial Attitudes and Opinions of Obama." *Sabato's Crystal Ball*. http://www.centerforpolitics.org/crystalball/articles/AIA2011051201/.

———. 2013. "Partisan Nation: The Rise of Affective Partisan Polarization in the American Electorate." Unpublished manuscript.

———. 2014. "How Race and Religion Have Polarized American Voters." *Monkey Cage*. http://www.washingtonpost.com/blogs/monkey-cage/wp/2014/01/20/how-race-and-religion-have-polarized-american-voters/.

———. 2008. "Forecasting the 2008 Presidential Election with the Time-for-Change Model." *PS: Political Science and Politics* 41 (4): 691–95.

Abramson, Paul R., John H. Aldrich, and David W. Rohde. 2011. *Change and Continuity in the 2008 and 2010 Elections*. Washington, DC: Congressional Quarterly Press.

Acharya, Avidit, Matthew Blackwell, and Maya Sen. 2014. "The Political Legacy of American Slavery." Unpublished manuscript.

Adams, Greg D. 1997. "Abortion: Evidence of an Issue Evolution." *American Journal of Political Science* 41:718–37.

Aldrich, John H., Bradford H. Bishop, Rebecca S. Hatch, D. Sunshine Hillygus, and David W. Rohde. 2014. "Blame, Responsibility, and the Tea Party in the 2010 Midterm Elections." *Political Behavior* 36 (3): 471–91.

Alford, John R., Peter K. Hatemi, John R. Hibbing, Nicholas G. Martin, and Lindon J. Eaves. "The Politics of Mate Choice." *Journal of Politics* 73: 362–79.

Alter, Jonathan. 2013. *The Center Holds: Obama and His Enemies*. New York: Simon and Schuster.

Ambinder, Marc. 2009. "Race Over?" *Atlantic*, January–February. http://www
.theatlantic.com/magazine/archive/2009/01/race-over/307215/.

Ansolabehere, Stephen D., and Bernard L. Fraga. 2014. "Just a Matter of Party?
The Impact of Race on House Incumbent Evaluations." Unpublished manuscript.

Ansolabehere, Stephen, and Douglas Rivers. 2013. "Cooperative Survey Research." *Annual Review of Political Science* 16: 307–29.

Atkinson, Matthew D. 2012. "Political Alignments in America." Ph.D. diss., UCLA.

———. 2013. "The Bigger Sort: Partisanship, Residential Choice, and Political Polarization." Unpublished manuscript.

Bafumi, Joseph, and Christina M. Greer. 2014. "President Obama and the Intensi-
fication of Black Threat from 2008 to 2012." http://papers.ssrn.com/sol3/papers
.cfm?abstract_id=2409226.

Banks, Antoine J. 2014. *Anger and Racial Politics: The Emotional Foundation of
Racial Attitudes in America*. Cambridge: Cambridge University Press.

Banks, Antoine J., and Nicholas A. Valentino. 2012. "Emotional Substrates of
White Racial Attitudes." *American Journal of Political Science* 56 (2): 286–97.

Baron, Reuben M., and David A. Kenny. 1986. "The Moderator-Mediator Variable
Distinction in Social Psychological Research: Conceptual, Strategic, and Statistical Considerations." *Journal of Personality and Social Psychology* 51: 1173–82.

Barreto, Matt A. 2010. *Ethnic Cues: The Role of Shared Ethnicity in Latino Political
Participation*. Ann Arbor: University of Michigan Press.

Barreto, Matt A., Luis R. Fraga, Sylvia Manzano, Valerie Martinez-Ebers, and
Gary M. Segura. 2008. "'Should They Dance with the One Who Brung 'Em?'
Latinos and the 2008 Presidential Election." *PS: Political Science and Politics*
61 (4): 753–61.

Barreto, Matt A., and Ricardo Ramirez. 2013. "Anti-Immigrant Politics and
Lessons for the GOP from California." *Latino Decisions Blog*. http://www
.latinodecisions.com/blog/2013/09/20/anti-immigrant-politics-and-lessons-for
-the-gop-from-california/.

Bartels, Larry. M. 2000. "Partisanship and Voting Behavior, 1952–1996." *American
Journal of Political Science* 44 (1): 35–50.

———. 2002. "Beyond the Running Tally: Partisan Bias in Political Perceptions."
Political Behavior 24 (2): 117–50.

———. 2006. "Three Virtues of Panel Data for the Analysis of Campaign Effects."
In *Capturing Campaign Effects*, edited by Henry E. Brady and Richard Johnston, 134–63. Ann Arbor: University of Michigan Press.

———. 2008. *Unequal Democracy: The Political Economy of the New Gilded Age*.
New York: Russell Sage Foundation.

———. 2012. "Our Own Facts." *Model Politics*. http://today.yougov.com/news/2012
/03/12/our-own-facts/.

———. 2013. "Obama Toes the Line." *Monkey Cage*. http://themonkeycage.org
/2013/01/08/obama-toes-the-line/.

———. 2014. "Can the Republican Party Thrive on White Identity?" *Monkey Cage*. http://www.washingtonpost.com/blogs/monkey-cage/wp/2014/04/16/can-the-republican-party-thrive-on-white-identity/.

Baum, Matthew A., and Tim J. Groeling. 2009. *War Stories: The Causes and Consequences of Public Views of War*. Princeton: Princeton University Press.

Berinsky, Adam J. 2007. "Assuming the Costs of War: Events, Elites, and American Public Support for Military Conflict." *Journal of Politics* 69 (4): 975–97.

———. 2009. *In Time of War: Understanding American Public Opinion from World War II to Iraq*. Chicago: University of Chicago Press.

———. 2012. "The Birthers Are Back." *Model Politics*. http://today.yougov.com/news/2012/02/03/birthers-are-back/.

———. 2015. "Rumors and Health Care Reform: Experiments in Political Misinformation." *British Journal of Political Science*, June 19. http://dx.doi.org/10.1017/S0007123415000186.

Bishop, Bill. 2009. *The Big Sort: Why the Clustering of Like-Minded America Is Tearing Us Apart*. Boston: Houghton Mifflin Harcourt.

Blumenthal, David, and James A. Morone. 2010. *The Heart of Power: Health and Politics in the Oval Office*. Berkeley: University of California Press.

Bobo, Lawrence. 2000. "Race and Beliefs about Affirmative Action: Assessing the Effects of Interests, Group Threat, Ideology, and Racism." In *Racialized Politics: The Debate about Racism in America*, edited by David O. Sears, Jim Sidanius, and Lawrence Bobo, 137–64. Chicago: University of Chicago Press.

Bobo, Lawrence, and James R. Kluegel. 1993. "Opposition to Race-Targeting: Self-Interest, Stratification Ideology, or Racial Attitudes?" *American Sociological Review* 58: 443–64.

———. 1997. "Status, Ideology, and Dimensions of Whites' Racial Beliefs and Attitudes: Progress and Stagnation." In *Racial Attitudes in the 1990s: Continuity and Change*, edited by Steven A. Tuch and Jack K. Martin, 93–120. Westport: Praeger.

Bobo, Lawrence, James R. Kluegel, and Ryan A. Smith. 1997. "Laissez Faire Racism: The Crystallization of a 'Kinder, Gentler' Anti-Black Ideology." In *Racial Attitudes in the 1990s: Continuity and Change*, edited by Steven A. Tuch and Jack K. Martin, 93–120. Westport: Praeger.

Bowler, Shaun, Stephen P. Nicholson, and Gary M. Segura. 2006. "Earthquakes and Aftershocks: Race, Direct Democracy, and Partisan Change." *American Journal of Political Science* 50 (1): 146–59.

Bowler, Shaun, and Gary Segura. 2012. *The Future Is Ours: Minority Politics, Political Behavior, and the Multiracial Era of American Politics*. Washington, DC: CQ Press.

Brady, David W., Morris P. Fiorina, and Arjun S. Wilkins. 2011. "The 2010 Elections: Why Did Political Science Forecasts Go Awry?" *PS: Political Science & Politics* 44 (2): 247–50.

Brewer, Mark D., and Jeffrey M. Stonecash. 2007. *Split: Class and Cultural Divides in American Politics*. Washington, DC: CQ Press.

Brody, Richard A. 1991. *Assessing the President: The Media, Elite Opinion, and Public Support*. Stanford: Stanford University Press.

Brownstein, Ronald. 2013. "Bad Bet: Why the Republicans Can't Win with Whites Alone." *National Journal*, September 5. http://www.nationaljournal.com /magazine/bad-bet-why-republicans-can-t-win-with-whites-alone-20130905.

———. 2015. "White-Out: Where Democrats Lost the House." *National Journal*, January 13. http://www.nationaljournal.com/next-america/newsdesk/white-out -where-democrats-lost-the-house-20150113.

Bullock, John G., Alan S. Gerber, Seth J. Hill, and Gregory A. Huber. 2013. "Partisan Bias in Factual Beliefs about Politics." Working Paper No. 19080, National Bureau of Economic Research, Cambridge.

Campbell, Angus, Philip E. Converse, Warren E. Miller, and Donald Stokes. 1960. *The American Voter*. Chicago: University of Chicago Press.

Campbell, James E. 2010a. "Forecasts of the 2010 Midterm Elections." 2010. *PS: Political Science & Politics* 43 (4): 625–26.

Campbell, James E. 2010b. "The Seats in Trouble Forecast of the 2010 Elections to the US House." *PS: Political Science & Politics* 43 (4): 627–30.

Carmines, Edward G., Paul M. Sniderman, and Beth C. Easter. 2011. "On the Meaning, Measurement, and Implications of Racial Resentment." *Annals of the American Academy of Political and Social Science* 634 (1): 98–116.

Carmines, Edward G., and James A. Stimson. 1980. "The Two Faces of Issue Voting." *American Political Science Review* 74 (1): 78–91.

———. 1989. *Issue Evolution: Race and the Transformation of American Politics*. Princeton: Princeton University Press.

Chong, Dennis. 1991. *Collective Action and the Civil Rights Movement*. Chicago: University of Chicago Press.

Citrin, Jack, Donald Phillip Green, and David O. Sears. 1990. "White Reactions to Black Candidates: When Does Race Matter?" *Public Opinion Quarterly* 54 (1): 74–96.

Citrin, Jack, and David O. Sears. 2014. *American Identity and the Politics of Multiculturalism*. Cambridge: Cambridge University Press.

Coe, Kevin, and Michael Reitzes. 2010. "Obama on the Stump: Features and Determinants of a Rhetorical Approach." *Presidential Studies Quarterly* 40 (3): 391–413.

Coe, Kevin, and Anthony Schmidt. 2012. "America in Black and White: Locating Race in the Modern Presidency, 1933–2011." *Journal of Communication* 62 (4): 609–27.

Cohen, Geoffrey L. 2003. "Party over Policy." *Journal of Personality and Social Psychology* 85 (5): 808–22.

Collingwood, Loren, Matt A. Barreto, and Sergio I. Garcia-Rios. 2014. "Revisiting

Latino Voting: Cross-Racial Mobilization in the 2012 Election." *Political Research Quarterly* 67 (3): 632–45. doi:10.117/1065912914532374.

Converse, Philip E. 1964. "The Nature of Belief Systems in Mass Publics." In *Ideology and Discontent*, edited by D. E. Apter, 206–61. New York: Free Press.

Converse, Phillip E., Angus Campbell, Warren E. Miller, and Donald E. Stokes. 1961. "Stability and Change in the 1960: A Reinstating Election." *American Political Science Review* 55: 269–80.

Converse, Philip E., and Gregory Markus. 1979. "Plus ça change . . . : The New CPS Panel Study." *American Political Science Review* 73: 32–49.

Craig, Maureen A., and Jennifer A. Richeson. 2014a. "More Diverse Yet Less Tolerant? How the Increasingly Diverse Racial Landscape Affects White Americans' Racial Attitudes." *Personality and Social Psychology Bulletin* 40: 750–61. doi:10.17177/0146167214524993.

Craig, Maureen A., and Jennifer A. Richeson. 2014b. "On the Precipice of a 'Majority-Minority' America Perceived Status Threat from the Racial Demographic Shift Affects White Americans' Political Ideology." *Psychological Science* 25 (6): 1189–97.

Crist, Charlie. 2014. *The Party's Over: How the Extreme Right Hijacked the GOP and I Became a Democrat*. New York: Penguin.

Dawson, Michael. 1994. *Behind the Mule: Race and Class in African American Politics*. Princeton: Princeton University Press.

———. 2001. *Black Visions: The Roots of Contemporary African American Political Ideologies*. Chicago: University of Chicago Press.

DeSante, Christopher D. 2013. "Working Twice as Hard to Get Half as Far: Race, Work Ethic, and America's Deserving Poor." *American Journal of Political Science* 57 (2): 342–56.

DeSante, Christopher D., and Candis Watts Smith. 2012. "New Attitudes or Old Measures?" Unpublished manuscript.

DeSipio, Louis. 1996. *Counting on the Latino Vote: Latinos as a New Electorate*. Charlottesville: University of Virginia Press.

Ditonto, Tessa M., Richard R. Lau, and David O. Sears. 2013. "AMPing Racial Attitudes: Comparing the Power of Explicit and Implicit Racism Measures in 2008." *Political Psychology* 34 (4): 487–510.

Ditto, Peter H., and David F. Lopez. 1992. "Motivated Skepticism: Use of Differential Decision Criteria for Preferred and Nonpreferred Conclusions." *Journal of Personality and Social Psychology* 63 (4): 568–84.

Domke, David. N.d. "Elite Messages: The Role of Race as a Source Cue." Unpublished manuscript.

Dovidio, John F., Kerry Kawakami, and Samuel L. Gaertner. 2002. "Implicit and Explicit Prejudice and Interracial Interaction." *Journal of Personality and Social Psychology* 82 (1): 62–68.

Dovidio, John F., Kerry Kawakami, Craig Johnson, Brenda Johnson, and Adaiah

Howard. 1997. "On the Nature of Prejudice: Automatic and Controlled Processes." *Journal of Experimental Social Psychology* 33 (5): 510–40.

Druckman, James N. 2013. "The Politics of Motivation." *Critical Review* 24 (2): 199–216.

Druckman, James N., Cari Lynn Hennessy, Kristi St. Charles, and Jonathan Weber. 2010. "Competing Rhetoric over Time: Frames versus Cues." *Journal of Politics* 72 (1): 136–48.

Dudziak, Mary L. 2011. *Cold War Civil Rights: Race and the Image of American Democracy*. Princeton: Princeton University Press.

Edsall, Thomas B. 2006. *Building Red America: The New Conservative Coalition and the Drive for Permanent Power*. New York: Basic Books.

———. 2013. "Should the Republican Party Just Focus on White Voters?" *New York Times*, op-ed, July 3.

Edsall, Thomas B., and Mary D. Edsall. 1992. *Chain Reaction: The Impact of Race Rights and Taxes on American Politics*. New York: Norton.

Enos, Ryan D. 2014. "Causal Effect of Intergroup Contact on Exclusionary Attitudes." *Proceedings of the National Academy of Sciences* 111 (10): 3699–704.

———. 2015. "What Tearing Down Public Housing Projects Teaches Us about the Effect of Racial Threat on Political Participation." *American Journal of Political Science* 59. doi:10.1111/ajps.12156.

Erikson, Robert S., Michael B. MacKuen, and James A. Stimson. 2002. *The Macro Polity*. New York: Cambridge University Press.

Erikson, Robert S., and Christopher Wlezien. 2012. *The Timeline of Presidential Elections: How Campaigns Do (and Do Not) Matter*. Chicago: University of Chicago Press.

Fazio, Russell H., Joni R. Jackson, Bridget C. Dunton, and Carol J. Williams. 1995. "Variability in Automatic Activation as an Unobtrusive Measure of Racial Attitudes: A Bona Fide Pipeline?" *Journal of Personality and Social Psychology* 69 (6): 1013.

Federico, Christopher M. 2004. "When Do Welfare Attitudes Become Racialized? The Paradoxical Effects of Education." *American Journal of Political Science* 48 (2): 374–91.

Festinger, Leon. 1957. *A Theory of Cognitive Dissonance*. Stanford: Stanford University Press.

File, Thom. 2013. "The Diversifying Electorate Voting Rates by Race and Hispanic Origin in 2012 and Other Recent Elections." Washington, DC: US Government Printing Office.

Filindra, Alexandra, and Noah Kaplan. 2014. "A Call to Arms: Racial Prejudice and White Opinion on Gun Control." Paper presented at the annual meeting of the American Political Science Association, Washington, DC, August.

Finkel, Steven E., Thomas M. Guterbock, and Marian J. Borg. 1991. "Race-of-Interviewer Effects in a Preelection Poll." *Public Opinion Quarterly* 55: 313–30.

Fiorina, Morris P. 1981. *Retrospective Voting in American National Elections*. New Haven: Yale University Press.

————. 2006. *Culture War? The Myth of a Polarized America*. New York: Pearson Longman.

Fiorina, Morris P., and Samuel J. Abrams. 2008. "Political Polarization in the American Public." *Annual Review of Political Science* 11:563–88.

Franklin, Charles H. 1989. "Estimation across Data Sets: Two-Stage Auxiliary Instrumental Variables Estimation (2SAIV)." *Political Analysis* 1 (1): 1–23.

Fredrickson, George M. 1971. *The Black Image in the White Mind: The Debate on Afro-Americans' Character and Destiny, 1817–1914*. New York: Harper and Row.

Frymer, Paul. 1999. *Uneasy Alliances: Race and Party Competition in America*. Princeton: Princeton University Press.

Gelman, Andrew. 2010. *Red State, Blue State, Rich State, Poor State: Why Americans Vote the Way They Do*. Princeton: Princeton University Press.

Gelman, Andrew, and Gary King. 1993. "Why Are American Presidential Election Campaign Polls So Variable When Votes Are So Predictable?" *British Journal of Political Science* 23: 409–51.

Gerstle, Gary. 2002. *American Crucible: Race and Nation in the Twentieth Century*. Princeton: Princeton University Press.

Gilens, Martin. 1999. *Why Americans Hate Welfare: Race, Media, and the Politics of Antipoverty Policy*. Chicago: University of Chicago Press.

Gilens, Martin, Paul M. Sniderman, and James H. Kuklinski. 1998. "Affirmative Action and the Politics of Realignment." *British Journal of Political Science* 28 (1): 159–83.

Gilliam, Frank, and Shanto Iyengar. 2000. "Prime Suspects: The Impact of Local Television News on Attitudes about Crime and Race." *American Journal of Political Science* 44: 560–73.

Gillion, Daniel Q. 2012. "The Paradox of Descriptive Representation in the Executive Office: Racial Rhetoric and Presidential Approval." Unpublished manuscript, University of Pennsylvania.

Glaser, James M. 1998. *Race, Campaign Politics, and the Realignment in the South*. New Haven: Yale University Press.

Goldman, Seth K. 2012. "Effects of the 2008 Obama Presidential Campaign on White Racial Prejudice." *Public Opinion Quarterly* 76 (4): 663–87.

Goldman, Seth K., and Diana C. Mutz. 2014. *The Obama Effect: How the 2008 Campaign Changed White Racial Attitudes*. New York: Russell Sage Foundation.

Goren, Paul. 2014. "Race-Coded Myths." Unpublished manuscript, University of Minnesota.

Green, Donald, Shang Ha, and John Bullock. 2010. "Enough Already about Black Box Experiments: Studying Mediation Is More Difficult Than Most Scholars Suppose." *Annals of the American Academy of Political and Social Science* 628: 200–208.

Green, Donald, Bradley Palmquist, and Eric Schickler. 2002. *Partisan Hearts and Minds*. New Haven: Yale University Press.

Greenwald, Anthony G., and Mahzarin R. Banaji. "Implicit Social Cognition: Attitudes, Self-Esteem, and Stereotypes." *Psychological Review* 102 (1): 4–27.

Greenwald, Anthony G., Colin Tucker Smith, N. Sriram, Yoav Bar-Anan, and Brian A. Nosek. 2009. "Implicit Race Attitudes Predicted Vote in the 2008 US Presidential Election." *Analyses of Social Issues and Public Policy* 9 (1): 241–53.

Gurin, Patricia, Shirley Hatchett, and James Jackson. 1989. *Hope and Independence: Blacks' Response to Electoral and Party Politics*. New York: Russell Sage Foundation.

Hajnal, Zoltan. L. 2007. *Changing White Attitudes toward Black Political Leadership*. Cambridge: Cambridge University Press.

Hajnal, Zoltan L., and Taeku Lee. 2011. *Why Americans Don't Join the Party: Race, Immigration, and the Failure (of Political Parties) to Engage the Electorate*. Princeton: Princeton University Press.

Harris-Lacewell, Melissa. 2004. *Barbershops, Bibles, and BET: Everyday Talk and Black Political Thought*. Princeton: Princeton University Press.

Henderson, Michael, and D. Sunshine Hillygus. 2011. "The Dynamics of Health Care Opinion, 2008–2010: Partisanship, Self-Interest and Racial Resentment." *Journal of Health Politics, Policy, and Law* 36 (6): 945–60.

Henry, P. J., and David O. Sears. 2002. "The Symbolic Racism 2000 scale." *Political Psychology* 23: 253–83.

———. 2009. "The Crystallization of Contemporary Racial Prejudice across the Lifespan." *Political Psychology* 30 (4): 569–90.

Hetherington, Marc J. 2001. "Resurgent Mass Partisanship: The Role of Elite Polarization." *American Political Science Association* 95 (3): 619–31.

Hetherington, Marc J., and Jonathan D. Weiler. 2009. *Authoritarianism and Polarization in American Politics*. Cambridge: Cambridge University Press.

Highton, Benjamin. 2011. "Prejudice Rivals Partisanship and Ideology When Explaining the 2008 Presidential Vote across the States." *PS: Political Science and Politics* 44 (3): 530–35.

Hill, Seth, James Lo, Lynn Vavreck, and John Zaller. 2007. "The Opt-In Internet Panel: Survey Mode, Sampling Methodology and the Implications for Political Research." Working paper, University of California, Los Angeles

Hillygus, D. Sunshine, and Simon Jackman. 2003. "Voter Decision Making in Election 2000: Campaign Effects, Partisan Activation, and the Clinton Legacy." *American Journal of Political Science* 47: 583–96.

Holbrook, Thomas M. 2008. "Economic Considerations and the 2008 Presidential Election." *PS: Political Science and Politics* 42 (3): 473–78.

Hopkins, Daniel. 2009. "No More Wilder Effect, Never a Whitman Effect: When and Why Polls Mislead about Black and Female Candidates." *Journal of Politics* 71: 769–81.

Hopkins, Daniel. 2010. "Politicized Places: Explaining Where and When Immigrants Provoke Local Opposition." *American Political Science Review* 104 (1): 40–60.

Howell, Susan E. 1994. "Racism, Cynicism, Economics, and David Duke." *American Politics Quarterly* 22: 190–207.

Huber, Gregory A., Seth J. Hill, and Gabriel S. Lenz. 2012. "Sources of Bias in Retrospective Decision Making: Experimental Evidence on Voters' Limitations in Controlling Incumbents." *American Political Science Review* 106 (4): 720–41.

Huber, Gregory A., and John Lapinski. 2006. "The 'Race Card' Revisited: Assessing Racial Priming in Policy Contests." *American Journal of Political Science* 50: 421–40.

———. 2008. "Testing the Implicit-Explicit Model of Racialized Political Communication." *Perspectives on Politics* 6 (1): 125–34.

Huckfeldt, Robert, and Carol W. Kohlfeld. 1989. *Race and the Decline of Class in American Politics*. Urbana: University of Illinois Press.

Huddy, Leonie, and Stanley Feldman. 2009. "On Assessing the Political Effects of Racial Prejudice." *Annual Review of Political Science* 12: 423–47.

Hughes, Michael. 1997. "Symbolic Racism, Old-Fashioned Racism, and Whites' Opposition to Affirmative Action." In *Racial Attitudes in the 1990s: Continuity and Change*, edited by Steven A. Tuch and Jack K. Martin, 45–75. Westport: Praeger.

Hurwitz, Jon, and Mark Peffley. 1997. "Public Perceptions of Race and Crime: The Role of Racial Stereotypes." *American Journal of Political Science* 41: 375–401.

———. 1998. "Introduction." In *Perception and Prejudice: Race and Politics in the United States*, edited by J. Hurwitz and M. Peffley, 1–16. New Haven: Yale University Press.

———. 2005. "Playing the Race Card in the Post–Willie Horton Era: The Impact of Racialized Code Words on Support for Punitive Crime Policy." *Public Opinion Quarterly* 69: 99–112.

Hutchings, Vincent L. 2009. "Change or More of the Same? Evaluating Racial Attitudes in the Obama Era." *Public Opinion Quarterly* 73 (5): 917–42.

Hutchings, Vincent L., and Nicholas A. Valentino. 2004. "The Centrality of Race in American Politics." *Annual Review of Political Science* 7: 383–408.

Iyengar, Shanto, Kyu Hahn, Christopher Dial, and Mahzarin R. Banaji. 2009. "Explicit and Implicit Attitudes: Black-White and Obama-McCain Comparisons." Prepared for presentation at the annual meeting of the International Society of Political Psychology, Dublin, July 15–18.

Iyengar, Shanto, and Donald Kinder. 1987. *News That Matters: Television and American Opinion*. Chicago: University of Chicago Press.

Iyengar, Shanto, Gaurav Sood, and Yphtach Lelkes. 2012. "Affect, Not Ideology a Social Identity Perspective on Polarization." *Public Opinion Quarterly* 76 (3): 405–31.

Iyengar, Shanto, and Sean J. Westwood. 2015. "Fear and Loathing across Party

Lines: New Evidence on Group Polarization." *American Journal of Political Science.* doi:10.1111/ajps.12152.

Jackman, Simon D., and Lynn Vavreck. 2009. *The 2007–2008 Cooperative Campaign Analysis Project (CCAP).* Palo Alto: YouGov/Polimetrix.

———. 2010. "Primary Politics: Race, Gender, and Age in the 2008 Democratic Primary." *Journal of Elections, Public Opinion and Parties* 20 (2): 153–86.

———. 2012. "How Does Obama Match-Up? Counterfactuals and the Role of Obama's Race in 2008." Unpublished manuscript.

Jacobson, Gary C. 2004. *The Politics of Congressional Elections.* 6th ed. New York: Pearson Longman.

———. 2007. *A Divider, Not a Uniter.* New York: Pearson Education.

———. 2011. "The Republican Resurgence in 2010." *Political Science Quarterly* 126 (1): 27–52.

———. 2013. "How the Economy and Partisanship Shaped the 2012 Presidential and Congressional Elections." *Political Science Quarterly* 128 (1): 1–38.

Jamieson, Kathleen Hall. 1993. *Dirty Politics: Deception, Distraction, and Democracy.* Oxford: Oxford University Press.

Johnston, Richard, Michael G. Hagen, and Kathleen Hall Jamieson. 2004. *The 2000 Presidential Election and the Foundations of Party Politics.* New York: Cambridge University Press.

Jones, Jeffrey M. 2010. "Avg. Midterm Vote Loss 36 Seats for Presidents below 50% Approval." http://www.gallup.com/poll/141812/avg-midterm-seat-loss-presidents-below-approval.aspx.

———. 2014. "U.S. Whites More Solidly Republican in Recent Years: Party Preferences More Polarized by Race and Ethnicity under Obama." http://www.gallup.com/poll/168059/whites-solidly-republican-recent-years.aspx.

Judis, John B., and Ruy Teixeira. 2004. *The Emerging Democratic Majority.* New York: Simon and Schuster.

Kalkan, Kerem Ozan, Geoffrey C. Layman, and Eric M. Uslaner. 2009. "'Bands of Others?' Attitudes toward Muslims in Contemporary American Society." *Journal of Politics* 71: 847–62.

Kalmoe, Nathan P., and Spencer Piston. 2013. "Is Implicit Prejudice against Blacks Politically Consequential: Evidence from the AMP." *Public Opinion Quarterly* 77 (1): 305–22.

Kam, Cindy D., and Donald R. Kinder. 2007. "Terror and Ethnocentrism: Foundations of American Support for the War on Terrorism." *Journal of Politics* 69 (2): 320–38.

———. 2012. "Ethnocentrism as a Short-Term Force in the 2008 American Presidential Election." *American Journal of Political Science* 56 (2): 326–40.

Kaufmann, Karen M., and John R. Petrocik. 1999. "The Changing Politics of American Men: Understanding the Sources of the Gender Gap." *American Journal of Political Science* 43: 864–87.

Kellstedt, Paul M. 2003. *The Mass Media and the Dynamics of American Racial Attitudes*. Cambridge: Cambridge University Press.

Kenski, Kate, Bruce W. Hardy, and Kathleen Hall Jamieson. 2010. *The Obama Victory: How Media, Money, and Message Shaped the 2008 Election*. Oxford: Oxford University Press.

Kenski, Kate, and Daniel Romer. 2006. "Analyses of Panel Data." In *Capturing Campaign Dynamics 2000 and 2004*, edited by D. Romer, K. Kenski, K. Winneg, C. Adasiewicz, and K. H. Jamieson, 150–64. Philadelphia: University of Pennsylvania Press.

Kinder, Donald R. 1998. "Opinion and Action in the Realm of Politics." In *Handbook of Social Psychology*, edited by Daniel T. Gilbert, Susan T. Fiske, and Gardner Lindzey, 778–867. Oxford: Oxford University Press

———. 2003. "Communication and Politics in the Age of Information." In *Oxford Handbook of Political Psychology*, edited by David O. Sears, Leonie Huddy, and Robert Jervis, 357–93. Oxford: Oxford University Press.

———. 2013. "Prejudice and Politics." In *Oxford Handbook of Political Psychology*, 2nd ed., edited by Leonie Huddy, David O. Sears, and Jack S. Levy, 812–51. Oxford: Oxford University Press

Kinder, Donald R., and Jennifer Chudy. 2014. "Accommodation or Backlash? Obama's Rise to Power and American Attitudes on Race." Paper presented at the annual meeting of the American Political Science Association, Washington, DC, August.

Kinder, Donald R., and Allison Dale-Riddle. 2012. *The End of Race?* New Haven: Yale University Press.

Kinder, Donald R., and Katherine W. Drake. 2009. "Myrdal's Prediction." *Political Psychology* 30 (4): 539–68.

Kinder, Donald R., and Cindy D. Kam. 2009. *Us against Them: Ethnocentric Foundations of American Opinion*. Chicago: University of Chicago Press.

Kinder, Donald R., and D. Roderick Kiewiet. 1981. "Sociotropic Politics: The American Case." *British Journal of Political Science* 11 (2): 129–61.

Kinder, Donald R., and Corrine M. McConnaughy. 2006. "Military Triumph, Racial Transcendence, and Colin Powell." *Public Opinion Quarterly* 70 (2): 139–65.

Kinder, Donald R., and Timothy J. Ryan. 2012. "Prejudice and Politics Re-Examined: The Political Significance of Implicit Racial Bias." Paper prepared for the annual meeting of the American Political Science Association, New Orleans, August.

Kinder, Donald R., and Lynn M. Sanders. 1996. *Divided by Color: Racial Politics and Democratic Ideals*. Chicago: University of Chicago Press.

Kinder, Donald R., and David O. Sears. 1981. "Prejudice and Politics: Symbolic Racism Versus Racial Threats to the Good Life." *Journal of Personality and Social Psychology* 40 (3): 414–31.

Kinder, Donald, and Nicholas Winter. 2001. "Exploring the Racial Divide: Blacks,

Whites, and Opinion on National Policy." *American Journal of Political Science* 45: 439–56.

King, Desmond S., and Rogers M. Smith. 2011. *Still a House Divided: Race and Politics in Obama's America*. Princeton: Princeton University Press.

———. 2014. "Without Regard to Race": Critical Ideational Development in Modern American Politics." *Journal of Politics* 76 (4): 958–71.

Klinkner, Philip A., and Rogers M. Smith. 2002. *The Unsteady March: The Rise and Decline of Racial Equality in America*. Chicago: University of Chicago Press.

Knowles, Eric. D., Brian Lowery, and Rebecca L Schaumberg. 2010. "Racial Prejudice Predicts Opposition to Obama and His Health Care Reform Plan." *Journal of Experimental Social Psychology* 46: 420–23.

Kramer, Gerald H. 1971. "Short-Term Fluctuations in US Voting Behavior, 1896–1964." *American Political Science Review* 65 (1): 131–43.

Kriner, Douglas L., and Andrew Reeves. 2014. "Responsive Partisanship: Public Support for the Clinton and Obama Health Care Plans." *Journal of Health Politics, Policy and Law* 39 (4): 717–49.

Krugman, Paul. 2009. "Town Hall Mob." *New York Times*, August 6.

Kuklinski, James H., and Norman L. Hurley. 1994. "On Hearing and Interpreting Political Messages: A Cautionary Tale of Citizen Cue-Taking." *Journal of Politics* 56: 729–51.

Kunda, Ziva. 1987. "Motivated Inference: Self-Serving Generation and Evaluation of Causal Theories." *Journal of Personality and Social Psychology* 53 (4): 636–47.

———. 1990. "The Case for Motivated Reasoning." *Psychological Bulletin* 108 (3): 480.

Kuo, Alexander, Neil A. Malhotra, and Cecilia Hyunjung Mo. 2014. "Why Do Asian Americans Identify as Democrats? Testing Theories of Social Exclusion and Intergroup Solidarity." Unpublished manuscript, Vanderbilt University.

Kuziemko, Iylana, and Ebonya Washington. 2015. "Why Did the Democrats Lose the South? Using New Data to Resolve an Old Debate." Paper presented at the annual meeting of the Center for the Study of American Politics, Yale University, June 9.

Lavine, Howard G., Christopher D. Johnston, and Marco R. Steenbergen. 2012. *The Ambivalent Partisan: How Critical Loyalty Promotes Democracy*. Oxford: Oxford University Press.

Layman, Geoffrey C. 2001. *The Great Divide: Religious and Cultural Conflict in American Party Politics*. New York: Columbia University Press.

Layman, Geoffrey C., and Thomas M. Carsey. 2002. "Party Polarization and 'Conflict Extension' in the American Electorate." *American Journal of Political Science* 46 (4): 786–802.

Lee, Taeku. 2002. *Mobilizing Public Opinion: Black Insurgency and Racial Attitudes in the Civil Rights Era*. Chicago: University of Chicago Press.

Leege, David C., Kenneth D. Wald, Brian S. Krueger, and Paul D. Mueller. 2002.

The Politics of Cultural Differences: Social Change and Voter Mobilization Strategies in the Post–New Deal Period. Princeton: Princeton University Press.

Lenz, Gabriel S. 2009. "Learning and Opinion Change, Not Priming: Reconsidering the Evidence for the Priming Hypothesis." *American Journal of Political Science* 53: 821–37.

———. 2012. *Follow the Leader? How Voters' Respond to Politicians' Policies and Performance.* Chicago: Chicago University Press.

Levendusky, Matthew. 2009. *The Partisan Sort: How Liberals Became Democrats and Conservatives Became Republicans.* Chicago: University of Chicago Press.

Lewis-Beck, Michael S., William Jacoby, Helmut Norpoth, and Herbert Weisberg. 2009. *The American Voter Revisited.* Ann Arbor: University of Michigan Press.

Lewis-Beck, Michael S., Charles Tien, and Richard Nadeau. 2010. "Obama's Missed Landslide: A Racial Cost?" *PS: Political Science and Politics* 43 (1): 69–76.

Lien, Pei-Te, M. Margaret Conway, and Janelle Wong. 2004. *The Politics of Asian Americans.* New York: Routledge.

Lodge, Milton, and Charles Taber. 2013. *The Rationalizing Voter.* Cambridge: Cambridge University Press.

Lopez, Ian Haney. 2014. *Dog Whistle Politics: How Coded Racial Appeals Have Reinvented Racism and Wrecked the Middle Class.* Oxford: Oxford University Press.

Luks, Samantha, and Laurel Elms. 2005. "African American Partisanship and the Legacy of the Civil Rights Movement: Generational, Regional, and Economic Influences on Democratic Identification, 1973–1994." *Political Psychology* 26: 735–54.

Lupia, Arthur, and Mathew D. McCubbins. 1998. *The Democratic Dilemma: Can Citizens Learn What They Really Need to Know?* New York: Cambridge University Press.

Malhotra, Neil, and Jon A. Krosnick. 2007. "The Effect of Survey Mode and Sampling on Inferences about Political Attitudes and Behavior: Comparing the 2000 and 2004 ANES to Internet Surveys with Nonprobability Samples." *Political Analysis* 15 (3): 286–323.

Mann, Thomas E., and Norman J. Ornstein. 2012. *It's Even Worse Than It Looks: How the American Constitutional System Collided with the New Politics of Extremism.* New York: Basic Books.

Masuoka, Natalie, and Jane Junn. 2013. *The Politics of Belonging: Race, Public Opinion, and Immigration.* Chicago: University of Chicago Press.

Mayer, Jeremy D. 2002. *Running on Race: Racial Politics in Presidential Campaigns, 1960–2000.* New York: Random House.

McCarty, Nolan, Keith T. Poole, and Howard Rosenthal. 2006. *Polarized America: The Dance of Ideology and Unequal Riches.* Cambridge: MIT Press.

———. 2013. *Political Bubbles: Financial Crises and the Failure of American Democracy.* Princeton: Princeton University Press.

McConahay, John B. 1986. "Modern Racism, Ambivalence, and the Modern

Racism Scale." In *Prejudice, Discrimination, and Racism*, edited by John F. Dovidio and Samuel L. Gaertner, 91–126. New York: Academic Press.

McConahay, John B., Betty B. Hardee, and Valerie Batts. 1981. "Has Racism Declined in America? It Depends upon Who Is Asking and What Is Asked." *Journal of Conflict Resolution* 254: 563–79.

McConahay, John B., and Joseph C. Hough Jr. 1976. "Symbolic Racism." *Journal of Social Issues* 322: 23–45.

McCright, Aaron M., and Riley E. Dunlap. 2011. "The Politicization of Climate Change and Polarization in the American Public's Views of Global Warming, 2001–2010." *Sociological Quarterly* 52 (2): 155–94.

McGinniss, Joe. 1969. *The Selling of the President, 1968*. New York: Trident Press.

McIlwain, Charlton, and Stephen M. Caliendo. 2011. *Race Appeal: How Candidates Invoke Race in US Political Campaigns*. Philadelphia: Temple University Press.

McThomas, Mary, and Michael Tesler. Forthcoming. "The Growing Influence of Gender Egalitarianism on Public Support for Hillary Clinton." *Politics & Gender.*

Mendelberg, Tali. 1997. "Executing Hortons: Racial Crime in the 1988 Presidential Campaign." *Public Opinion Quarterly* 61 (1): 134–57.

———. 2001. *The Race Card*. Princeton: Princeton University Press.

———. 2008. "Racial Priming Revived." *Perspectives on Politics* 6:109–23.

Miller, Warren Edward, and J. Merrill Shanks. 1996. *The New American Voter*. Cambridge: Harvard University Press.

Morone, James A. 2010. "Presidents and Health Reform: From Franklin D. Roosevelt to Barack Obama." *Health Affairs* 29: 1096–1100.

Moskowitz, David, and Patrick Stoh. 1994. "Psychological Sources of Electoral Racism." *Political Psychology* 15 (2): 307–29.

Motyl, Matt, Ravi Iyer, Shigehiro Oishi, Sophie Trawalter, and Brian A. Nosek. 2014. "How Ideological Migration Geographically Segregates Groups." *Journal of Experimental Social Psychology* 51: 1–14.

Mueller, John E. 1973. *War, Presidents and Public Opinion*. New York: Wiley.

Myrdal, Gunnar. 1944. *An American Dilemma*. New York: Harper and Row.

Nadeau, Richard, and Michael S. Lewis-Beck. 2001. "National Economic Voting in U.S. Presidential Elections." *Journal of Politics* 63:159–81.

Newman, Benjamin J. 2013. "Acculturating Contexts and Anglo Opposition to Immigration in the United States." *American Journal of Political Science* 57 (2): 374–90.

Newport, Frank. 2013. "Democrats Racially Diverse; Republicans Mostly White: Democrats and Independents Grow More Diverse since 2008." http://www .gallup.com/poll/160373/democrats-racially-diverse-republicans-mostly- white .aspx.

Nosek, Brian A., Frederick L. Smyth, Jeffrey J. Hansen, Thierry Devos, Nicole M. Lindner, Kate A. Ranganath, and Colin Tucker Smith. 2007. "Pervasiveness and

Correlates of Implicit Attitudes and Stereotypes." *European Review of Social Psychology* 18 (1): 36–88.

Nyhan, Brendan, Eric McGhee, John Sides, Seth Masket, and Steven Greene. 2012. "One Vote out of Step? The Effects of Salient Roll Call Votes in the 2010 Election." *American Politics Research* 40 (5): 844–79.

O'Reilly, Kenneth. 1995. *Nixon's Piano: Presidents and Racial Politics from Washington to Clinton*. New York: Free Press.

Page, Benjamin I., and Robert Y. Shapiro. 1992. *The Rational Public: Fifty Years of Trends in Americans' Policy Preferences*. Chicago: University of Chicago Press.

Parker, Christopher S., and Matt A. Barreto. 2013. *Change They Can't Believe In: The Tea Party and Reactionary Politics in America*. Princeton: Princeton University Press.

Parlett, Martin A. 2014. *Demonizing a President: "The Foreignization" of Barack Obama*. Santa Barbara: Praeger.

Pasek, Josh, Tobias H. Stark, Jon A. Krosnick, Trevor Tompson, and B. Keith Payne. 2014. "Attitudes toward Blacks in the Obama Era Changing Distributions and Impacts on Job Approval and Electoral Choice, 2008–2012." *Public Opinion Quarterly* 78 (S1): 276–302.

Pasek, Josh, Alexander Tahk, Yphtach Lelkes, Jon A. Krosnick, B. Keith Payne, Omair Akhtar, and Trevor Tompson. 2009. "Determinants of Turnout and Candidate Choice in the 2008 US Presidential Election Illuminating the Impact of Racial Prejudice and Other Considerations." *Public Opinion Quarterly* 73 (5): 943–94.

Payne, B. Keith, Clara Michelle Cheng, Olesya Govorun, and Brandon D. Stewart. 2005. "An Inkblot for Attitudes: Affect Misattribution as Implicit Measurement." *Journal of Personality and Social Psychology* 89 (3): 277–93.

Payne, B. Keith, Jon A. Krosnick, Josh Pasek, Yphtach Lelkes, Omair Akhtar, and Trevor Tompson. 2010. "Implicit and Explicit Prejudice in the 2008 American Presidential Election." *Journal of Experimental Social Psychology* 46 (2): 367–74.

Peffley, Mark, and Jon Hurwitz. 2010. *Justice in America: The Separate Realities of Blacks and Whites*. New York: Cambridge University Press.

Petrocik, John R. 1987. "Realignment: New Party Coalitions and the Nationalization of the South." *Journal of Politics* 49: 347–75.

Pettigrew, Thomas F., and R. W. Meertens. 1995. "Subtle and Blatant Prejudice in Western Europe." *European Journal of Social Psychology* 25: 57–75.

Petty, Richard E., and Jon A. Krosnick, eds. 1995. *Attitude Strength: Antecedents and Consequences*. Mahwah: Laurence Erlbaum Associates.

Pew Research Center. 2009a. "No Increase in 'Too Much Obama' Despite Media Blitz." September 23. http://www.people-press.org/files/legacy-pdf/547.pdf.

———. 2009b. "Top Stories of 2009: Economy, Obama, Health Care." December 29. http://people-press.org/report/575/.

————. 2010. "A Year after Obama's Election: Blacks Upbeat about Black Progress, Prospects." January 12. http://www.pewsocialtrends.org/files/2010/10/blacks-upbeat-about-black-progress-prospects.pdf.

————. 2011. "GOP Makes Big Gains among White Voters." July 22. http://www.people-press.org/2011/07/22/gop-makes-big-gains-among-white-voters/.

————. 2012a. "Hillary Clintons Career of Comebacks." June 4. http://www.people-press.org/2012/12/21/hillary-clintons-career-of-comebacks/.

————. 2012b. "Partisan Polarization Surges in Bush and Obama Years." June 4. http://www.people-press.org/files/legacy-pdf/06-04-12%20Values%20Release.pdf.

————. 2013a. "Big Racial Divide over Zimmerman Verdict. July 22. http://www.people-press.org/2013/07/22/big-racial-divide-over-zimmerman-verdict/.

————. 2013b. "King's Dream Remains Elusive as Many Americans See Racial Disparities." August 22. http://www.pewsocialtrends.org/2013/08/22/kings-dream-remains-an-elusive-goal-many-americans-see-racial-disparities/.

————. 2013c. "The Rise of Asian Americans." April 4. http://www.pewsocialtrends.org/files/2013/04/Asian-Americans-new-full-report-04-2013.pdf.

————. 2014a. "Public Sees Religion's Influence Waning." September 22. http://www.pewforum.org/2014/09/22/public-sees-religions-influence-waning-2/.

————. 2014b. "Sharp Racial Divisions in Reactions to Brown and Garner Decisions." December 8. http://www.people-press.org/2014/12/08/sharp-racial-divisions-in-reactions-to-brown-garner-decisions/.

————. 2014c. "Stark Racial Divisions in Reactions to Ferguson Police Shooting." August 18. http://www.people-press.org/2014/08/18/stark-racial-divisions-in-reactions-to-ferguson-police-shooting/.

Piston, Spencer. 2010. "How Explicit Racial Prejudice Hurt Obama in the 2008 Election" *Political Behavior* 32:431–51.

————. 2014. "Lighter-Skinned Minorities Are More Likely to Support Republicans." *Monkey Cage*. http://www.washingtonpost.com/blogs/monkey-cage/wp/2014/09/17/lighter-skinned-minorities-are-more-likely-to-support-republicans/.

Poole, Keith. 2014. "An Update on the Presidential Square Wave." https://voteviewblog.wordpress.com/page/2/.

Popkin, Samuel, and Douglas Rivers. 2008. "The Unmaking of President McCain." *Economist*/ YouGov. November 4. http://www.pollster.com/blogs/Popkin%20Rivers%20Campaign%20Analysis%2011-04%20w%20graphs.pdf.

Price, Vincent, and David Tewksbury. 1997. "News Values and Public Opinion: A Theoretical Account of Media Priming and Framing." In *Progress in Communication Sciences: Advances in Persuasion*, edited by George A. Barnett and Franklin J. Boster, 13:173–212. Cambridge: MIT Press.

Price, Vincent, and John Zaller. 1993. "Who Gets the News: Alternative Measures of News Reception and Their Implications for Research." *Public Opinion Quarterly* 57 (2): 133–64.

Putnam, R. D., and D. E. Campbell. 2010. *American Grace: How Religion Divides and Unites Us*. New York: Simon and Schuster.

Reeves, Keith. 1997. *Voting Hopes or Fears? White Voters, Black Candidates, and Racial Politics in America*. Oxford: Oxford University Press.

Rivers, Douglas. 2006. "Sample Matching: Representative Sampling from Internet Panels." Polimetrix White Paper Series.

Sanchez, Gabriel R. 2006. "The Role of Group Consciousness in Latino Public Opinion." *Political Research Quarterly* 59 (3): 435–46.

Schaller, Thomas F. 2006. *Whistling Past Dixie: How Democrats Can Win without the South*. New York: Simon and Schuster.

Schmidt, Kathleen, and Brian A. Nosek. 2010. "Implicit (and Explicit) Racial Attitudes Barely Changed during Barack Obama's Presidential Campaign and Early Presidency." *Journal of Experimental Social Psychology* 46 (2): 308–14.

Schuman, Howard. 2000. "The Perils of Correlation, the Lure of Labels and the Beauty of Negative Results." In *Racialized Politics: The Debate about Racism in America*, edited by David O. Sears, James Sidanius, and Lawrence Bobo, 302–23. Chicago: University of Chicago Press.

Schuman, Howard, Charlotte Steeh, Lawrence Bobo, and Maria Krysan. 1997. *Racial Attitudes in America: Trends and Interpretations*. Cambridge: Harvard University Press.

Sears, David O. 1975. "Political Socialization." In *Handbook of Political Science*, edited by Fred I. Greenstein and Nelson W. Polsby, 2:93–150. Reading: Addison-Wesley.

———. 1983. "The Persistence of Early Predispositions." In *Review of Personality and Social Psychology*, edited by L. Wheeler and P. Shaver, 4:79–116. Beverly Hills: Sage.

———. 1988. "Symbolic Racism." In *Eliminating Racism: Profiles in Controversy*, edited by Phyllis A Katz and Dalmas A. Taylor, 53–84. New York: Plenum Press.

———. 1993. "Symbolic Politics: A Socio-Psychological Theory." In *Explorations in Political Psychology*, edited by Shanto Iyengar and William J. McGuire, 113–49. Durham: Duke University Press.

Sears, David O., and Jack Citrin. 1985. *Tax Revolt: Something for Nothing in California. Enlarged Edition*. Cambridge: Harvard University Press.

Sears, David O., Jack Citrin, and Richard Kosterman. 1987. "Jesse Jackson and the Southern White Electorate in 1984." In *Blacks in Southern Politics*, edited by Robert P. Steed, Laurence W. Moreland, and Tod A. Baker, 209–25. New York: Praeger.

Sears, David O., and Carolyn L. Funk. 1999. "Evidence of the Long-Term Persistence of Adults' Political Predispositions." *Journal of Politics* 61:1–28.

Sears, David O., and P. J. Henry. 2005. "Over Thirty Years Later: A Contemporary Look at Symbolic Racism and Its Critics." In *Advances in Experimental Social Psychology*, edited by Mark P. Zanna, 95–150. New York: Academic Press.

Sears, David O., P. J. Henry, and Rick Kosterman. 2000. "Egalitarian Values and Contemporary Racial Politics." In *Racialized Politics: The Debate about Racism in America*, edited by David O. Sears, James Sidanius, and Lawrence Bobo, 75–117. Chicago: University of Chicago Press.

Sears, David O., and Donald R. Kinder. 1971. "Racial Tensions and Voting in Los Angeles." In *Los Angeles: Viability and Prospects for Metropolitan Leadership*, edited by Werner Z. Hirsch, 51–88. New York: Praeger.

Sears, David O., Richard R. Lau, Tom R. Tyler, and Harris M. Allen Jr. 1980. "Self-Interest vs. Symbolic Politics in Policy Attitudes and Presidential Voting." *American Political Science Review* 74 (3): 670–84.

Sears, David O., and Sheri Levy. 2003. "Childhood and Adult Development." In *Handbook of Political Psychology*, edited by David O. Sears, Leonie Huddy, and Robert L. Jervis, 60–109. New York: Oxford University Press.

Sears, David O., and Victoria Savalei. 2006. "The Political Color Line in America: Many Peoples of Color or Black Exceptionalism? *Political Psychology* 27: 895–924.

———. 2009. "Sharp or Blunt Instruments? Measuring Affect toward Ethnic and Racial Groups in Contemporary America." Paper presented at the annual meeting of the International Society for Political Psychology, Dublin, July 17.

Sears, David O., Jim Sidanius, and Lawrence Bobo, eds. 2000. *Racialized Politics: The Debate about Racism in America*. Chicago: University of Chicago Press.

Sears, David O., and Michael Tesler. 2009. "Are We There Yet? White Youths, Symbolic Racism and the Obama Victory." Paper prepared for presentation at the annual meeting of the International Society for Political Psychology, Dublin, July 17.

Sears, David O., Colette van Laar, Mary Carillo, and Richard Kosterman. 1997. "Is It Really Racism? The Origins of White Americans' Opposition to Race-Targeted Policies." *Public Opinion Quarterly* 61 (1): 16–53.

Shani, Danielle. 2006. "Knowing Your Colors: Can Knowledge Correct for Partisan Bias in Political Perceptions?" Paper presented at the annual meeting of the Midwest Political Science Association, Chicago, April.

Sidanius, Jim, Shana Levin, Joshua L. Rabinowitz, and Christopher M. Federico. 1999. "Peering into the Jaws of the Beast: The Integrative Dynamics of Social Identity, Symbolic Racism, and Social Dominance." In *Cultural Divides: Understanding and Overcoming Group Conflict*, edited by D. A. Prentice and D. T. Miller, 80–132. New York: Russell Sage Foundation.

Sides, John. 2009. "How Much Did Racial Prejudice Affect the 2008 Election?" *Monkey Cage*. http://themonkeycage.org/2009/03/10/how_much_did_racial_prejudice/.

———. 2010. "How Much Did the Tea Party Help GOP Candidates." *Monkey Cage*. http://themonkeycage.org/2010/11/04/how_much_did_the_tea_party_hel/.

————. 2013a. "Group-Centrism in American Public Opinion." Unpublished manuscript, George Washington University. Paper prepared for the 2013 annual meeting of the Midwest Political Science Association, Chicago. http://home.gwu .edu/~jsides/groupcentrism.pdf.

————. 2013b. "What If a Party Re-branded Itself and Americans Never Noticed?" *Monkey Cage*. http://themonkeycage.org/2013/06/13/what-if-a-party-re -branded-itself-and-americans-never-noticed/.

Sides, John, and Kimberly Gross. 2012. "Stereotypes of Muslims and Support for the War on Terror." *Journal of Politics* 75 (3): 583–98.

Sides, John, and Lynn Vavreck. *The Gamble: Choice and Chance in the 2012 Presidential Election*. Princeton: Princeton University Press, 2013.

Sigelman, Carol K., Lee Sigelman, Barbara J. Walkosz, and Michael Nitz. 1995. "Black Candidates, White Voters: Understanding Racial Bias in Political Perceptions." *American Journal of Political Science* 39: 243–65.

Sitkoff, Harvard. 1978. *A New Deal for Blacks: The Emergence of Civil Rights as a National Issue*. New York: Oxford University Press.

Skocpol, Theda, and Vanessa Williamson. 2012. *The Tea Party and the Remaking of Republican Conservatism*. Oxford: Oxford University Press.

Sniderman, Paul M., Richard A. Brody, and Phillip Tetlock. 1991. *Reasoning and Choice: Explorations in Political Psychology*. Cambridge: Cambridge University Press.

Sniderman, Paul M., and Edward G. Carmines. 1997. *Reaching beyond Race*. Cambridge: Harvard University Press.

Sniderman, Paul M., Gretchen C. Crosby, and William G. Howell. 2000. "The Politics of Race." In *Racialized Politics: The Debate about Racism in America*, edited by David O. Sears, Jim Sidanius, and Lawrence Bobo, 236–79. Chicago: University of Chicago Press.

Sniderman, Paul M., and Thomas Piazza. 1993. *The Scar of Race*. Cambridge: Harvard University Press.

————. 2002. *Black Pride and Black Prejudice*. Princeton: Princeton University Press.

Sniderman, Paul M., and Edward H. Stiglitz. 2008. "Race and the Moral Character of the Modern American Experience." *Forum* 6 (4): art. 1.

Sniderman, Paul M., and Philip E. Tetlock. 1986a. "Reflections on American Racism. *Journal of Social Issues* 42:173–87.

————. 1986b. "Symbolic Racism: Problems of Motive Attribution in Political Debate." *Journal of Social Issues* 42 (2): 129–50.

Stephens-Davidowitz, Seth. 2013. "The Effects of Racial Animus on a Black Presidential Candidate: Using Google Search Data to Find What Surveys Miss." http://papers.ssrn.com/sol3/papers.cfm?abstract_id=2050673.

Stimson, James A. 2004 *Tides of Consent: How Public Opinion Shapes American Politics*. Cambridge: Cambridge University Press.

Taber, Charles S., and Milton Lodge. 2006. "Motivated Skepticism in the Evaluation of Political Beliefs." *American Journal of Political Science* 50 (3): 755–69.

Tate, Katherine. 1994. *From Protest to Politics: The New Black Voters in American
Elections*. Cambridge: Harvard University Press.

Taylor, Paul. 2013. "The Growing Electoral Clout of Blacks Is Driven by Turnout,
Not Demographics." March 10. http://www.pewsocialtrends.org/2012/12/26/the
-growing-electoral-clout-of-blacks-is-driven-by-turnout-not-demographics/.

Tesler, Michael. 2011. "President Obama and the Novel Influence of Anti-Muslim
Attitudes in the 2010 Midterms." Paper presented at the 2011 annual meeting
of the American Political Science Association, Seattle, September.

———. 2012a. "Did Racial Conservatives Fuel Newt's South Carolina Surge." January 30. http://today.yougov.com/news/2012/01/30/did-racial-conservatism-fuel
-newts-south-carolina-/.

———. 2012b. "The Racializing Influence of Romney's Welfare Ad." *Monkey Cage*.
http://themonkeycage.org/2012/08/20/the-racializing-influence-of-romneys
-welfare-ad/.

———. 2012c. "The Spillover of Racialization into Health Care: How President
Obama Polarized Public Opinion by Racial Attitudes and Race." *American
Journal of Political Science* 56 (3): 690–704.

———. 2013a. "Explaining President Obama's Minimal (Aggregate) Impact on
White Racial Attitudes." Paper presented at the annual meeting of the Midwest
Political Science Association, Chicago, April.

———. 2013b. "The Return of Old-Fashioned Racism to White Americans' Partisan Preferences in the Early Obama Era." *Journal of Politics* 75 (1): 110–23.

———. 2014. "Elite Domination and Public Doubts about Climate Change and
Evolution." Unpublished working paper, University of California Irvine.

———. 2015a. "The Conditions Ripe for Racial Spillover Effects." *Political Psychology* 36 (Supp. 1): 101–17.

———. 2015b. "Priming Predispositions and Changing Policy Positions: An
Account of When Mass Opinion Is Primed or Changed." *American Journal of
Political Science*, December 31. doi:10.1111/ajps.12157.

Tesler, Michael, and David O. Sears. 2010. *Obama's Race: The 2008 Election and the
Dream of a Post-Racial America*. Chicago: University of Chicago Press.

Tesler, Michael, and John Zaller. 2014. "The Power of Political Communications."
In *Oxford Handbook of Political Communications*, edited by Kathleen Hall
Jamison and Kate Kenski. New York: Oxford University Press. doi:10.1093
/oxfordhb/9780199793471.013.003.

Tomz, Michael, and Paul M. Sniderman. 2005. "The Organization of Mass Belief Systems." Paper presented at the annual meeting of the Midwest Political
Science Association, Chicago, April 7–10.

Trende, Sean. 2013. "The Case of the Missing White Voters Revisited." June 21.
Real ClearPolitics. http://www.realclearpolitics.com/articles/2013/06/21/the
_case_of_the_missing_white_voters_revisited_118893.html.

Tufte, Edward R. 1975. "Determinants of the Outcomes of Midterm Congressional Elections." *American Political Science Review* 69: 812–26.

———. 1978. *Political Control of the Economy*. Princeton: Princeton University Press.

Valentino, Nicholas A. 1999. "Crime News and the Priming of Racial Attitudes during Evaluations of the President." *Public Opinion Quarterly* 63: 293–320.

Valentino, Nicholas A., Vincent L. Hutchings, and Ismail K. White. 2002. "Cues That Matter: How Political Ads Prime Racial Attitudes during Campaigns. *American Political Science Review* 96: 75–90.

Valentino, Nicholas A., Kosuke Imai, L. Matthew Vandenbroek, and Teppei Yamamoto. 2013. "Obama and the End of Racial Priming." Unpublished manuscript, University of Michigan.

Valentino, Nicholas A., and David O. Sears. 2005. "Old Times There Are Not Forgotten: Race and Partisan Realignment in the Contemporary South." *American Journal of Political Science* 49: 672–88.

Vanneman, Reeve D., and Thomas F. Pettigrew. 1972. "Race and Relative Deprivation in the Urban United States." *Race* 13: 461–86.

Vavreck, Lynn. 2009. *The Message Matters: The Economy and Presidential Campaigns*. Princeton: Princeton University Press.

———. 2014. "It's Not Too Late for Republicans to Win Latino Votes." *Upshot*. August 11. http://www.nytimes.com/2014/08/12/upshot/its-not-too-late-for -republicans-to-win-latino-votes.html?_r=0&abt=0002&abg=0.

Vavreck, Lynn, and Douglas Rivers. 2008. "The 2006 Cooperative Congressional Election Study." *Journal of Elections, Public Opinion, and Parties* 18 (4): 355–66.

Virtanen, Simo, and Leonie Huddy. 1998. "Old-Fashioned Racism and New Forms of Racial Prejudice." *Journal of Politics* 60 (2): 311–32.

Weisberg, Herbert F. 2014. "The Decline in the White Vote for Barack Obama in 2012: Racial Attitudes or the Economy?" *Electoral Studies*. doi:10.1016/j .electstud.2014.09.014.

Weisberg, Herbert F., and Christopher J. Devine. 2010. "Racial Attitude Effects on Voting in the 2008 Presidential Election: Examining the Unconventional Factors Shaping Vote Choice in a Most Unconventional Election." *Electoral Studies* 29 (4): 569–81.

Weisberg, Herbert F., and Jerrold G. Rusk. 1970. "Dimensions of Candidate Evaluation." *American Political Science Review* 64 (4):1167–85.

Weiss, Nancy Joan. 1983. *Farewell to the Party of Lincoln: Black Politics in the Age of FDR*. Princeton: Princeton University Press.

White, Ismail K. 2007. "When Race Matters and When It Doesn't: Racial Group Differences in Response to Racial Cues." *American Political Science Review* 101: 339–54.

Williamson, Vanessa, Theda Skocpol, and John Coggin. 2011. "The Tea Party and the Remaking of Republican Conservatism." *Perspectives on Politics* 9 (1): 25–43.

Windett, Jason H., Kevin K. Banda, and Thomas M. Carsey. 2013. "Racial Stereotypes, Racial Context, and the 2008 Presidential Election." *Politics, Groups, and
Identities* 3: 349–69.

Winter, Nicholas J. G. 2006. "Beyond Welfare: Framing and the Racialization of
White Opinion on Social Security." *American Journal of Political Science* 50
(2): 400–420.

———. 2008. *Dangerous Frames: How Ideas about Race and Gender Shape Public
Opinion*. Chicago: University of Chicago Press.

Zaller, John R. 1992. *The Nature and Origins of Mass Opinion*. Cambridge: Cambridge University Press.

———. 1994. "Elite Leadership of Mass Opinion." In *Taken by Storm: The Media,
Public Opinion and US Foreign Policy in the Gulf War*, edited by W. Lance Ben-
nett and David L. Paletz, 250–74. Chicago: University of Chicago Press.

———. 2004. "Floating Voters in US Presidential Elections, 1948–2000." In *Studies
in Public Opinion: Attitudes, Nonattitudes, Measurement Error, and Change*, edited by Willem E. Saris and Paul M. Sniderman, 166–212. Princeton: Princeton
University Press.

Index

Chicago Studies in American Politics

A SERIES EDITED BY BENJAMIN I. PAGE, SUSAN HERBST,
LAWRENCE R. JACOBS, AND ADAM J. BERINSKY

Lightning Source UK Ltd.
Milton Keynes UK
UKOW01f0240150817
307316UK00001B/124/P